Visitor's Guide
SWEDEN

*The author would like to thank Scandinavian Seaways and
Stena Sealink for their help in making this book possible
and staff at the many regional tourist offices in
Sweden for their unfailing good humour and patience.*

'To my mother'

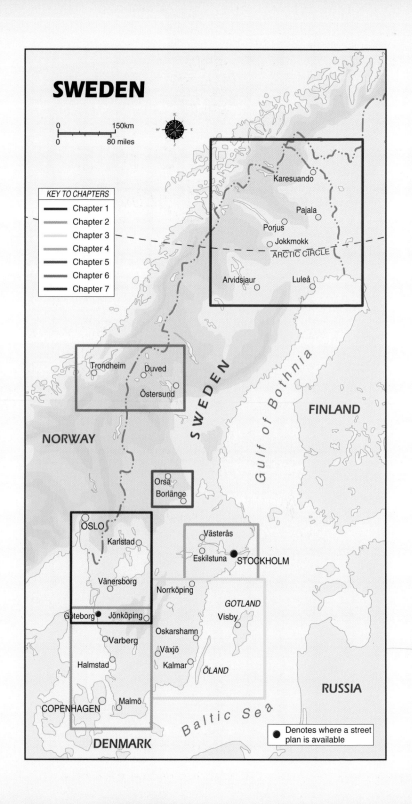

SWEDEN

0   150km
0   80 miles

KEY TO CHAPTERS
— Chapter 1
▧ Chapter 2
▧ Chapter 3
▧ Chapter 4
— Chapter 5
▧ Chapter 6
— Chapter 7

Karesuando

Pajala

Porjus

Jokkmokk

ARCTIC CIRCLE

Arvidsjaur   Luleå

Trondheim   Duved

Östersund

SWEDEN

FINLAND

Gulf of Bothnia

NORWAY

Orsa
Borlänge

OSLO

Karlstad

Vänersborg

Västerås

Eskilstuna   STOCKHOLM

Norrköping

GOTLAND

Visby

Goteborg   Jönköping

Oskarshamn

Varberg

Växjö

Halmstad

Kalmar   ÖLAND

RUSSIA

COPENHAGEN

Malmö

Baltic Sea

● Denotes where a street
plan is available

DENMARK

VISITOR'S GUIDE
SWEDEN

Ingrid Morris

MPC

HUNTER

Published by:
Moorland Publishing Co Ltd,
Moor Farm Road West, Ashbourne,
Derbyshire DE6 1HD
England

Published in the USA by:
Hunter Publishing Inc,
300 Raritan Center Parkway,
CN 94, Edison, NJ 08818

ISBN 086190 389 7

British Library Cataloguing in Publication Data:
A catalogue record for this book is available from the British Library.

Colour origination by: Sele & Color, Bergamo, Italy

Printed in Hong Kong by: Wing King Tong Co Ltd

Cover photograph: Mariefred church *(International Photobank)*
Rear cover: Överkalix *(Swedish Tourist Board)*
Page 3: Sollerön *(Ingrid Morris)*

The illustrations have been supplied by A. J. Emery pp143, 146;
Swedish Tourist Board pp10, 43, 46, 134, 138, 139, 175, 215, 218, 226, 234,
235; S. M. Wragg pp11, 14, 26, 27, 30, 31, 50, 134, 139; the remainder by
Ingrid Morris

MPC Production Team:
Editor: Tonya Monk
Designer: Ashley Emery
Cartographer: Alastair Morrison
Typesetting & Editorial Assistant: Christine Haines

CONTENTS

KEY TO SYMBOLS USED IN TEXT MARGIN AND ON MAPS

🏃	Recommended walks	🏛	Church/Ecclesiastical site
🌼	Garden	⊞	Building of interest
🏰	Castle/Fortification	⊤	Archaeological site
✳	Other place of interest	🖼	Museum/Art Gallery
🎿	Winter sports	🏔	Beautiful view/Scenery, Natural phenomenon
🦌	Nature reserve/Animal interest	🦆	Birdlife
🌳	Parkland	🦢	Beach/Bathing
⛵	Water sports	🐟	Aquatic interest

KEY TO MAPS

▬▬▬▬	Motorway		City/Town
▬▬▬▬	Main Road	⬤	Town /Village
▬▬▬▬	Secondary Road		River/Lake
▬▬▬▬	Minor Road	⌐·⌐··⌐·⌐	Country Boundary
··········	Rail line		Regional Boundary

HOW TO USE THIS GUIDE

This MPC Visitor's Guide has been designed to be as easy to use as possible. Each chapter covers a region or itinerary in a natural progression which gives all the background information to help you enjoy your visit. MPC's distinctive margin symbols, the imortant places printed in bold and a comprehensive index enable the reader to find the most interesting places to visit with ease.

At the end of each chapter an Additional Information section gives specific details such as addresses and opening times, making this guide a complete sightseeing companion.

At the back of the guide the Fact File, arranged in alphabetical order, gives practical information and useful tips to help you plan your holiday before you go and while you are there.

The maps of each region show the main towns, villages, roads and places of interest, but are not designed as route maps and motorists should always use a good recommended road atlas.

INTRODUCTION

'I had no idea we had such an enormous amount of forest!' The chance remark by a leading Swedish politician as he surveyed the countryside from a train window caused a good deal of local hilarity. Every Swedish schoolchild knows that half of the country, the fourth largest in Europe, is covered in forest. It stretches northwards into a vast, unspoilt wilderness, one of Europe's last, providing sanctuary for elk, lynx, wolves and even brown bear. Among the pine and silver birch trees lie many of Sweden's 96,000 lakes; small watery oases often flanked by cheerful red or yellow wooden houses. In the more densely populated south there are fertile farmlands while in the north-west a long mountain chain reaches up past the Arctic Circle to the world of the Midnight Sun.

Sweden is described by its inhabitants as 'our oblong land' because it stretches 1,574km (976 miles) from the far north to the province of Skåne, a short ferry ride from Denmark, in the south. To put it in perspective, a journey from one end of the country to the other would be the equivalent of driving from Calais in northern France to Gibraltar. The widest part however is just 499km (309 miles) across, flanked by the Baltic and the Gulf of Bothnia to the east and a long, rugged boundary with Norway to the north-west. At its most northerly point a remote Arctic monument marks the spot where Sweden, Finland and Norway meet, while the south-west of the country faces Denmark and the British Isles across Kattegat and the North Sea.

Sweden lies on approximately the same latitude as Alaska, but enjoys a temperate climate with surprisingly warm summers and cold, crisp winters. Spring is slow to arrive in the far north of the country, but when it finally comes it brings the Midnight Sun which can be seen above the Arctic Circle from mid-May to mid-July. Conversely the 24-hour daylight is matched by 24-hour darkness in this region as, in mid-winter, the sun fails to rise at all.

Swedes make the most of the long warm summer days when they take to the coast in their thousands to swim, sail and work on their suntans. There are unspoilt beaches and countless small islands some lush and green, others windswept and barren. Sweden has long been a leader in environmental protection and is justifiably proud of the fact that you can even swim and catch salmon in the waterways of Stockholm.

Blessed with a landmass about the size of Spain and a population like that of London it is not surprising that most of Sweden is sparsely populated. More than 80 per cent of the population lives in the southern third of the country and visitors driving off the beaten track are almost as likely to meet an elk as they are another vehicle! In fact the tall fences along major routes are not there to keep people out of the forest — they are there to keep elks off the road! These huge (they can stand up to 2m/7ft high) ungainly looking creatures are the unwitting cause of dozens of accidents every year as they stroll into the path of oncoming vehicles.

Sweden's unspoilt environment has become a magnet for nature lovers. There are thousands of marked walks and long distance trails which double up as ski tracks in winter. The lakes and rivers attract amateur anglers, canoeists and even white-water enthusiasts and an unwritten Swedish law called *allemansrätten* (literally 'everyone's right') allows unusually free access across private terrain provided environmental codes of practice are strictly adhered to. The Swedes themselves make the most of their surroundings and the stereotype of a healthy-looking sun-tanned blonde is no coincidence. They are a nation of sports enthusiasts, more likley to be found out walking or running than slumped infront of their television sets or propping up a local bar. Many city dwellers are the proud owners of small remote holiday cottages or *sommar stugor* to which they retreat at every opportunity.

Sweden enjoys one of the highest standards of living in the world with life expectancy of about 80 years for women, 74 for men, and extensive social welfare benefits. Over 90 per cent of its teenagers go on to further education, old-age pensions are generous and the statutory paid annual holiday is 5 weeks. Public transport is clean, efficient and suprisingly inexpensive and the road network.

The cost of these and other benefits inevitably led to a draconian tax system, so steeply progressive that high earners could in some cases be faced with 'negative' income. The Swedish children's author Astrid Lindgren, presumably falling into that category herself, was driven to write a modern 'fairy story' called *Pomperipossa* about the government's fiscal policies. It became something of a best seller. High levels of VAT and other indirect taxes on goods and services have given Sweden a reputation as an expensive and even exotic holiday destination, especially for those keen on top-notch restaurants and elegant bars. The price of a large round of drinks may be hard to swallow, but there have recently been political moves to change the tax structure and put greater emphasis on market forces.

As a comparatively expensive country Sweden has traditionally competed on the basis of quality and efficiency rather than on price. Mindful of the effect on tourism however, hotel chains, city corporations and other services now provide a useful crop of incentives and discounts to help keep down costs for visitors. There are, for example, thousands of log cabins, picturesque on the outside and full of Nordic high tech on the inside, available for holiday lets at reasonable prices. Camping sites are modern and efficient while farm holidays, bed and breakfast and other private accommodation (signposted 'Rum' the Swedish for 'rooms') are in the ascendancy. The large cities offer discount cards and long journeys by rail or coach can be surprisingly cheap. Swedes today are far removed from the old Ingmar Bergman film stereotype where they were all too frequently portrayed as a reserved, humourless and unapproachable lot. Most will go out of their way to help a visitor and will probably be only too delighted to practice their near-fluent English.

The Regions At A Glance

For the purposes of this book Sweden has been divided into seven areas, each with its own sights and character. It is a large country (449,964sq km/ 173,731 sq miles) and distances, especially in the north, can be deceptively long. Every year brings its crop of battered Citroens and Renaults, sporting thousands of miles worth of dust, a pair of antlers as a trophy inscribed with the words 'Nordcap or bust' (North Cape). A frantic dash through the length of Sweden and Norway to mainland Europe's most northerly point may sound exciting but is probably not the best way to get to know the country. Independent travellers with limited time would do better to concentrate on one or two smaller, but no less interesting areas.

Many visitors travelling by car arrive first in the south where the the provinces of Skåne, Blekinge and Halland form the breadbasket and garden of Sweden. Here are rolling fertile fields with long, low half-timbered farmhouses, historic towns and miles of safe, sandy beaches which attract thousands of holidaymakers every year. This part of Sweden used to belong to Denmark and there are plenty of reminders in the local architecture. The broad dialect spoken in Skåne sounds distinctly uncouth to refined Stockholm ears and many locals regard Copenhagen, just across the water, as their local 'capital' instead. Skåne is jokingly referred to as 'Madariket', dialect for 'the Kingdom of Food' so it is no coincidence that Sweden has these southern bon viveurs to thank for the famous Swedish *smörgåsbord*.

Anyone travelling the direct sea route from Britain will arrive first in Sweden's second city, Göteborg (Gothenburg) in the west. It is an elegant, bustling place which became known as 'Little London' because of its close trading links with the British Isles. It also houses one of the country's most popular tourist venues, a landscaped amusement park called Liseberg. North of the city the sandy beaches of Halland give way to a weatherbeaten, rocky coastline that tails off into hundreds of skerries and islands. All along are small fishing communities, tiny jumbles of timber houses scattered among the smooth granite rocks. The sheltered coves and inlets are a favourite haunt of sailing enthusiasts. The meadows and forest further inland give way to Sweden's largest lake, Vänern and to one

Rocky coastlines and sheltered coves are a local haunt of sailing enthusiasts

Relaxing in the sun, a favourite Swedish pastime

of its most historically interesting areas recently referred to as the 'Cradle of the Kingdom'.

To the south-east lies the country's second largest lake, Vättern and the province of Småland which, with its boulder-strewn pine forests, is perhaps more typical of the traditional image of Sweden. Life was harsh in this part of Sweden and at the end of the last century hundreds of thousands of people emigrated to the USA in search of a better life. One industry which has flourised in the area and become a major tourist attraction is the manufacture of Swedish crystal. What may be less well-known is that the world-wide Ikea furniture chain was founded here. Just off the east coast is the island of Öland. It is linked to Kalmar on the mainland by a 6km (4 mile) long bridge and is a popular holiday spot, not least with the Swedish royal family which has its summer residence there. The Baltic island of Gotland further to the east is another popular holiday destination among the Swedes themselves — perhaps partly because it feels like going 'abroad' without the passport formalities.

Stockholm, built on fourteen different islands linked by a network of waterways, is described as one of the most beautiful capital cities in Europe. Sometimes known as the 'Venice of the North', it has successfully retained its character while operating as a clean, modern city, proud of the high quality of life it offers. As one might expect, it also contains the greatest concentration of sights including the Royal Palace, the seventeenth-century warship *Vasa* and the celebrated open-air museum, Skansen. Much of the sightseeing can be done by boat, and while afloat,

The old Opera House, Stockholm

do not miss a visit to the lush green islands of its archipelago. Distances seem longer and towns and villages further apart as you travel north and west past the forests, lakes and rolling plains of central Sweden. But the journey is well worth it because on reaching Dalarna you will have arrived in its traditional heartland. Nowhere has folklore and culture been better preserved than in this colourful province where north and south meet. The famous painted Dala Horse, symbol of all things Swedish, is just one of the many arts and crafts which still survive while the arrival of mid-summer, in particular, is marked by festivals and folk dancing to traditional fiddle music.

Further north in the provinces of Härjedalen and Jämtland the gentle hills are transformed into a chain of mountains which, unlike the Alps, were left smooth and rounded after the Ice Age. Here there are well-developed ski centres and marked cross country trails, fast flowing rivers, spectacular waterfalls and forests full of wild flowers, mushrooms and berries. Wild animals such as beaver, lynx and wolverine inhabit these regions and you can even join a bear safari. Anyone not satisfied with that can look for Sweden's version of the Loch Ness Monster, *Storsjö Odjuret* or 'the Big Lake Monster', rumoured to skulk in the waters of Lake Storsjö.

And so finally to Lappland and the world beyond the Artic Circle where in summer there is no night and in winter the northern lights flicker across the sky. It is a region of wide open spaces, mountains (including Kebnekaise, the highest in Sweden) fast flowing rivers and rugged National Parks. It has justifiably earned a reputation as 'Europe's last wilderness' and attracts walkers and nature lovers from all over the world. But it is also a vital part of the Swedish economy with huge ore mines, hydroelectric projects and timber reserves. Kiruna, a remote mining community is billed as the largest town in the world because it covers an area approximately the size of Corsica. Lappland is of course also home, but by no means the only one, to thousands of Lapps or Sami as they prefer to be called. Many still live off traditional reindeer husbandry although modern methods now include the use of snow scooters and helicopters. Do not be surprised to see reindeer wandering along the main road, they really are as common up here as sheep or cows elsewhere in Europe.

A Brief History

Modern Sweden has an enviable reputation for stability both in domestic affairs and in international relations. It has traditionally shunned involvement in the hurly-burly of twentieth-century international politics, preferring to take the high, maybe even slightly smug, moral ground. Its position as a quiet, safe and neutral backwater was enhanced by men like Dag Hammarskjöld, the gifted UN Secretary General and Raoul Wallenberg, a diplomat who saved thousands of Hungarian Jews during World War II. The murder in 1986 of another internationally known Swede, Prime Minister Olof Palme, not only shocked the nation, but forced it reluctantly into the world spotlight. Sweden has not always been such a tranquil place. Swedish Vikings once controlled the seaways to Constantinople (now Istanbul) and the East. There were countless squabbles between the Scandinavian neighbours and, during the seventeenth century, a period of expansion when Sweden became a great power encompassing Finland, part of Russia, the Baltic States and even pockets of what is now Germany.

Sweden is believed to have been populated from around 10,000BC and artefacts from the Stone, Bronze and Iron Ages have been found. It is generally believed that by AD500 Uppsala and the area around Lake Mälaren had become the focus of an emerging nation which slowly expanded across central and southern Sweden. Ancient tales tell of terrible battles in which the Svear who came from that area, overpowered the Götar, or Goths in the West. They became the heirs to the Swedish kingdom and gave Sweden its name, *Svea-rike* literally the Svea Kingdom, or simply Sverige today.

It is difficult to separate fact and fiction when it comes to the Vikings, those Scandinavian warriors who left an indelible and often unwanted mark on much of Europe and Asia between 800 and AD1050. The Swedish Vikings appear to have headed mainly eastwards on expeditions with the dual purposes of plunder and trade. They used the rivers stretching deep into Russia to establish trading stations and travelled as far as the Black and Caspian Seas where they acquired links with the Byzantine Empire and the Arabs. Christianity first reached Sweden at about this time and the first Christian church was founded in AD830. But it took at least two more centuries before pagan sacrifices to gods like Freya and Frö finally disappeared. Olof Skötkonung became Sweden's first Christian monarch when he was baptised by an English monk in the eleventh century. Another English monk named Stephen was made the country's first archbishop with a seat at Uppsala.

Two families, the Sverker and the Eriks held the Swedish Crown alternately for much of the twelfth and thirteenth centuries although local assemblies or *ting* carried out most of the administration. It was not until the latter part of the thirteenth century that the Crown gained real influence. By the time Magnus Ladulås became king in 1275 Swedish expansion had engulfed Finland and royal power was firmly established. King Magnus was given the name Ladulås (Barn Lock) because of decrees which stopped travelling noblemen living off the local peasants.

Trade, especially with the German Hansa towns, increased during the fourteenth century and many Swedish communities were founded over the next 200 years as copper and iron ore mining grew in importance. Agricultural techniques also improved, but the Black Death, which reached Sweden in 1350, led to a long period of comparative decline as whole parishes were wiped out leaving abandoned farmland and labour shortages.

In 1389 the Crowns of Denmark, Norway and Sweden were united under the Danish Queen Margareta. Her nephew Erik of Pomerania was

Colourful flowers brighten the streets of Göteborg

(below)
The natural environment of Sweden's largest predator, the brown bear, at Björnpark, Grönklitt

crowned king of all three at the so-called Union of Kalmar in 1397 although it was Margareta who retained the real power until her death in 1412. The period was marked by conflict both at home and abroad. Erik, married to Philippa, the sister of the English King Henry V, was not the most popular of Scandinavian rulers. He raised taxes to fight a war against the Hanseatic League while squabbles with rebellious aristocrats continued at home. The infighting went on through the fifteenth century as unionists clashed with nationalists and in 1520 the Danish King Christian II, then presiding over the un-

A friendly Swedish Smile

ion, ordered the execution of eighty eminent Stockholm men in what became known as 'Stockholm Bloodbath'. A young nobleman, Gustav Vasa, tried and at first failed, to stir up a popular revolt against Danish superiority. He headed for exile in Norway but, in one of the best known episodes from Swedish history, was overtaken by two messengers on skis from the town of Mora in Dalarna who persuaded him to return. The 90km (56 mile) chase is now re-run annually by thousands of skiers and called the Vasalopp. Gustav Vasa was elected to the Swedish throne in 1523 and as king laid the foundations of the modern Swedish state. He turned it into a hereditary monarchy, strengthened the power of the Crown and confiscated church estates in what became the start of the Protestant Reformation. The Crown passed to his son Erik XIV, one of many suitors to Elizabeth I of England. Highly educated but mentally unstable he was on the throne for just 8 years before his brother, Johan deposed him. Erik ended his days in prison where he is said to have been poisoned with a bowl of pea soup. Johan was succeeded by his son Sigismund who ruled over Sweden and Poland. He tried to reintroduce Catholicism but was deposed by his uncle Karl X, a popular character known as the Peasants' King.

The last of the famous Vasa dysnasty was Gustav II Adolf, Gustav Vasa's grandson. He was still a teenager when he was crowned in 1611 but despite his youth he helped turn Sweden into a great regional power, concluding peace treaties and securing vital trade routes. He did much to promote education, the sciences and industry and set up a new form of municipal self-government. But in 1630 his determination to ensure that Sweden remained protestant, and the need to preserve its growing regional influence edged the nation into the Thirty Years War. The conflict claimed its royal victim, perhaps Sweden's greatest monarch, at the battle of Lutzen in 1632 — a date which, like Britain's 1066, is etched in the memory of every Swedish schoolchild.

Kristina, Gustav Adolfus's only child and brought up by him as a boy, became queen. But she abdicated in 1654 and, ironically in view of her father's protestant loyalties, travelled to Rome where she converted to Catholicism. Her life has been immortalised on celluloid by actress Greta Garbo. After the dissolution of the union with Denmark and Norway, Swedish foreign policy was aimed at domination of the Baltic. Sweden defeated Denmark in two wars and incorporated the Danish provinces of Skåne, Halland, Blekinge and Gotland in the south as well as a number of Norwegian territories in the west and north-west. The Peace of Roskilde, signed with Denmark in 1658, marked the peak of Swedish expansionism and the country could truly be counted a great northern power. Domestically the arts and literature flourished and a great university was established at Lund. But the Caroleans who were now on the throne were faced with the problem of having to enforce the country's extensive borders. Sweden, basically an agrarian economy, was unable to maintain its position as a great power and was defeated in the Great Nordic War of 1700-1721 against the combined forces of Denmark, Poland and Peter the Great of Russia. Even the well documented courage of the 'warrior king' King Karl XII, who had succeeded to the throne at the age of 15, could do nothing to stop the disintegration. He spent most of his life in battle abroad and after he was killed by a snipers' bullet in 1718 the Swedish Parliament (Riksdag) introduced a new form of constitutional government in which the four estates, the nobility, clergy, burghers and peasants were represented and the power of the throne was reduced.

The so-called Era of Liberty spawned two political parties, press freedom and progress in science, agriculture and industry. Carl von Linne, the botanist introduced his plant classification system, Anders Celcius invented the centigrade scale and Carl Bellman wrote his famous poetry. Gustav III managed to reduce parliamentary power through a bloodless coup in 1772, re-kindling the authority of the throne. But Europe was in turmoil with the French Revolution at its height and in 1792 he was shot by an assassin during a masked ball in Stockholm. Verdi turned the dramatic incident into an opera.

Gustav's son was deposed after military defeats and ended his days abroad as plain 'Colonel Gustavsson'. By now Sweden had lost most of its overseas territories and had been reluctantly sucked into the Napoleonic Wars. The king, Karl XIII (Gustav VI's uncle) was childless and the Swedish throne had no heir. Napoleon's armies were feared and admired and in what appears to have been an extraordinary move one of his Generals, Jean Baptiste Bernadotte, was chosen to become king. He was officially adopted by Karl and crowned king of Sweden and Norway in 1818 taking the name Karl XIV Johan.

What the down-to-earth Swedes thought of having a French king who could speak no Swedish is a matter for conjecture. There is a famous story that when his wife Desiree eventually arrived to join her husband, curious locals at the port of Helsingborg were encouraged to shout 'We want rain' as enthusiastically as they could. The Swedish words, when part of a large motley chorus sounded like a passable version of 'Vive la Rein' or Long Live the Queen in French. The new arrival was apparently impressed that peasantry of such a remote and, to her Parisian taste, uncivilised land could speak French. No doubt she discovered the truth before too long and it quickly became apparent that life in this Nordic outpost did not suit her. She returned to France and stayed there for 12 years, leaving her husband to rule Sweden alone. Fortunately he managed it with some success. His son and grandson (Oscar I and Karl XV) presided over a period of prosperity with the introduction of compulsory education, elementary schools, the abolition of the guild system, free trade, the reform of parliament and introduction of local self government. Sweden's present king, Carl XVI Gustav is a direct descendant of the French general. The nineteenth century also saw the emergence of the Labour movement which grew with industrialisation. But life was hard for the great majority of Swedes who still worked on the land and mass emigration to the USA began in 1850. Over the next 80 years more than a million Swedes left the old country in search of a better life in the new. The exodus is chronicled in Vilhem Moberg's moving novel, *The Emigrants*.

Trade unions began to appear at the end of the nineteenth century as the struggle for better working conditions grew apace with industrialisation. Feminist and temperance movements were also in the ascendancy as heavy drinking and alcoholism reached epidemic proportions among the working class. In 1889 the Social Democratic Party which was to govern Sweden for much of the twentieth century was founded. Many great figures in Swedish culture made their mark at this time. Alfred Nobel left the money he made from inventing dynamite to finance his annual Nobel

The Swedes are immensely proud of their natural environment. They established their first National Park at the beginning of the twentieth century and now have twenty ranging from a lush deciduous forest in the deep south to bare mountain scenery in the north. Here are some of the best known.

1 Stenshuvud
The highest point on the southeastern tip of Sweden. It was formerly believed to be haunted by trolls and giants but is now a 4 acre national park with a visitors centre and a hiking trail specially adapted for the handicapped.

2 Dalby Söderskog
A tiny National Park by Swedish standards comprising a lush deciduous wood with a colourful carpet of wild flowers in spring and early summer. It is situated near the busy southern towns of Lund and Malmö and planks have had to be laid on some paths to reduce wear on the ground.

3 Blå Jungfrun
A legendary granite island off the coast of Öland with boulders, caves, a stone labyrinth and a rich variety of lichen. The name means the 'Blue Maiden' and she can be reached by boat tour from Oskarshamn or Öland.

4 Tiveden
The source of fairytales, and superstitious troll stories. This dark forest north of Lake Vättern has ancient trees and enormous boulders that were left behind when the Ice Age glaciers retreated. There are trails, but the terrain can be demanding.

5 Töfsingdalen
An eerie boulder-strewn wilderness covering 16sq km (6sq miles) near the Norwegian border in northern Dalarna.

6 Sånfjället
In the province of Härjedalen and best known for its indigenous bear population. The park covers 103sq km (40sq miles) of highland and is surrounded by forest. There are hiking trails and shelters.

7 Skuleskogen
Part of the so-called 'High Coast' along the Ångermanland seaboard. The coastal highlands are separated by deep ravines, stretches of treeless shingle, bogs and lakes. There is a nature information centre on the E4.

8 Muddus
Also in Lappland, but on the eastern lowlands north of Jokkmokk. It covers 510sq km (196sq miles) of great bogs and untouched primeval forest. There are deep gorges, a lake and unusually varied bird and wildlife population. Access is comparatively easy and there are trails and cabins.

9 Sarek
Has an almost legendary status in Sweden as the great untouched wilderness. It covers a massive 1,970sq km (757sq miles) of mountain massifs, plateaux, deep valleys and more than 100 glaciers in western Lappland. The terrain supports bear, lynx, Arctic fox and many other species and makes no concessions to man. It is being preserved as the ultimate wilderness and therefore has no facilities and no walking trails. It is not recommended for novices.

Sweden's National Parks

10 Padjelanta

The third of three neighbouring parks in western Lappland and, at 1,984sq km (763sq miles), one of Europe's largest. It has vast mountain moors, nearly all of them above the treeline, reindeer pastures and rare vegetation. There are no public roads, but there are trails and overnight cabins.

11 Stora Sjöfallet

A more accessible neighbour of Sarek, a road leads through part of it and there are a number of marked walking trails and one or two places to stay. The mountain scenery covers 1,278sq km (491sq miles) and is centred around lakes in the Stora Lule river system. The south is dominated by Mount Akka, known as Lappland's Queen.

12 Abisko

Almost as northerly as Vadvetjåkka but easy to reach and very popular. It has been described as 'an Arctic garden' because of its rich flora. There is more about Abisko in Chapter 7, Lappland.

13 Vadvetjåkka

One of the most isolated parks situated in the far north-eastern corner of Sweden. It is dominated by a mountain ridge and large delta area with lakes, willow brush, bogs and rich birdlife. It also has some of Sweden's largest limestone caves but is comparatively inaccessible.

13

12 KARESUANDO

10 **11**

9 **8** GÄLLIVARE

ARCTIC CIRCLE

LULEÅ

ÖSTERSUND **7**

6

5

MORA

FALUN

KARLSTAD VÄSTERÅS

STOCKHOLM

4

NORRKÖPING

GÖTEBORG

JÖNKÖPING

KALMAR **3**

2

MALMÖ

1

Prizes. Works by the artists Anders Zorn and Carl Larsson are worth small fortunes today while writers Selma Lagerlof and August Strindberg won critical acclaim.

In 1905 Norway became independent for the first time since the four-teenth century and the map of Scandinavia took on the form that it still holds today. Sweden had not been involved in a war since a short skirmish with Norway in 1814 and continued to pursue its policy of non-alignment and neutrality during World War I. The conflict inevitably took its toll on the economy as Sweden trod a perilous path between the warring parties. There were problems on its northern borders with Finland too as the Russian Revolution in 1917 brought civil war and paved the way for Finnish independence. Sweden got its first Labour government under Prime Minister Hjalmer Branting in 1920 and had adopted universal suffrage for both men and women over 23 by 1921. Plans for its much acclaimed welfare society were laid during the 1930s. Sweden again declared neutrality in 1939, a delicate business as both Denmark and Norway were occupied by Hitler's troops.

That neutrality was underlined by a decision not to follow Denmark and Norway and join NATO when the organisation was founded in 1948. Post war politics were marked by great stability, growing prosperity and consensus politics. The Social Democrats, elected to government in 1932, held or shared power for all but 7 years until 1991 when they were ousted by a centre right coalition. The increasing cost of living and the tax burden caused by the huge and often unwieldy welfare state led to demands for a change and murmerings of discontent.

Sweden's application to join the European Union sparked fierce public debate. While many Swedes believe the nation's future lies 'in Europe', others feel that its traditional neutrality and independence has served it well and should continue to do so. There is little doubt however that Sweden is being drawn inexorably into the mainstream of European political and social life. One very concrete sign of this are the plans for a 16km (10 mile) bridge and tunnel project across the narrow sound be-tween Malmö and Copenhagen. Meanwhile Sweden has continued to live up to its reputation as a safe haven for refugees and admitted 80,000 people from the former Yugoslavia.

More pragmatic market orientated policies during the early 1990s effec-tively reduced a number of taxes including, most importantly for readers of this book, VAT on tourist services. This was cut from 21 per cent to 12 per cent in July 1993 and resulted in lower domestic fares and hotel prices. Taxes on some alcoholic drinks also fell bringing price tags closer to those in the rest of Europe.

There was more good news for foreign visitors, if not for the Swedes themselves, in 1993 when the value of the *krona* declined sharply on the foreign exchange markets. At one point it had fallen by some 20 per cent against major currencies. The effect of these developments has been to boost Sweden's beleaguered tourist industry after a dismal few years dogged by dauntingly high prices. Local tourist authorities seem justified in suggesting that there has never been a better time to visit Sweden.

1

GÖTEBORG AND THE SOUTH-WEST

For many visitors their first glimpse of Sweden is a lonely, windswept piece of granite, so smooth and flat that it seems in permanent danger of losing its battle with the sea. As the ferry slides past, a few buildings and a lighthouse come into view. This is the island of Vinga, a barren outpost known to generations of Swedish seamen. Ballads have been written in its honour, not least because it was for a time the childhood home of Evert Taube, a popular Swedish folksinger whose father was in charge of the lighthouse there. Vinga lies at the western edge of the archipelago of islands which guard the approaches to Sweden's second largest city, Göteborg (Gothenburg). It is believed to have been an important landmark even in Viking times and there is an engraving on a rock dated 1381 to show there were people on Vinga even then.

Between Vinga and the mainland the sea is dotted with dozens of islands, some of them deserted outcrops of rock, others sprinkled with shrubbery and cheerful-looking wooden houses. **Göteborg** has the larg- ❋ est harbour in Sweden and huge cargo and passenger ships ply a cautious route between the maze that makes up the city's northern and southern archipelagos. The small white island ferries which form a local commuter service for the offshore communities look more at home. Their passenger load multiplies in summer when thousands of holidaymakers flock to the archipelago to enjoy some of the best swimming and sailing in the area. There is usually a dash for seats up on deck as the boats pick their way through narrow channels calling in at pint-sized harbours and landing stages. The water here is clear, sheltered and non-tidal but in summer be prepared to share the voyage with a noisy mêlée of day-trippers clutching picnic baskets and beach towels while hanging onto children with sticky ice creams.

Unfortunately many of the islands in Göteborg's archipelago are out of bounds to foreigners because they lie in a military security zone. For more details on this, and where to take the ferries, look in the section entitled Island Hopping Off The Bohuslän Coast (page 50-51).

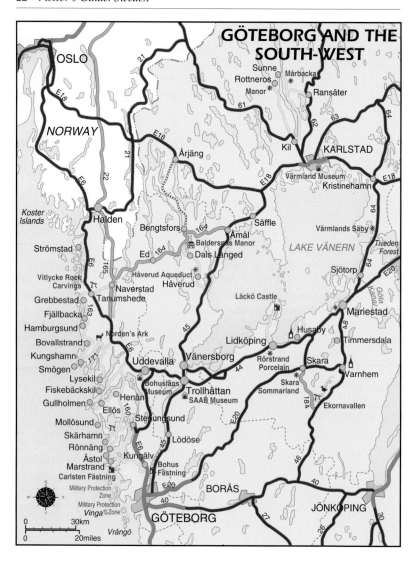

Göteborg is Sweden's main commercial gateway, a city which has flourished on international maritime trade but which, like many others has seen the decline of its shipyards in recent years. It lies in a rocky landscape at the mouth of the Göta River, its harbour dominated by the impressive span of Älvsborgsbron, one of Europe's longest suspension bridges. Apart from the important docks, container and ferry terminals, Göteborg is also the home of Volvo cars which started production in 1927 and of the famous Hasselblad cameras.

Fortunately Göteborg's commercial backdrop does not detract from its pleasant boulevards and squares. It is known as 'Little London' because

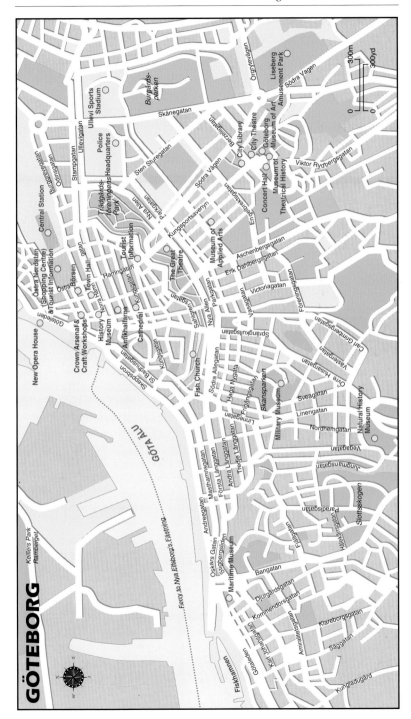

GÖTEBORG

GÖTA ALV

Keillers Park
Ramberget

New Opera House

Göteleden

Crown Arsenal &
Craft Workshops

Central Station

Östra Nordstan
(Shopping Centre)
& Tourist Information

Burggrevegatan

Odinsgatan

Stampgatan

Ullevigatan

Ullevi Sports
Stadium

Police
Headquarters

Skånegatan

Burgårds-
parken

Örgrytevägen

Liseberg
Amusement Park

Södra Vägen

300m
300yd

Skanegatan

Sten Sturegatan

Södra Vägen

City Library

City Theatre

Göteborg
Museum of Art

Viktor Rydbergsgatan

Berzeliigatan

Concert Hall

Museum of
Theatrical History

Engelbrektsgatan

Aschenbergsgatan

Erik Dahlbergsgatan

Victoriagatan

Vasagatan

Föreningsgatan

Carl Grimbergsgatan

Östra Hamn

Norra Hamn

Tourist
Information

Town Hall

Börsen

Östra

Hamngatan

Kungsgatan

The Great
Theatre

Museum of
Applied Arts

Kungsportsavenyn

Nya Allén

Parkgatan

Språngkullsgatan

Västergatan

Övre Husargatan

Sveagatan

Linnégatan

Nordhemsgatan

Natural History
Museum

Vegagatan

Jungmansgatan

Paradisgatan

Slottsskogen

History
Museum

Antikhallarna

Cathedral

St Badhusgatan

Kungsgatan

Skeppsbron

Fish Church

Södra Allégatan

Haga Nygata

Fridhemsgatan

Linnégatan

Skansparken

Military Museum

Linnégatan

Andreegatan

Masthamnsgatan

Första Långgatan

Andra Långgatan

Tredje Långgatan

Oskars Gatan

Sylbergsliden

Maritime Museum

Fiskhamnen

Färjor Nya Elfsborg's Fästning

Karl Johansgatan

Bangatan

Djurgårdsgatan

Kommendörsgatan

Amiralitetsgatan

Filllgatan

Halakärrsgatan

Klareborgsgatan

Såggatan

Kungsladugård

Sahlgren

Fästung

Ostra Allén

Trädgårds-
föreningens
Park

of its close links with Britain but it has the Dutch to thank for its layout and design. The main legacy of these seventeenth-century masters of town planning is a ringed canal system. They would not be too pleased to learn that some of the canals have since been filled in to make way for the Göteborg traffic, but you can still enjoy a waterborn view of the city from the Paddan sightseeing boat moored near the main tourist office. The blue and cream trams (among Sweden's last) that clank through the traffic are a cheap and efficient if somewhat bone-shaking way of seeing the city as the locals do. Try tram number 4 which will take you through the centre and out to the small ferry and yacht harbour at Saltholmen or number 5 which heads along Göteborg's most impressive boulevard, Kungsportsavenyn and past one of Sweden's prime tourist attractions, the Liseberg amusement park. But central Göteborg can really best be explored on foot. The avenues have broad pavements, there are plenty of pedestrian shopping streets, squares and parks and most of the main sights are not too far apart.

Göteborg was founded at the beginning of the seventeenth century by the then king, Gustav II Adolfus who is said to have climbed to the top of a rock by the river, pointed and said; 'The city shall be there!' A fortress had stood on the site since the 1300s but it was twice taken by the invading Danes. The Swedes suffered the indignity of having to buy it back on each occasion in order to retain vital access to the sea at a time when Denmark and Norway held almost all of the coast. The second occasion was apparently the last straw. The price was one million pieces of silver, an enormous amount in the early 1600s and taxes had to be levied around the country in order to pay. Even church bells were melted down for extra cash. In 1670 a new fortress, called **Nya Elfsborg's Fästning** (sometimes spelt Älvsborg) was built on an island in the harbour, its aim — to keep the Danes out once and for all. It was at the centre of a fierce sea battle in 1719 and a cannon ball from that time is still lodged in the wall of the fortress church. It was later turned into a prison for 'lifers' and particularly awkward inmates were draped from head to toe in 160lb of iron which became known as the 'Elfsborg review dress'. The fortress is a rather jollier place now with a cafeteria and a museum and can be reached by a regular ferry service from Stenpiren (Stone Pier) in Göteborg. There are lovely views of the harbour and part of the island has been used as a base for diving expeditions to the *Göteborg*, an East India Company ship which sunk nearby in 1745 with its cargo of porcelain.

The ruins of the earlier fourteenth-century fortress **Gamla Elfsborg**, a few crumbling stones protected by a makeshift wooden roof are not really much to see. They lie on a cramped hill, hemmed in by a modern hotel and warehouses in an area near the river which is now a cultural reservation called **Klippan's Kultur Reservat** (Heritage Centre). It includes a good fish restaurant in a former East India Company house and an old anchor smithy.

Göteborg owes much to the influence of British, especially Scottish merchants who founded many of its major businesses and institutions and built some of the elegant houses which line its boulevards and canals. A good place to start a sight seeing tour is at **Götaplatsen** where Carl Milles huge statue of Poseidon has become something of a symbol of the city. The square is dominated by the rather severe façade of the city art gallery, **Göteborg's Konstmuseum**, the second largest in Sweden with a formidable collection ranging from Rembrandt to the Impressionists as well as Scandinavian artists such as the Skagen painters and Carl Larsson whose homely family scenes have adorned cards and decorative writing paper the world over. An annex and a gallery (**Konsthallen**) at the foot of the main museum usually show the most avant-garde art. Also at Götaplatsen is the ivy-covered city theatre, the concert hall and the main library which was founded in 1861 with the help of a donation from the Scottish merchant James Dickson. Just around the corner the **Teaterhistoriska Museet** (Museum of Theatrical History), has models of stage sets, scenery designs and play manuscripts.

From Götaplatsen the city's broadest boulevard **Kungsportsaveyn** (Kings Gate Avenue) takes a direct line toward the old centre of the city. This has always been one of the places to be seen in Göteborg and a favourite place for summer strolls. The pavement cafés and brasseries still attract the local 'smart set' who are drawn by the shops and expensive boutiques which dot the side streets. The boulevard still has some fine old pastel coloured houses which have managed to survive the onslaught of modern development and the shopping culture. About halfway down on a sidestreet lies **Röhsska Konst-Slöjdmuseet**, the only museum in Sweden totally devoted to crafts and industrial design. There are exhibitions of Swedish furniture, textiles, silver and glass alongside collections from the Far East and Ancient Greece. The Avenue, as it is called by the locals, continues through a strip of greenery before it reaches the canal. The old opera house, Stora Teatern, was being replaced during 1994, but people still joke that the near-naked men on sculptor Johan Peter Molin's statue *The Knife Wrestlers* which stands opposite, are fighting over tickets for the evening performance. The new Göteborg opera house, a modern glass and concrete construction, lies about 1km (½ mile) away near the harbour. Behind the statue is **Trädgårdsföreningen**, one of three large parks in Göteborg. There is a restaurant and music throughout the summer as well as a rose garden with some 3,500 varieties and a nineteenth-century Palm House. Cross the canal to Kungsportsplatsen and you are in the old centre of the city, although you could be forgiven for not realising it. One of three city gates once stood here, but it is now a busy shopping area with the Tourist Information Centre (Turistbyrå) in one corner and a large market hall in another. This is Göteborg's main shopping area with pride of place going to the pedestrianised Kungsgatan and its many offshoots. Set at a strange angle to Kungsgatan is **Domkyrkan**, Göteborg's cathedral dating from 1825. It looks a little uninviting from the outside but is pleasantly uncluttered inside and a peaceful sanctuary away from the shopping

An efficient way of seeing Göteborg is by tram

Göteborg was originally planned around a ringed canal system

Ship building in Göteborg harbour

A pilot boat passes the early morning ferry from Göteborg, bound for Denmark

mania nearby. Continue down Kunsgatan and turn right onto Västra Hamngatan and you will come to **Antikhallarna**, once an old bank building but now containing small antique stalls which blend well with the slightly faded grandeur of its marble halls.

If the shops beckon but the weather is bad head from Kungsportsplatsen, along Östra Hamngatan and past Stora Hamnkanal, Göteborg's widest canal, to **Östra Nordstan**. This is a huge covered shopping complex housing just about every major retail outlet and an expensive, but handy carpark. It is a favourite place for people to 'hang out' and meet others doing the same and there is usually a harmless, but hopeful gaggle of drunks hovering around the entrance to the Systembolag, the state-owned liquor store. A different sort of crowd can often be found queuing up for ice-cream, a favourite snack no matter how cold the weather. Right in the middle is a useful Tourist Information Centre.

Across the road from Östra Nordstan lies the slightly bleak but elegant **Gustaf Adolf Torg** (Square) named after Göteborg's founder and complete with his statue. To one side is the Rådhuset (Town Hall) and behind him, the colonnaded **Börsen** Stock Exchange with statues depicting affluence, commerce, industry and other essentials for a successful city. The Town Hall bears an interesting little plaque to the memory of a British admiral named Saumarez. He had been ordered to bombard the town when, during the Napoleonic Wars, the French tried to stop it trading with Britain. The Admiral apparently refused to do so. He had become rather fond of Göteborg, not least according to some, because of its attractive young ladies.

A little further along the Stora Hamnkanal which flanks the square and in among some narrow streets lies **Kronhuset**, the city's oldest secular building dating from the mid-1600s. It was constructed in Dutch style for ordnance purposes and its cobbled courtyard has been fairly tastefully turned over to small arts and crafts workshops. There is an old-fashioned general store where you can still buy sweets in a paper cone and of course the inevitable café. Just a block or two away is the Göteborgs **Historiska Museum** (Historical Museum) housed in the old headquarters of the East India Company and containing furniture and decorative art as well as ethnological and archaeological collections. Another small museum worth mentioning, as much for its location as for its contents is **Skansen Kronan**, a stocky round stone construction, once part of the city's defences which now houses a military museum. It sits on top of a rocky knoll and the climb up is rewarded with a good view over the city. The area north of the knoll is the old working class quarter known as Haga which has in recent years become more of a place for the upwardly mobile with smart apartments and boutiques. Fortunately many of the old wooden houses have been preserved and renovators now have to tread cautiously. While on the subject of property, it is worth mentioning the characteristic design of many Göteborg apartment houses which typically have two upper floors in wood and the bottom floor in stone. These were the crafty invention of a former Lord Lieutenant of Göteborg to get round official regulations, because of the fire risk, that timber houses should be no more than two floors high. They are now called Lord Lieutenants' Houses.

Göteborg has a thriving fishing industry and the local catch can be admired in the city's most unusual 'church', **Fiskekyrkan** (Known as Feskekörkan in local dialect). Although the name means 'Fish Church' it is in reality a fish market hall. It has never been a church and got its name because the 1873 design bears more than a passing ecclesiastical resemblance. Inside the spotless, refrigerated stalls — a tribute to Swedish efficiency and hygiene—would perhaps be more at home in an expensive fishmongers than a market. But what they lack in atmosphere they make up for with their piles of fresh prawns, crab and other shellfish, mackerel, cod, herring as well as home-made herring (*sill*) in marinades. Early risers can see an altogether noisier contrast at the fish auction held in **Fiskehamnen**, the fish harbour on weekday mornings at 7am. Overlooking the harbour is the **Sjöfartsmuseet** (Maritime Museum), which also houses an aquarium containing assorted tropical and local fish and even the odd crocodile. The 5m (16ft) high plinth surmounted by the figure of a fisherman's wife looking wistfully out to sea awaiting her husband's return has become another symbol of the city. Back toward the centre, but also by the harbour a strange red and cream confection crowned with tubes and pipework rises above the **Maritima Centrum** (Maritime Centre). Whatever your opinion of the architecture of this office development hemmed in between the river and several lanes of traffic, it has one saving grace — a good viewing area at the top which is open to the public in summer. Far below, the Maritima Centrum boasts a floating museum of elderly ships ranging from a four-masted sail training ship to a submarine, an old fire boat, a lightship and more. In summer you can go aboard several and there is an indoor museum too. The centre is reached by pedestrian bridge from the Östra Norstan shopping centre.

For many visitors, especially the younger ones, Göteborg's undisputed number one attraction is the **Liseberg** amusement park, the biggest in Sweden and one of the country's most popular venues. There are open-air theatres, restaurants, gardens and, most important of all, an assortment of rides ranging from the Liseberg loop to the flume ride in which victims shoot down rapids in artificial logs. The roller coaster is claimed to be Europe's longest and the latest offering is a 'spaceport' said to give the sensation of 'galactic travel'. The park is a few minutes walk from Götaplatsen, otherwise take tram number 5.

Two other parks are worth mentioning. The first, **Slottskogen** is a patch of wilderness in the heart of the city. It rises high above the surrounding office blocks and flats and some of its walks give splendid views over the harbour. There is a spacious animal park with Scandinavian species, including elk and Arctic fox and the children's zoo which is open in summer is a real delight. This is a favourite place for a Sunday stroll and

Old meets new in Göteborg — a modern office block with sailing ship at the Maritime Centre

Lisebergstornet revolving tower stands tall in Liseberg park, Göteborg

Getting Around Göteborg

Göteborg is perhaps not the easiest of cities to drive in. Its one-way systems have a habit of whisking you in the wrong direction with no apparent means of escape and the trams can seem quite a hazard to the uninitiated. Outside the metropolis, a system of motorways and dual carriageways speed through-traffic past rather dreary looking modern suburbs and industrial areas. Parking although not cheap is fairly easy. There are plenty of meters and parking ticket machines in the centre, especially toward the river and harbour area. The multi-storey carpark at Östra Nordstan is one of the most convenient, but the entrance is at the back of the complex near the river and can be difficult to find.

By far the best value for anyone staying in the city for a day or more and wanting to see the sights is the Göteborg Card available from the Tourist Information Centres, hotels, campsites and from Liseberg or the Pressbyran newspaper kiosks. The card, valid for one, two or three days entitles the holder to free parking and free travel on all local trams and buses, including the lovely old vintage trams that make round trips in the summer. You also get a free boat trip to the Vinga lighthouse, to the Elfsborg fortifications and even a ferry trip to Denmark if you have the time. The card gives free admission to nearly all the museums and to Liseberg, a sight-seeing tour by coach and a trip on the Paddan boat. It also entitles holders to a number of concessions including free admission to a local football league match.

for disposing of the weeks' old bread and biscuits. Look out for the large fish lurking around the feet of the pink flamingoes in the main lake. For yet another panoramic view, go to the Masthuggs Kyrka on its rocky hill near the harbour. The red-brick church is not especially interesting architecturally, but its stocky tower dominates the city skyline. The

 Naturhistoriska Museum (Natural History Museum) at the edge of Slottskogen boasts the remains of a giant blue whale which was once beached near Göteborg and is so enormous that at the beginning of the twentieth century visitors could have coffee inside its stomach. This slightly macabre practice did little for the creature's conservation and was

 stopped. It would be a shame not also to include Göteborg's **Botaniska Trädgård** (Botanical Gardens) — a pleasant place for a stroll with grounds continuing up a sharp rise to give a taste of some of the wooded wilderness that surrounds the city.

Much of Göteborg is built on a rough hewn terrain of rock and forested hills. Away from the centre the ground rises and falls and the construction of new housing frequently involves blasting away large chunks of granite. Layers of clay on top of bedrock have, in the last 50 years, caused two serious landslides in outlying areas. The most recent in a commuter community called Tuve claimed a number of lives when modern homes were effectively carried off down a slope because the clay on which they stood slipped on the bedrock beneath. Strict building regulations are now in force to prevent such a tragedy re-occurring.

The surrounding landscape may give construction engineers a headache but not sports enthusiasts or keen walkers for whom there are marked trails, golf courses, riding, canoeing and other activities. One of the best and most popular recreation areas near Göteborg is the **Delsjö** tract. Centred on Lake Delsjö it stretches inland for miles — and it is wild enough to make a foray from the marked paths seem a daunting prospect. The recreation centre at **Skatås** on the edge of the area marks the beginning of five trails ranging from an illuminated 2km (1 mile) one to an 18km (11 mile) circuit and finally a 40km (25 mile) one called Vildmarksleden which heads off inland to another leisure area called Hindås and does not return to the centre. In winter these tracks double up as ski trails. But be warned, no matter how fast you go you will probably be overtaken along the way by some tall, healthy looking Swede who has barely had to work up a sweat. He will be sitting at the recreation centre when you get back, drinking a glass of milk and tucking into a second portion of *pytt i panna* — a popular fry-up of chopped potato, onion and meat topped with a fried egg. The trails head through pine and birch woods and past areas of rock with heather, juniper and other shrubs. The rough ridges which cross the area have names like 'magpie fell' and 'the big goats back'. Look out for juniper bushes which appear to have had a trim by a keen topiarist. The gardener in question is undoubtedly an elk as juniper is one of the creatures favourite winter diets. You have the best chance of actually seeing the culprit at dawn or dusk which is when elks are at their most active.

Apart from its wildlife — which also includes deer, badger, fox and more than 70 species of bird, the Delsjö area boasts an 18 hole golf course, a riding stables, a canoe hire depot, fishing and fitness facilities. There is a small beach at Lake Delsjö which is popular with young families, a cafeteria and a campsite at nearby Kärralund.

Göteborg has its ups and downs, and for what many claim to be the very best view of the city and its surroundings you have to cross to the north side of the Göta River and climb the 100m (328ft) high **Ramberget**. In clear weather you can see not only the city, but its two archipelagos and perhaps even the lighthouse on Vinga far out to sea. There are pleasant walking trails here too. The area around Ramberget is called Keillers Park because the land was given to Göteborg at the beginning of the century by James Keiller, the Scottish marmalade manufacturer.

From Göteborg follow the signs for Oslo and the E6 motorway but beware of the notoriously difficult Tingstads Tunnel with its complicated interchange which seems designed to send the unwary off on a tour of the city's less appealing suburbs. After leaving Göteborg the E6 follows the flat, industrial Göta River valley north. A long, strangely sloping bridge links commuter areas on either side of the valley and before long the rounded turret of the **Bohus Fästning** (fortress) comes into view. The turret is affectionately known as Father's Hat (the remains of another is called Mother's Bonnet) and is the best preserved part of a crumbling fortification said to be Scandinavia's largest ruin. The fortress can be forgiven for looking a little down-at-heel, it came under siege fourteen times but never surrendered. It was founded in 1308 in what was then border country between Denmark, Sweden and Norway and was at the centre of continual feuding between the rival powers. It was extended over the years and nearly succumbed to an invading army (this time the Swedes) in 1566 when a gang of 250 enemy managed to occupy one of the towers. A Danish defender crept into the cellar which happened to contain the garrison's gun-powder supply and lit the fuse. The tower and the invaders went up in giant explosion which became known as the Bohus bang. The invaders were hurled 'like crows into the sky' according to one contemporary report.

The labyrinthine battlements, grassy, uneven courtyards and dark archways are open to the public and give commanding views over the Göta River Valley and the river's tributary, Nordre Älv. The courtyard is sometimes used for concerts and plays in the summer and next to the fortress is a tourist office and a stone monument commemorating the meeting of three Scandinavian kings there in 1101. The town of **Kungälv** nearby has had a similarly unsettled history. It is the successor of an ancient Norwegian town called Kongahella and has over the years, been burnt and looted by the Vikings, the Swedes and the Danes. In desperation the town was moved closer to the fortress for additional protection, but even that did not help and it was burnt to the ground again. The reigning king finally cancelled the town's international trade licence and

Festively decorated doors in Kungälv

A painted timbered building in Kungälv

ordered the inhabitants to leave. They refused and rebuilt Kungälv across the river from the fortress where it still stands today. The short road to Kungälv from the E6 takes you straight to the old square with its quaint pastel coloured timber houses and a wooden church from 1679 whose plain exterior conceals a masterful Baroque interior. Västra Gatan which leads from the square used to clatter to the sound of horse-drawn carriages and tradesmen pushing their carts across the cobbles but is now strangely quiet. The crooked eighteenth- and nineteenth-century houses remain however, mainly converted into apartments or offices. The real life of the town has moved ½ km down the road where the old world charm abruptly gives way to a new department store and a shopping centre that could be just about anywhere in Sweden.

For a pleasant detour from Kungälv take route 168 to the medieval town of **Marstrand** perched on its own traffic-free island off the coast. Until recently the journey involved two ferry crossings, but now there is a bridge which has reduced this to a short hop from the unglamorously named Koön or 'Cow Island' to Marstrand. Today the town is a smart summer resort, and especially popular with the sailing fraternity who hold regular regattas there. Historically however its main claim to fame is its fortress, Carlsten. Built in the seventeenth century for defensive purposes, it became a notorious prison whose best known inmate was 'Lasse-Maja', a kind of Swedish Robin Hood. He dressed as a woman to steal from the rich and give to the poor and is said to have been pardonned by the king after 25 years imprisonment having won considerable acclaim as the prison cook.

Rejoin the E6 and continue northward in the direction of Uddevalla. The terrain becomes rougher and more rural here with small farms eking out an existence among rocky tree-clad knolls. Turn onto route 160 toward the town of Stenungsund and the islands of Tjörn and Orust. Almost immediately the first of the many bridges which link these islands comes into view set in the granite scenery so typical of Bohuslän province. **Stenungsund** is a modern industrial town with little of note unless you are particularly interested in the petro-chemical industries that dominate the local economy. It does however have unrivalled surroundings and is as such an important commercial centre for summer visitors on the islands. Three bridges, in ascending order of size, take you onto Tjörn island. The last, a big suspension bridge with commanding views over the surrounding islands and inlets replaces one which collapsed in 1980 when a freighter struck one of its supports in thick fog.

Tjörn, Sweden's sixth largest island, was inhabited in prehistoric times and has a number of ancient rock carvings, burial mounds and graves to prove it. But for most people its charm lies in the salt-stained, weatherbeaten rocks and the old fishing communities that dot the coast defying both terrain and town-planning. A detour is well worth the effort and route 169 (a left turn signposted Rönnäng shortly after the Tjörn Bridge) heads for two of the most strangely picturesque villages. After a pleasant drive through mixed farm and woodland (some 18km/11 miles) the circling seagulls and fish conservation plants tell their own story. This is one of Sweden's premier coastlines for herring — the famous Swedish *sill* and historically its fortunes have come and gone with the herring shoals. It is a happy coincidence that local farms are known for their tasty potatoes as the combination of *sill* and potatoes is a classic culinary tradition. Just before Rönnäng, a right-hand turn takes travellers across a sort of granite moon-landscape to **Klädesholmen**, a tight jumble of pale wooden houses jostling for space on a small island. The need for fishing families to live as close to the harbour as possible meant that every bit of surrounding rock was built on. From a distance you could well imagine the odd house sliding into the sea on stormy days. The narrow thoroughfares have names like Herring Road and Steamboat Street and almost every house seems to boast a model ship in the window. Klädesholmen gets an influx of summer visitors but also retains its role as a busy year-round fishing community. These days the island can be reached by bridge which is not the case for neighbouring Åstol, said to be the most densely populated community in Sweden.

The island of **Åstol** can be seen from **Tjörnehuvud**, the southernmost point of Tjörn with one of the best views along the whole coast. From here its small wooden houses appear so tightly packed it is difficult to see what they are built on. Beyond is Carlsten Fortress at Marstrand and the Pater Noster lighthouse which has played a vital role for shipping since 1868. To get to Åstol and its neighbouring islands Tjörnekalv and Dyrön, take the ferries from Rönnäng harbour. The detour can be lengthened by taking the road to **Skärhamn** (a left turn off the 169) where a little maritime museum tells something of Tjörn's sea-faring history. Skärhamn, the main community on Tjörn once played host to one of Sweden's largest fleets of small cargo boats. These are now outnumbered by yachts and pleasure craft, but in summer you can still see *Lutfisk*, the speciality fish Swedes eat at Christmas, drying on large wooden frames. Even this traditional industry is in decline as competition and more modern techniques take their toll.

There are numerous places on Tjörn to swim and sunbathe, far more than can be marked along the road or on a map. This is true of the entire West Coast. You have only to nip off the main route and the chances are that you will find a smooth, secluded bit of rock on which to sunbathe. But do not expect sandy beaches, they are few and far between in this part of the country.

Tjörn's prehistoric sites are also well-marked, the most interesting of which is perhaps the Pilane burial field with about 100 Iron Age graves and the 3,000-year-old rock carvings at Baseröd depicting fifteen ship figures. The whole area is well-endowed with Stone, Bronze and Iron Age sites, burial grounds and rock drawings. They are all marked from the road with the standard 'site of interest' symbol and the better ones have parking nearby. Some, such as the extraordinary rock carvings at

Tanumshede (dealt with later in this chapter) are fascinating to all. Others comprising what to the untrained eye may seem little more than a few arbitrary stones require a more finely honed interest in ancient culture. The main route 160 leads through pleasant farmland dotted with rocky outcrops, pine forest and watery inlets before yet another bridge with lovely views crosses a deep channel onto the larger island of Orust. Once again, farming and fishing dominate the local economy.

The road passes small rural communities (some, even here, infiltrated by energetic Göteborg commuters) and low-key fjord scenery. There are two more bridges and a tunnel before finally returning to the mainland some 18km (11 miles) west of Uddevalla. To continue northwards without joining the trail of heavy goods vehicles on the E6 follow the ferry signs on route 161 toward Lysekil. Anyone interested in boat excursions or fishing and bathing trips along the coast may however find it useful to call in at the Tourist Information Centre in **Uddevalla** where staff are a mine of useful local information. The city, which confusingly boasts several *centrum* or centres on its approach signs, is a good point from which to explore the region but lacks the character to give it much appeal of its own. A bleak dual carriageway splits the tourist office (head for 'Centrum-Hamnar') and the museum from other parts of the centre, much of which burnt down in a devastating fire in the early nineteenth century. Apart from a highly acclaimed museum and Sweden's oldest seaside resort at Gustafsberg, there is little to see.

Back on the 161, the route to the Lysekil ferry heads across **Bokenäs** peninsula and past a twelfth-century church of the same name with an ill-fitting eighteenth-century wooden tower. The churchyard contains the grave of a British soldier killed in the battle of Jutland. Although Sweden was neutral in both wars, a number of bodies were washed ashore and buried in local churchyards under memorials erected by the parish. Later efforts to move the graves to the official cemetery near Göteborg apparently met with some resistance because the locals were proud of their old soldiers and did not want to lose them. The car ferry to Lysekil, a modest but serviceable vessel which shuttles continuously from one side of the Gullmarn inlet to the other, is free. In Sweden the cost of ferries forming part of major road networks are funded by the state while other smaller operations can be privately owned. Gullmarn, meaning God's Sea is incidentally Sweden's only true fjord. Just 35m (115ft) deep at its mouth it then plunges to 125m (410ft) further inland. The crossing takes about 15 minutes but there can be queues in summertime.

An alternative and more leisurely way of getting to this spot would be to take a brief tour around Orust first. In this case turn left at Varekil and head for the pretty, but isolated fishing village of **Mollösund** where the local museum is housed in an old fishermans' cottage. The road passes signs for a 4,000-year-old grave, **Hagadösen**, its five stone slabs propped together to form an ancient tomb. From Mollösund the route north has a turnoff toward the island of **Gullholmen**, one of the province's oldest fishing communities with yet another museum, this time the well-heeled home of a nineteenth-century shipping family. A couple of kilometres further on at **Ellös** car ferries (for which you pay) make the 15 minute crossing to Rågardsvik and from there the road skirts picturesque **Fiskebäckskil** where the west coast's most famous artist, Carl Willhelmson lived and worked. There are good views across the fjord to the town of Lysekil before the detour joins the main route a little way along the coast at the car ferry terminal near Bokenäs.

The **Lysekil** skyline is dominated by its huge turn-of-the century granite church which towers over the surrounding residential areas, harbour life and fish canneries. At 95m (317ft) above sea-level it is also an important landmark for shipping and is one of a number of rather pompous looking churches built around 1900 to satiate demand for religion in the fishing communities. On Sundays fishing vessels were turned into temporary 'church boats' ferrying believers from outlying islands to services on the mainland. But superstition as well as religion used to play an important role in these parts. Clergy were thought to bring bad luck if they went onboard a fishing vessel and while at sea even the most God fearing fisherman was superstitious about using a priests' official title, preferring references like 'the blackcoat'. Eggs and poultry were banned because they were considered inauspicious and the catch would almost certainly suffer if anyone brought a woman onboard!

Residential streets of timber houses, some with intricate carving, lead up a short rise to the church from where there are commanding views across the town and the surrounding area. There is a marine laboratory at Lysekil and plenty of opportunity for deep-sea fishing trips and excursions to the local archipelago to view seal colonies and other wildlife.

Lysekil lies at the end of one of many rocky peninsulas and the main road back toward the ever present E6 is really the only route to take. It is one of the few communities along this coast which is also served by a railway line. The road is flat and rather uninteresting, but turn left along the 171 toward Kungshamn and Smögen and among the fjord scenery you will find **Nordens Ark** or the Nordic Ark, an animal park for endangered species. Here both Scandinavian and exotic animals are housed in parkland around an old manor house and cafeteria. The project, the only one of its kind in northern Europe, includes Red Panda from China, Przewalskis Horse from Mongolia, snow leopards, wild reindeer, otter, Arctic fox, rare wolves and many other species suited to the climate. Its aim is to breed and if possible reintroduce animals to their native surroundings. The park also has a batch of ancient stone carvings. Route 171 continues across yet another peninsula winding first through farmland, then across rocks and water to **Smögen**, one of the best known and most scenic coastal communities. Smögen has a lively fish auction every weekday evening except Fridays — 5pm for fish, 8pm for prawns. The village is famous for its fresh prawns which are served unpeeled and 'as many as you can eat' for a fixed — but not necessarily bargain — price in local

Fishing boats and fishermen's huts in Smögen

hotels and restaurants. You can also buy a bag to munch as you walk down the kilometre-long wooden jetty. Many of the pint-sized fishermen's huts along the jetty which once used to store nets and equipment have become upmarket summer residences and property prices in general are high. Parts of the village are inaccessible to cars, but you can drive around the harbour from where there is a good view of some typical fishermen's huts set against a sheer cliff face. Smögen is one of the smartest coastal communities and its population swells during June, July and August with the arrival of holidaymakers. The village is joined to the mainland by bridge across which are panoramic views of the barren landscape and islands with groups of neat houses scattered here and there. The adjacent community of Kungshamn suffers from living in the shadow of its smarter, more popular neighbour across the bridge.

A pleasant country road follows the sea northwards past more fishing villages to Bovallstrand and immediately after, a left turn to Hamburgstrand continues the coastal route. The tiny white stone church at **Svenneby** dates from the 1100s and inside a ship suspended from the ceiling is believed to spin around to warn of coming winds. The bell tower is perched separately on top of a nearby cliff with the bell ringers rope hanging temptingly down the rock face.

There are good views of the miriad islands which guard the coastline as the road continues past Hamburgsund and into **Fjällbacka**. The actress Ingrid Bergman spent more than twenty summers on a nearby island and a bust of her in the aptly named Ingrid Bergman Square by the harbour recalls her connections with the village. Fjällbacka, an old seaside resort, is still popular today thanks in part to its picturesque archipelago. Some 5km (3 miles) beyond the coastal islands lies another group of 370 rocky outcrops called Väderöarna (The Weather Isles) with crystal clear water and rich birdlife. The nearby Kungsklyftan (King's Wedge), a 200m (656ft) long and 20m (66ft) deep gulley between sheer rocks was used as a location for a popular Swedish film *Ronja Rövardotter*. Further up the coast is **Grebbestad**, another old fishing port popular with the bathing fraternity since the days when it was believed that a dose of seaweed and salt water cured all ills. Today it boasts 90 per cent of Sweden's oyster catches and is also renowned for its lobster, crab, mussels and of course the prawns for which the whole coastline is justly famous. The coastal route continues its course northward, but just inland around **Tanumshede** lie Sweden's most important rock carvings believed to be between 2,500 and 3,500 years old. Prehistoric carvings have been found in some 1,200 locations along the Bohuslän coast and like the many other ancient remains they bear witness to settlements in the area going back 5,000 years. The most impressive carvings are to be found in the administrative district of Tanum. The main road from Grebbestad first passes one of Sweden's most interesting Iron Age burial grounds at **Greby** where 200 stones, many of them standing upright like ancient daggers stuck into the ground, dot an eerie heather-strewn slope just off the main road. Further on at Tanumshede road signs point to the various carvings in four main locations of which the ones at **Vitlycke** — take the turn at the church signposted carvings and museum — are the crème de la crème. Here no less than 100 ancient figures and symbols jostle for space on a large flat rock situated conveniently close to the road at the edge of some trees. The drawings include several ships and figures, including a famous carving of a man and woman called *The Bridal Couple* which leaves little to the imagination. The area is riddled with smaller groups of drawings and across the road is a museum, cafeteria and, perhaps predictably, a Bronze Age house. The area is believed to owe its wealth of carvings to the fact that the sea once reached up here and the land has since risen. Why these Bronze Age artists hacked away at the hard granite can only be guessed at, but the carvings are thought to have religious or magical significance. The other main sites are nearby at Listleby, where a 2m (7ft) tall man wields a spear, and at Aspeberget. There is yet another set of carvings at Fossum on route 163 about 3km (2 miles) from its junction with the E6.

From Tanumshede the main E6 beats a busy, lorry-laden path north-ward toward the Norwegian border and on to Oslo. To continue this itinerary however take the pleasantly rural route 163 from Tanumshede toward the Bullare Lakes; long, thin fingers of water that stretch some 30km (19 miles) south from Norway through farmland and forest. Spare a thought for the young priest who according to legend placed the in-scribed stone outside **Naverstad**'s twelfth-century church in memory of his wife and child. She is said to have thrown herself into the lake with the child after being damned and persecuted by the old vicar for giving birth sooner after her wedding than early nineteenth-century morals would allow.

Follow the main road first north and then east toward the town of Ed in the province of Dalsland. The forests and lakes are typical of this small, unspoilt county which has adopted the forget-me-not as its provincial flower. The rugged country is broken by narrow bands of water serving as reminders that Norway and its fjords lie just a few kilometres to the north. **Ed** occupies a narrow spit of land between the big and little Le lakes. Relations with its northern neighbour are rather more cordial today than in the 1700s when it was used as a base for a 30,000 strong Swedish army during a campaign against Norway. Memorial stones commemorate the events and every year a version of them are performed on an outdoor stage. But it is the countryside rather than the town that attracts visitors and Ed is best used as a base from which to explore the surrounding wilderness. There are summer boat excursions on the lake and the forests are rich in wildlife such as elk and beaver. Both can be hunted under strictly controlled terms at certain times of year. Route 164 heads east past **Steneby** where hollowed out rocks near the church are known as Jätte Grytor or 'Giant Cauldrons'. The formations were caused by the Ice Age. Continue on the 164 toward Bengtsfors, then after 2km (1 mile) turn right to Dals Långed. If on the other hand you have ever fancied yourself as a

railroad pioneer and feel in need of some exercise you may enjoy a brief
✳ detour to **Bengtsfors**. The paper industry dominates the local economy in
this quiet corner of Sweden and the route there first passes Billingsfors
where a rather unappealing industrial complex brings nature lovers
abruptly down to earth. Fortunately Bengtsfors is well away from the
billowing smoke and offers a novel mode of transport for people wanting
to explore the countryside — railway inspection trolleys. They can be
hired from the local station which long ago abandoned uneconomic
northbound train services and now operates southbound only. The trains
that ply a picturesque single-track route to Mellerud on Lake Vänern stop
at Bengtsfors leaving the line to the north free for pedal power. In summer
the station does a brisk trade in inspection trolley hire and on a good day
the unused line is dotted with these strange looking contraptions known
as Dressin cycles in Sweden. They can take two people, some luggage and
go at an average speed of about 10km (6 miles) per hour. Visitors can
peddle the full 50km (31 miles) along the track to Årjang in the neighbouring province of Värmland or just rent a trolley for a few hours. Local maps
show suitable picnic or camping sites, shops and other facilities along the
way and there is a definite code of practice to avoid collisions.

Picturesque country roads head south from Dals Långed to an impressive aqueduct at Håverud which has become Dalsland's best known
tourist attraction. It has to be said that this route is narrow, undulating and
winding in parts and anyone with a particularly large caravan may prefer
to continue east on the 164 Bengtsfors road joining the itinerary again at
Åmal.

The smaller route follows the Dalsland Kanal and passes signs on the
⌂ left for **Baldersnäs Manor**, an Italian style mansion in pleasant parkland
on a lakeside peninsula. It now houses a restaurant and café in summer
and the grounds have craft shops, a yacht harbour and pleasant walking
trails. **Dals Långed** is an industrial community whose fortunes were once
Π closely linked with those of the canal. Further south at **Högsbyn** is another
batch of rock carvings and although they might not quite be up to the ones
at Tanumshede, their location near a lakeshore is pleasant. After Högsbyn
the road deteriorates but the scenery improves as it takes a roller-coaster
route over uninhabited fell. There are good views across the forested hills
and lakes, but do not get too carried away as the tight bends are no
deterrent to determined Swedish lorry drivers. This is also a popular
✳ tourist route because on the other side of the fell is the **Håverud Aqueduct**,
a piece of engineering described as a 'technological miracle' when it was
inaugurated in 1868. The aqueduct links two lakes which form part of the
canal system by carrying sizeable boats over a section of turbulent water
on a 32m (105ft) long metal channel. A road bridge and rail viaduct cross
here also and the ultimate souvenir photograph involves getting a shot of
all three modes of transport crossing at once. The aqueduct which is
reached by a series of locks, was built for the benefit of local industry but
is now the exclusive preserve of tourists and pleasure craft. In summer

A tribute to Sola,
Karlstad's most
popular 'barmaid'

Bridging the gap,
a passenger boat
crossing the Håverud
Aqueduct in Dalsand

boat services run from Köpmannebro on Vänern to Baldersnäs. Just after Håverud, a small road to the left passes the attractive red-painted church at **Skållerud** dating from 1680. The wrought iron crosses in the graveyard are reminders of the iron working that once dominated the economy along the canal.

The road joins the 45 trunk route on the shores of Vänern, Sweden's largest lake and heads north to the small provincial town of **Åmål**. There are some pleasant eighteenth-century timber buildings, parkland and a river running through the centre, but otherwise not a great deal to see. Continue around the lake, crossing into the province of Värmland and on to **Karlstad**, a sizeable city spread out across the nine arms of the Klarälv (Clear River) delta. As the name implies Karlstad was founded by a king, Karl XI to be precise, although it was a meeting place for the old Ting or parliament long before then. Today it is a large industrial and harbour town with broad boulevards and squares, elegant buildings and a sprinkling of municipal statues to underline its importance. It also has one distinctly odd claim to fame. Ask any Swede to describe something that gleams and they will probably reply that it 'shines like the sun in Karlstad'. Karlstad does not have significantly more sun than anywhere else. The source of this saying was an exceptionally attractive waitress at the local inn who had such a cheerful personality that she was known all around the region as 'Sola', or 'The Sun'. She died in 1818 but there is a statue of her in the city centre. Local residents are rather less complimentary about a statue in the main square (Stora Torget) commemorating the 1905 break-up of the union with Norway. The work is called *The Peace Monument* but the figure with her foot on a helmeted skull has been dubbed by locals as 'the old hag in the old square'.

Very little remains of historic Karlstad because of a devastating fire in 1845 although there are some attractive old wooden houses in the Almen district. The cathedral, built in 1730 also survived the fire as did the Bishop's Residence (Biskopsgården) thanks largely to the efforts of the bishop himself it is said. According to one account of the inferno the Lord Mayor cried and prayed while the bishop swore like a trooper and got on with putting out the fire! Karlstad has an extravagantly decorated city theatre and the Värmland Museum which houses a series of visiting exhibitions. It also plays host to one of the largest government buildings in Sweden, known to locals as the 'Pentagon' because of its links with the Defence Ministry. An old prison has been turned into a luxury hotel called Bilan where guests pay five star prices to sleep in former cells. The city is effectively shaped by the powerful Klarälven and linked together by a series of bridges. The river annually dumps thousands of tons of mud and sand into its estuary and the Hammarö peninsula to the south has become a popular local recreation area with some good beaches. Boat trips on Lake Vänern leave from the Inner Harbour south-east of the main station.

The Klarälven river is 500km (310 miles) long in total and was once a vital transport artery for people and goods travelling north into otherwise inaccessible wilderness. Pilgrims made their way along its banks to the grave of St Olof at Trondheim while logs were, until recently, floated in the other direction from the forests of Värmland to Lake Vänern. River logging ceased a few years ago, making way for a new holiday activity — rafting. Holidaymakers can rent ready-built timber rafts from a variety of operators upstream and then sit back and relax while the river carries them gently down to Karlstad and into the estuary.

Anyone familiar with the works of Sweden's Nobel Prize winning author Selma Lagerlöf may enjoy a detour north to her former home and the area from which she drew her inspiration. Take the E18 west and then follow road 61/62 north, quickly turning off onto the 234 toward the town of Sunne at the northern end of Lake Fryken. There are pleasant views of the finger-shaped lake to the right and, just before Sunne, signs for **Rottneros Manor**. Rottneros is known to generations of Swedes as the fictional 'Ekeby Manor' in Lagerlöfs *Story of Gösta Berling* and is one of many local landmarks that are fictionalised in her books. After her death in 1940, tourists and Lagerlöf fans began to descend on the area and the owner of Rottneros Manor cannily turned his home into a leading sculpture park as an added attraction. Dozens of fine works litter the formal gardens and if you get bored looking at them all, there is an enclosure housing wolves. A handful still roam free in the forests of Värmland, much to the annoyance of local farmers and the delight of conservationists. There is also a small children's zoo near the entrance to the grounds.

Just north of the park lies the small but prosperous community of **Sunne** with an array of modern hotels and camp sites along the lake shore. There are lovely views from the 350m (1,142ft) high Tossebergs Klätten 12km (7 miles) further north. From Sunne follow signs for **Mårbacka**, Lagerlöf's former home on the eastern side of Lake Fryken. The modest country house is a sort of time capsule from the author's lifetime and has attracted more than a million visitors since it was opened to the public. Tourists are greeted by the sight of a stuffed goose in the hall, a reminder that one of her best known books is an imaginative children's story about a boy who flies over Sweden on the back of a goose. The boy came from Skåne and so does the stuffed goose. It was sent to the venerable old lady by a couple of young admirers there.

Selma Lagerlöf did not actually write her most famous literature at Mårbacka. Her family had been forced to sell her childhood home and it was not until many years later that she had earned enough money to buy it back. Lagerlöf's grave can be seen in the churchyard at Östra Ämtervik a few kilometres to the south. Head south past the village on a country road that follows the lake shore or cut across to the main route 62 eventually re-joining the E18. Continue east around the lake passing industrial **Kristinehamn**, an important nineteenth-century iron-ore shipment centre. The local economy once depended on the ore that was mined just to the north of here from mineral seams with exotic names like Tasmania, Manchuria and Abyssinia. A number of old iron works have now been

Göta Kanal

Göta Kanal, fondly known as Sweden's 'blue band' is something of an anachronism in these days of high speed trains and air shuttles. The journey between Göteborg and Stockholm can be completed in just a few hours — but on the Göta Kanal it takes 4 days or more. It is this leisurely pace of travel that has endeared the canal to generations of Swedish holidaymakers and continues to attract more than 6,500 leisure boats and hundreds of thousands of visitors each summer.

Göta Kanal was built between 1810 and 1832 by a labour force of some 58,000 men. Its driving force, a naval officer called Count Baltzar von Platen intended it to be a short-cut between the North Sea and the Baltic but its commercial use waned as the railway network expanded. Instead the picturesque canal with fifty-eight locks became a fashionable way to travel between Sweden's two largest cities. It still is today, and for those who do not have their own boat a number of companies operate passenger services along small stretches or the full length of the waterway. The best known canal boats are the old steamers *Diana*, *Juno* (dating from 1874) and *Wilhelm Tham* run by the Göta Kanal Steamship Company which make regular trips between Göteborg and Stockholm from May to September.

They take about sixty passengers on the all-inclusive three night journey although the fare it has to be said, would fund many return rail trips. The old steamers have limited cabin space but compensate for that with a turn-of-the-century charm. The maximum speed is just 5 knots so passengers can easily get off at one lock, walk or cycle along the canal bank and hop back on at the next one. Göta Kanal uses natural waterways for much of its length and the route crosses many lakes including the two largest, Vänern and Vättern. The latter was deemed highly dangerous in the old days and boats were often blessed before setting out.

The canal rises to more than 90m (295ft) above sea level and journeys pass a number of popular tourist attractions such as Läckö Castle, Vadstena and Karlsborg fortress as well as numerous towns and villages. It is open to general traffic from the beginning of May to mid-October although precise dates vary from year to year. Fees are charged per boat and depend on its length and the distance being travelled. Boat hire is available; contact AB Göta Kanalbolag, Box 3, 591 21 Motala ☎ 0141 53510.

turned into tourist attractions. There is little to tempt the tourist in Kristinehamn however. Perhaps Picasso sympathised. Encouraged by a friend who knew the area he gave the community a 15m (49ft) tall stylised Indian head now said to be the largest Picasso sculpture in the world.

Head south from Kristinehamn on route 64 passing near Järsberg's rune stone, one of the oldest runes in Sweden. On the right lies the elegant eighteenth-century **Värmland Säby** manor house which is open to the  public in summer. Leaving Värmland behind the road now crosses into the province of Västergötland with the wild, forbidding and formerly robber-infested Tiveden forest to the east of it. The dark pines, moss

The impressive Varnhem church   *Rörstrand Museum, Lidköping*

covered stones and hidden lakes (one of them, Fagertärn, is famous for red waterlilies which flower in July and August) are the stuff that troll sagas are made of. It is not difficult to imagine the hairy little creatures peering out from behind a tree stump as dusk falls. But Tiveden is far from threatening these days. Much of it has been turned into a national park; there are well marked walking trails, campsites, holiday cottages and plenty of 'watering holes' for hungry humans as well as for the many wild animals who share the forest.

At Sjötorp the road crosses the Göta Kanal, a nineteenth-century engineering feat which took 58,000 men 22 years to build (see Feature Box opposite). Boats can be hired at Sjötorp. The road joins the busy E20 and

✳ arrives at the well-preserved lakeside town of **Mariestad**, 'the pearl of Vänern' according to locals. The quaint old centre has seventeenth-century timber buildings and cobbled streets sloping down toward the water — among them an ancient tannery turned youth-hostel. But like most provincial Swedish towns there is also a utilitarian modern centre just along the road and a lively twice weekly market. The large red brick church is referred to as a cathedral even though it does not have its own bishop. Ferry services operate to the island of Torsö, the largest in a small archipelago which is popular in summer for swimming and other watersports.

South of Mariestad, just off route 48 is **Lake Hornborg** (Hornborgarsjön), a wide marshy expanse famous for its rich birdlife and in particular for the annual dance put on by thousands of migrating cranes. The springtime spectacle predictably attracts flocks of birdwatchers so roadsigns are placed along major routes indicating where you have the best chance of seeing the cranes (the Swedish word is *Tranor*). Every year some 4,000 birds are attracted to this marshy area, their appetites whetted by special 'crane potatoes' grown for them around the lake. Unfortunately the elegant visitors are temperamental performers and can only be seen in late March or April — but the little Bird Museum and Information Centre built on wooden poles over the marshland at Fågeludden highlights the lake's other less flighty feathered inhabitants. It has a number of fixed displays, simulated examples of bird calls and a so-called 'crane discoteque' showing a video of the star attraction. Helpful staff wax lyrical about their favourite subject and will gladly sell you a wooden 'duck' pencil case or a crane coffee mug. As always, there is a cafeteria close at hand.

This is also one of Sweden's most culturally important areas. A country road from route 48 toward Timmersdala and Varnhem follows the eastern side of the Lake Hornborg through farmland and undulating deciduous woods dotted with small lakes. The region known as Valle is one of the oldest cultivated parts of the country. A nature reserve has now been established, protecting local flora like the Lady's Slipper Orchid and anemonae which thrive in the area. Swedish tourists inevitably call in at the thirteenth-century Cistercian monastery church in **Varnhem**. The size and elaborate design make it appear rather ostentatious amid simple farming communities. So much so that the aesthetically inclined King Gustav III wanted to move the whole church and adjacent monastery ruins to Stockholm because he deemed them too grand to be stuck in an obscure rural village. Fortunately he either forgot about the scheme or thought better of it. The church, which contains the graves of a number of Swedish kings was built by Cistercian monks from France. All that now remains of the monastery, which fell into disrepair during the Reformation, is a maze of waist high stone walls with descriptive plaques to fire the imagination. Recent finds have left little doubt about the skill and industriousness of the monks. But rumours that a few lovelorn inmates dug an underground tunnel so that they could secretly visit nuns at the nearby Gudhem convent remain just a good story.

About 10km (6 miles) south of Varnhem is the prehistoric burial ground of **Ekornavallen** with an assortment of stone formations set in a wind- 𝝥 swept meadow. There is a rough tomb, a stone circle and a burial cairn, a variety of ancient funereal styles that indicate the field was used over a 6 to 7,000 year period. Follow the narrow country road south and turn right onto the larger route 184 heading north to **Skara** whose imposing cathe- ♠ dral is the second oldest in Sweden. Scenes from the town's 1,000 year history decorate the unusual 'chronicle well' in the main square. Skara played an important role in Swedish Christianity as the seat of the country's first bishop, but today the area offers diversions of a rather more wordly kind. A few kilometres to the east along route 49 lies the Sommarland (Summerland) amusement park, one of the area's top family ❋ attractions. It is centred on a series of pools and waterslides and activities include 'bunji jumping', water skiing, various fun rides and a pirate ship. Sommarland charges a set entrance fee which includes a number of attractions and use of the pools while a separate 'ride ticket' gives unlimited access to the other amusements. There is a well-equipped campsite nearby. Skara's museum (Länsmuseet) has a separate section for musical instruments which include the country's oldest flute, found in a prehistoric burial chamber.

Sweden's first bishop may have been installed at Skara, but **Husaby**, north on the E20 then west on route 44, has an even better ecclesiastical ♠ pedigree. Its twelfth-century stone church marks a spring where an English missionary called Sigfrid baptised Sweden's first Christian king, Olof Skötkonung. The event brought pilgrims flocking to this unremarkable bit of countryside believing the spring to have healing powers. Unfortunately the water that put an end to Sweden's pagan past has now dried up. Some say it was deliberately blocked by Lutheran priests who got fed up with all the pilgrims. It looks a little sad and deserted today, but a memorial stone above the source — it is called St Sigfrid's Spring in honour of the missionary — tells the story of the historic event. Two medieval graves at the church are said to be those of King Olof and his queen. North of Husaby the Kinnekulle hill gives panoramic views over 🌲 Lake Vänern. The area is famous for its flora and fauna and is perhaps best explored from a marked 45km (28 mile) long walking trail. From Kinnekulle the country road descends to **Lidköping**, an industrial town rescued from obscurity by the presence of the Rörstrand factory, one of the top names in Swedish porcelain. All signposts seem to point there so it is difficult to miss either the factory shop or museum with memorable pieces from Rörstrand's 250 year history. One of the most recent additions is a dinner service specially designed for the annual Nobel celebrations in Stockholm. Guided tours of the manufacturing process are arranged for groups but the highlight is usually the factory shop which does a roaring trade in seconds. An annual 'porcelain fair' is held in Lidköping each August.

Island Hopping Off The Bohuslän Coast

There are some 3,000 islands along the coast between Göteborg and the Norwegian border. Many are deserted bits of barren rock visited only by seabirds, while others support whole communities and attract boatloads of summer visitors. Few have sandy beaches, but the granite polished smooth by centuries of wind and sea is an acceptable substitute. Many islands have small coves with shallow water suitable for younger children. Some have shops and even hotels, while a picnic basket would be useful on the more deserted ones. The summer influx has spawned a confusing array of ferry routes and boating excursions all along the coast. Regular services for people who live there throughout the year are supplemented in peak season, but there can still be queues. Briefly, starting from the south, the entrance to Göteborg's harbour is guarded by two separate groups of islands, the northern and southern archipelagos which both have regular ferry services to and from the mainland. All but three of the main islands are out of bounds for foreigners because of military installations and visitors are warned off by big yellow noticeboards. It can be frustrating to have to remain onboard the ferry while your Swedish fellow passengers go ashore. To make things worse, there is hardly a military installation in sight and you may justifi-

Calm waters surround Göteborg harbour

ably wonder what all the fuss is about. Fortunately the journey is a pleasure in itself and takes 50 minutes to the island of Vrångö (accessible to foreign tourists — and good for swimming) in the southern archipelago. The ferries weave their way through narrow channels between the other islands and the whole trip costs no more than the price of a Göteborg tram ride. To get there take the number 4 tram from the city centre to the end stop, Saltholmen from where the ferries (foot passengers only) depart.

Foreign tourists can visit two islands in the northern archipelago, Hönö and Öckerö. They are more densely populated than the southern islands and the ferries take cars free. The islands are linked to each other by bridge, there is good swimming and, on Öckerö, an attractive old church dating from the 1400s. To get there take a bus or drive to the ferry harbour at Hjuvik on a peninsula north-west of Göteborg. Foreigners can visit the island of Vinga and boats (foot passengers only) depart regularly during the summer from Stenpiren in Göteborg. The ferry to Marstrand runs regularly and from the harbour it is possible to take an excursion to Åstol. You can travel by boat from Skärhamn on Tjörn to Kyrkesund and on to islands such as Käringön (literally 'Old Crone Island') and Gullholmen. There are direct boats from Orust to these islands as well and services go on to Fiskebäckskil. The town of Lysekil (linked to Fiskebäcksil by foot ferry) is a good starting point with regular excursion boats to Smögen in the north and to its own archipelago. Inland, the town of Uddevalla offers similar excursions as well as 'bathing boats' to popular spots in its fjord with some of the region's few sandy beaches. Further north scheduled foot passenger ferries ply between Fjällbacka and its archipelago, calling in at various islands on the way. Services forming part of a road network linking one peninsula with another are usually free as they are run by the government. Scheduled island ferries that belong to the local transport system are by far the best value.

There are deep sea and in-shore fishing trips from most of the larger communities along the coast. For the latest information on these and other boat excursions around the islands contact the local tourist offices. Anyone travelling up to Oslo can catch a boat from Strömstad to Norway or to Sweden's most westerly islands, Kosteröarna.

A picturesque scene off the Bohuslän Coast

Lidköping's old Town Hall, a former hunting lodge, was hauled on rollers to its present location in the 1600s. The removal was at the request of local aristocrat Magnus De La Gardie whose castle Läckö Slott lies on a ragged and beautiful peninsula 20km (12 miles) north of the town. Läckö is one of Sweden's most photogenic castles with unblemished white walls against a blue watery backdrop and is well worth a detour. It was originally used in the thirteenth century by the bishops of Skara but was later given to the De La Gardie family who spared no expense on its refurbishment. Magnus De La Gardie could certainly afford it—at one point he and his wife owned 1,000 properties including several castles. His extravagance seems to have been legendary. A De La Gardie mission to France went down in history not for its political results but for its sheer cost, prompting the Swedish chancellor to comment that he could have achieved the same result by writing a letter. Läckö went into decline after De la Gardie's death but was restored in the 1920s and 30s and opened to the public. It is now partly furnished in Baroque style and otherwise used for temporary exhibitions and cultural events. There are boat excursions around the islands, a small yacht harbour, restaurant and cafeteria.

Take route 44 to Trollhättan passing signs for **Sparlösa** where the local churchyard boasts an unusual rune stone with inscriptions from both the eighth and the eleventh century. Further west, a dark wall of rock topped with pines rises to the right and fencing isolates the road from the surrounding countryside. Such fencing is commonplace in Sweden. Its aim is not to keep people out of the forest, but to keep wild animals, especially elk, off the road. This stretch is meticulously fenced because the forested knolls on either side known as Halleberg and Hunneberg are believed to have the largest number of elks per square kilometre in Sweden. What is a bane for the local traffic department has proved a boon for tourism. Special 'elk safaris' some with 'elk sightings or your money back' guarantees take visitors into the wilds at dawn and dusk when the animals are at their most active. The drivers know where to look and passengers are rarely disappointed — the tourist office at Trollhättan should have more information. At **Trollhättan** a 32m (105ft) drop in the Göta Älv river, once the major obstacle to navigation from the west coast to Lake Vänern, is harnessed into four locks. Ships weighing up to 3,500 tons can now pass and some 13,000 vessels of all shapes and sizes use the locks each year. The river is however allowed its moment of glory on special 'waterfall days' in summer when the lock gates are opened and the water is allowed to thunder wildly down the rocky gorge as it did in the past. It has become a popular tourist attraction. There are good views from Kopparklinten on the west side of the river. Trollhättan is an important commercial centre and local industries include the motor and aircraft manufacturer Saab.

All that now remains is to follow the meandering Göta river back to Göteborg, the beginning and end of this itinerary. Choose the main route 45 on the left bank of the river for speed or the slower but more appealing country road on the right bank with pleasant views of the river valley and surrounding countryside.

Additional Information

Places to Visit

Göteborg
Botaniska Trädgård (Botanical Gardens)
Carl Skottsbergs Gata 22
☎ 031 412488
Open: daily 9am 'till dusk'.

Fiskekyrkan (The 'Fish Church')
Fisktorget
Open: Tuesday to Friday 9am-5pm,
Saturday 9am-1pm.

*Göteborg's Konstmuseum
(Göteborg Museum of Art)*
Götaplatsen
☎ 031 611000/612977
Open: Monday 12noon-4pm, Sunday
11am-5pm.

*Kronhuset (Crown Arsenal and Craft
Workshops)*
Kronhusgatan 1D
☎ 031 117377
Opening times vary, but generally
summers, Monday to Friday 12noon-
4pm, Saturday 11am-2pm. Kronhuset
exhibition hall, Monday to Saturday
12noon-4pm, Sunday 11am-5pm.

Liseberg (Amusement Park)
Örgrytevägen
☎ 031 400100
Open: mid-April to end September
(April and September, weekends only).

Maritima Centrum (Maritime Centre)
Lilla Bommen
☎ 031 101290
Open: weekends 11am-5pm April to
mid-November. Daily June to mid-
August.

*Museums of Ethnography/Archaeology/
History*
East India House
Norra Hamngatan 12
☎ 031 612776/612580/612770
Open: May to August Monday to
Saturday 12noon-4pm, Sunday 11am-
5pm. September to April Tuesday to
Saturday 12noon-4pm, Sunday 11am-
5pm.

*Naturhistoriska Museum
(Natural History Museum)*
Slottskogen
☎ 031 145609
Open: Monday to Saturday 9am-4pm,
Sunday 9am-5pm.

*Nya Älvsborg (New Älvsborg (Elfsborg)
Fortifications)*
By boat from Stenpiren
☎ 031 121025
Open daily mid-May to mid-September.

*Röhsska Konst-Slöjdmuseet
(Museum of Applied Art)*
Vasagatan 37-39
☎ 031 200605
Open: Monday to Saturday 12noon-
4pm, Sunday 11-5pm.

*Skansen Kronan (Museum of Military
History)*
Skansberget
Open: 12noon-3pm Saturday and
Sunday.

Sjöfartsmuseet (Maritime Museum)
Karl Johansgatan 1-3
☎ 031 611000
Open: Monday to Saturday 9am-4pm,
Sunday 9am-5pm.

*Teaterhistoriska Museet (Museum of
Theatrical History)*
Lorensbergsparken
☎ 031 209215
Open: Tuesday to Friday 10am-4pm.

*Trädgårdsföreningen (City Park with Palm
House)*
Open: daily from 7am. Palmhouse from
10am-4pm.

Dals Långed
Baldersnäs Manor
North of Dals Långed, Dalsland
☎ 0531 41213
Open: daily from 10am mid-May to end
August.

Karlstad
Värmland Museum
Sandgrundsudden, Karlstad
Open: Tuesday to Sunday 12noon-4pm
(June to August weekdays 11am-6pm,
Saturday and Sunday 12noon-4pm).

Mårbacka
Selma Lagerlöfs' Home
Östra Ämtervik
☎ 0565 31029
Open: daily 1 May to 1 September, 9am-6pm.

Värmlands Säby (Manor House Museum)
30km (19 miles) south of Kristinehamn
☎ 0551 10143
Open: daily 15 June to 1 September, 11am-5pm.

Informationshuset Hornborga (Lake Hornborg Ornithological Centre)
Fågeludden, Falköping
☎ 0500 91450
Open: early April to end August.

Marstrand
Carlsten Fortress (Fästning)
☎ 0303 60265
Open: June to August daily 12noon-4pm.

Nordens Ark
On route 171, 15km (9 miles) from Smögen
☎ 0523 52215
Open: October to April 11am-3pm, May to mid-June and mid-August to end September 11am-5pm, mid-June to mid-August 11am-7pm.

Lidköping
Läckö Castle
North of Lidköping
☎ 0510 67200
Open: daily mid-June to late August 10am-6pm.

Rörstrand Porcelain Factory Shop and Museum
☎ 0510 22030
Open: weekdays 9.30am-6pm, Saturday 9am-2pm, Sunday 12noon-4pm.

Skara
Skara Sommarland
(Summer amusement park)
Axvall, north-east of Skara
☎ 0511 64000
Open: daily end May to mid-August 10am-5pm (19 June to 1 August, 10am-6pm).

Sunne
Rottneros Park
On route 234, 4km (2 miles) south of Sunne ☎ 0565 60295
Open: early May to end August 9am-6pm.

Tanumshede
Hällristningsmuseet (Rock Carvings Museum)
Vitlycke, Tanum
☎ 0525 20950
Open: May to mid-September 10am-5pm. 1 July to 14 August, 10am-8pm.

Trollhättan
SAAB Museum
☎ 0520 84344
By Hjulkvarnelunds camping
Open: daily from early June to mid-August.

Uddevalla
Bohusläns Museum
Museigatan 1
☎ 0522 39200
Open: Tuesday to Friday 10am-8pm, Saturday and Sunday 10am-4pm (mid-June to mid-August also Monday 10am-8pm).

Useful Information: Göteborg

ACCOMMODATION

Hotels
SAS Park Avenue Hotel
Kungsportsavenyn 36-38
☎ (031) 176520

RESO Hotel Rubinen
Kungsportsavenyn 24
☎ (031) 810800

Sheraton Göteborg Hotel
S. Hamngatan 59-65
☎ (031) 806000

Scandic Crown Hotel
Polhemsplatsen 3
☎ (031) 800900

Hotel Kung Karl
Nils Ericssongatan 23
☎ (031) 805835

Hotel Lorensberg
Berzeliigatan 15
☎ (031) 810600

Novotel
Klippan 1
☎ (031) 149000

Hotel Opalen
Engelbrektsgatan 73
☎ (031) 8100300

Hotel Liseberg Heden
Sten Sturegatan
☎ (031) 200280

Panorama Hotel & Restaurant
Eklandagatan 51-53
☎ (031) 810880

Hotel Allén
Parkgatan 10
☎ (031) 101450

Spar Hotel
Karl Johansgatan 66-70
☎ (031) 420020

Hotel Eggers
Drottningtorget
☎ (031) 806070

Hotel Poseiden
Storgatan 33
☎ (031) 100550

Fogg's Hotel
Gamla Tingstadsgatan 1
☎ (031) 222420

Hotel Ritz
Burggrevegatan 25
☎ (031) 800080

Hotel Riverton
Stora Badhusgatan 26
☎ (031) 101200

Hotel Royal
Drottninggatan 67
☎ (031) 806100

Tidbloms Hotel & Restaurant
Olskroksgatan 23
☎ (031) 192071

Landvetter Airport Hotel
Landvetter
☎ (031) 946410

Guest Houses & Private Rooms
Contact the Göteborg Tourist Office

Youth Hostels (Vandrarhem)
STF Vandrarhem Ostkupan
Mejerigatan 2
☎ (031) 401050 (open summer only)

Kärralunds Gästhus and
Campingstugor
Olbergsgatan
☎ (031) 252761

STF Turiststation
Torrekulla
☎ (031) 951495

Partille Vandrarhem
Landvettervägen
☎ (031) 446163/446501

Campsites
Askim Camping
Askim Beach
☎ (031) 286261

Delsjö Camping
Delsjö Nature Reserve
☎ (031) 252909

Kärralund Camping
(See under Youth Hostels)

Lilleby Camping
Torslanda (about 20km/12 miles from
city centre)
☎ (031) 560867

Kronocamping
Åby
☎ (031) 878884

BANKS
Bank opening hours are Monday to Friday 9.30am-3pm. Some stay open till 5pm on Thursdays. There are three Forex currency exchange offices. They are in the Central Station, Östra Nordstan shopping centre and at Kungsportsavenyn 22. Open daily 8am-9pm.

CAR HIRE
Avis
Polhemsplatsen
☎ (031) 805780

Budget
Kristinelundsgatan 13
☎ (031) 200930

Hertz
Östra Nordstan Shopping Centre
☎ (031) 803730

Landvetter Airport
☎ (031) 946055

CONSULATES
British Consulate
Götgatan 15
Open: Monday to Friday 9am-1pm and 2-5pm.
☎ 031 151327 and 155820

There is no US Consulate in Göteborg. US citizens should contact the US embassy in Stockholm.

MEDICAL HELP

Emergency medical care is available from hospital casualty departments. For urgent medical help out of hours call the duty doctor on (031) 415500

Emergencies
For police, ambulance or firebrigade
☎ 90000

Doctor/Medical information
☎ (031) 415500

Dentist Stampg. 2 ☎ (031) 807800

Hospital Sahlgrenska ☎ (031) 601000

SIGHTSEEING

Paddan
Boats leave from the bridge at Kungsportsplatsen
Open: May to mid-September daily 10am-5pm. Tour takes 55 minutes.
☎ 031 133000

TOURIST INFORMATION CENTRE

Kungsportsplatsen 2 ☎ 031 100740

TRAVEL

Air
Landvetter Airport
(International and domestic flights)
☎ (031) 941000
Airport buses leave every 15 minutes from Drottningtorget next to the Central Station.

Bus and Train Information
Central Station
☎ (031) 104445
Tickets (020) 757575

Bus, Tram and Ferry Information (local services)
Tidpunkten, Central Station
☎ (031) 801235

Taxi
☎ (031) 650000 (No monopoly)

Ferry Services (international)
Scandinavian Seaways (to the UK and Holland)
Skandiahamnen
☎ (031) 172050

Stena Line (to Denmark)
Gögatan 14
☎ (031) 7750000

Seacat (high speed service to Denmark)
Östra Nordstan shopping centre
☎ (031) 7750800

Tourist Information Centres

Bengtsfors
(summer only)
Torget ☎ 0531 16105/16000

Karlstad
The Public Library
Tingvallagatan ☎ 054 195901

Kristinehamn
Västerlånggatan 22 ☎ 0550 88187

Kungälv
Fästningsholmen ☎ 0303 12035

Lidköping
Stadshuset ☎ 0510 83500

Lysekil
Hamngatan 6 ☎ 0523 13050

Mariestad
Hamnplan ☎ 0501 10001/16264

Marstrand
Båtellet
Summer only ☎ 0303 60087

Skara
Skolgatan 1 ☎ 0511 32580

Tanumshede
Affärsvägen 16 ☎ 0525 29770

Trollhättan
Summer only
Stranna, Karl Johans Torg
☎ 0520 14005
For information at other times call
☎ 0520 87886
(For 'Elk Safaris' contact Vänersborg Tourist Office ☎ 0521 71241).

Uddevalla
The Bus Terminal
Kampenhof
☎ 0522 11787

2

THE SOUTH

Every part of Sweden has its own character, but few are as distinctive as the southernmost province of Skåne — the starting point for this itinerary. Skåningar (Scanians in English) are known for their good food, their easy going nature and their broad dialect, a reminder that in common with the neighbouring provinces of Halland and Blekinge the area was Danish until 300 years ago. Skåne's own red and yellow flag often flies alongside the national colours and its rolling fertile fields, cosy villages and aristocratic castles are a far cry from the wild terrain of the north.

The ports of Helsingborg and Malmö are, along with the city of Göteborg on the west coast, the natural gateways for most visitors arriving by car or rail. Political changes in Eastern Europe have also increased the importance of ferry services from Poland and Germany to Trelleborg and Ystad and although Malmö airport has a few international services Copenhagen's busy Kastrup just across the Öresund channel is effectively treated as the major 'local' air gateway.

The shortest and most popular crossing point over the narrow sound that separates Sweden from Denmark is between Helsingør (better known as Elsinor in English) and Helsingborg. Hamlet's legendary castle, Kronborg, slides past on the left hand side as the ferries, many of which take trains as well as cars, squeeze out of Helsingør's cramped harbour. Some 18 million passengers make the 20-minute crossing annually and there have been all sorts of efforts to cut the lengthy queues during summer. A brand new ferry terminal which also houses the main railway station was opened in Helsingborg in 1991 to speed the process and reduce waiting time. Ferries run at least every 30 minutes and are supplemented by smaller foot-passenger-only boats called 'Sound Buses'.

Helsingborg is a pleasant town which, like so many ports and transport ✳ junctions, suffers from its role as a transit point. It is all too easy to charge off the ferry and straight onto the motorway ignoring it completely — a trend the local council is trying hard to combat. There are certainly a number of things which make a stop-over worthwhile and one of them, Kärnan, comes into view almost as soon as the ferry has departed Den-

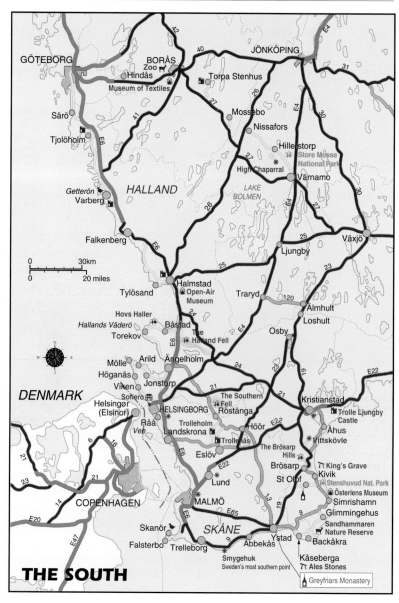

THE SOUTH

mark. The stocky 30m (98ft) high tower dating from the 1300s is all that remains of the fortress that once guarded the then Danish town of Helsingborg. It stands in a raised position above the main square, visible from far out to sea. Visitors who plod up the dark winding steps are rewarded with good views across the water to Denmark and even to Copenhagen on a clear day.

Kärnan, Helsingborg's main landmark, is a reminder that relations were not always so cordial between the Swedes and Danes

Ferries run several times an hour from Helsingborg harbour to Denmark

Helsingborg's strategic position at the narrowest point of Öresund resulted in a troubled and sometimes bloody history. It was first mentioned in a letter written by King Canute of Denmark 900 years ago and developed into an important military and administrative centre. But the city went into decline when its fortress proved defenceless against 'modern cannon'. The long suffering residents ended up right in the firing line during the seventeenth-century wars between Denmark and Sweden and their community was conquered and then lost by the Swedes no less than six times. At one stage the Danes demolished streets full of houses just to get a clear line of fire at their arch enemy. The fifteenth-century church, Maria Kyrkan is one of the few buildings that survived the destruction. It dominates a cramped square just a few minutes walk from Kärnan and its slightly gloomy façade conceals a surprisingly warm and welcoming interior and a fine collection of church silver.

Helsingborg has a compact centre and the best way to get a feel for it is on foot. Not far from the church is the town museum, Stadsmuseet, crammed from top to bottom with an eclectic mix of mementoes and zoological curiosities including an array of stuffed animals. It has one other star attraction which requires absolutely no interest in local artefacts. In summer the Möllebacken (Millhill) café behind the museum serves wonderful freshly baked waffles with whipped cream and conserve in a rustic setting. The steep steps to the café not only help to work up an appetite but reward visitors with a pleasant view across the rooftops. In common with most large Swedish towns Helsingborg has a pedestrianised shopping area. Most of the main stores are on Kullagatan although Stortorget (Big Square) has a number of upmarket boutiques and there is another shopping area to the south. The square also houses the most elegant of the local hotels, the Grand Hotel and, at the harbour end, a statue of Magnus Stenbock who triumphed over the Danes in one of the bloodiest battles ever fought on Swedish soil.

A few metres from the statue is the Town Hall, a grandiose turreted red brick building which has been the object of both love and loathing since its construction 90 years ago. The carved stone relief propped against the front façade commemorates the role played by the city as a haven for refugees escaping Nazi occupied Denmark during World War II. Running parallel with the main pedestrian shopping street is Norra Storgatan with some of Helsingborg's earliest buildings. The half-timbered Jacob Hansson's Hus built in 1641 is the oldest in town and lies somewhat incongruously behind a modern Åhlens department store. Local housewives make the most of their proximity to Denmark, treating a shopping trip to Helsingør rather as they would a weekly visit to the local superstore. Regular travellers can tell you down to the last few *öre* the difference in the price of butter or how much they save on a piece of cheese. Bulging shopping bags bear witness to current bargains. The ferries also provide a daily commuter service for people who live in Helsingør and work in Helsingborg or vice-versa while in the evenings they become a social focus as the source of what is, by Swedish standards at least, cheap beer. Revellers use the shuttle services as a sort of floating bar, consuming large quantities of aptly named 'elephant beer' (elefant ÖL) and often emerging somewhat worse for wear. Liquor is sold only for consumption onboard and the tax free shops stock neither alcohol nor bargain cigarettes although you can buy a small quantity of the latter by showing your ticket. Chocolates and sweets are however available at concessionary rates while the restaurant has good food at reasonable prices. Although the regular services are dominated by ferries to Helsingor smaller passenger boats (no cars) make crossings to the Danish village of Snekkersten, and there are regular services to Grenå on Jutland.

Helsingborg boasts a rather famous bottled beverage of its own — Ramlösa mineral water pumped from an underground source south-east of the town. Ramlösa was, in its heyday, one of Sweden's most elegant spa resorts and many of the old houses still remain. North-east of the centre is Fredriksdals Parken, an open-air museum in the grounds of an eight- eenth-century manor house with a nostalgic collection of old houses, manned shops and workshops dating back to the last century. There is also a popular summer theatre and a botanical garden. Just to the north of the town in a wooded area along the coast lies Sofiero, the much loved summer residence of the former Swedish king, Gustav VI Adolf. It had been a wedding present from his grandparents and when he died in 1973 he willed it to the town. The king was a keen gardener and the grounds are a riot of colour in spring when the rhododendrons blossom. Refreshments are served throughout summer on the castle terrace.

There are plenty of places to swim along this part of the coast, including a beach and bathing house less than a kilometre from the centre of Helsingborg. Between Sofiero castle and the town is Pålsjö Skog, a leafy wood and a popular spot for a stroll.

The simplest route south is undeniably the motorway toward Malmö, but by far the most pleasant is the country road which runs pretty well parallel. First follow the signs toward **Råå**, an old fishing community within Helsingborg's town boundary. The unpronounceable looking name sounds a bit like 'Roe', but even expert linguists may need practice if they want to order the local eel — it is called 'Råå å ålen', literally Råå River Eel. The long low fishermen's homes and cobbled streets are well preserved reminders of the time when this was Sweden's largest fishing community with a complement of 300 trawlers. There is a good restaurant by the harbour, a small fishing and maritime museum and, in summer, regular ferry services to the island of Ven (more information later in this chapter). Råå also has a large campsite and several narrow strips of sandy beach.

From Råå the coast road heads south towards Landskrona across rolling fields with open views of the sound and the Danish coast. The small village of **Ålabodarna**, meaning 'Eel Huts', nestles on a narrow strip of land between the sea and a steep escarpment. As the name implies, eel (usually smoked) is very much a local speciality although all sorts of fish can be bought from local suppliers and smoke houses along the coast.

The town of **Landskrona** is justly proud of its moated sixteenth-century Citadellet (the Citadel), one of Scandinavia's largest and best preserved fortifications. So important was the Citadel to Landskrona's security that the local church, the second largest in the whole province, was demolished during the 1700s, reportedly because it was feared that enemy agents could spy on the fortress from its tower. A new church, the existing Sofia Albertina, was built at a safe distance. Not satisfied with demolishing the church, the Swedish parliament ordered that the whole medieval town be razed in 1747 and a new one constructed on land reclaimed from the sea. In more recent years the Citadel became a prison and a wartime refugee centre. It is now open to the public and houses exhibitions and craft workshops. Landskrona has made up for the decline in its traditional shipbuilding industry by establishing a flourishing horticultural and plant breeding business. The local interest in gardening seems to have taken root at an early stage because this is also the home of Sweden's oldest allotments, dating from 1875 and situated next to the Citadel. These, like allotments elsewhere in Sweden, are no ordinary vegetable patches but deluxe gardens with immaculate miniature cottages that double up as summer homes for weary flat dwellers.

The radical town planning ordered by parliament in the 1700s has left central Landskrona with a classical eighteenth-century look of broad streets and open squares. The local museum housed in a military barracks building contains a permanent exhibition about life at the end of the nineteenth century. One of its most famous inhabitants who took up temporary residence around that time was writer Selma Lagerlöf, an elementary school teacher who went on to win the Nobel Prize for literature.

Landskrona's ferry terminal operates regular services to Copenhagen and to **Ven**, a lush green island with a population of 350 in the middle of Öresund. It has inspired ballads, poetry and a burgeoning bike-hire business. Pedal power (bicycles of all shapes and sizes can be hired near the harbour) is definitely the best way to explore the island, but horse-drawn carriages and tractor-powered wagons are also available in summer. In the late sixteenth century Ven was the home of Tycho Brahe, a leading astronomer. His statue can be seen gazing up at the sky. Some of his castle, Uranienborg and observatory have been reconstructed as part of the Tycho Brahe Museum. Apparently Brahe's academic virtues were not matched by his personal qualities. He lost part of his nose in a duel and wore a false golden proboscis for much of his life. He was also an unpopular landlord whose quarrels with the islanders and with the king of Denmark eventually caused him to leave Ven. He died in Prague where he is buried — reportedly minus his expensive nose.

Tycho Brahe's pew can still be seen in the white twelfth-century church of St Ibb which stands above a steep escarpment at Backafall. The area, a popular spot for an outing, is known throughout Sweden as the subject of a nostalgic ballad.

Back on the mainland, the next major port of call is the university city of Lund. But to see a little of Skåne's 'castle country' try a detour along route 17 from Landskrona toward Eslöv. About 5km (3 miles) before the town lies **Trollenäs** castle with roots from the fourteenth century. Although it is still a private residence it has a permanent exhibition of dolls and part of the castle is open for guided group tours during summer. The parkland and twelfth-century church is open to the public. Separated from the castle by a couple of kilometres and a good few hundred years are the Thule Stones at **Västra Strö**, a mysterious ring formation from Viking times with seven raised blocks, two of which bear runic inscriptions. It is one of a number of Iron Age and Viking remains in an area which forms a geographical border between the flat, fertile plains of central Europe and the primary Nordic rock. The scenery shifts suddenly from farmland to forest as if to counter irreverent quips by northerners that Skåne is too tame and 'as flat as a pancake'.

The next castle with the confusingly similar name of Trolleholm lies about 10km (6 miles) from Trollenäs past Västra Strö. **Trolleholm** was originally built in the 1500s and looks like an illustration from a Hans Christian Andersen fairy story with its green-spired turrets and moat. Romantics may be disappointed to know that it owes much of this fantasy appearance to an imaginative nineteenth-century architect. Trolleholm, like Trollenäs, is a private home and only the park with its rhododendron bushes is open to the public.

Take the road toward Stockamöllan which lies just south of an area dominated by a wooded ridge called Söderåsen. A left turn onto the main route 13 will take you to **Kopparhatten**, one of its most popular walking areas where a broad ravine cuts through the fell. It is signposted from the main road. Also on this stretch of route 13 is **Nackarpsdalen**, another area of nature trails with a small cafeteria and an allegedly bottomless lake. **Billinge**, a nondescript looking village just north of Stockamöllan has a culinary claim to fame thanks to a local bakery devoted to the making of a Skåne delicacy called *Spettkakor*. These very sweet crispy cakes are made by spinning egg yokes and sugar around a central cone to form an edible latticework which can grow to enormous proportions. To continue the itinerary however turn right along the main road in the direction of **Höör** and one of the provinces most popular family attractions, the Skåne's Djurpark (Skåne Zoo) housing some seventy Nordic species. There is also a children's zoo and a Stone Age village which comes complete with a group of live Stone Age residents in summer. A pleasant 2½km (1½ mile) walking trail runs through the grounds and in winter a ski track links the park with the sports centre at nearby Frostavallen. This undulating forested area generally enjoys more snow than other parts of Skåne and has been developed as something of a winter and summer recreation area. There are 250km (155 miles) of marked tracks and paths through the forest which are popular with skiers in winter and walkers and joggers for the rest of the year.

The 'Gästgifvaregård' or local inn at Höör has roots going back to the 1600s and is typical of many in Skåne, a province which prides itself on being the true home of the Swedish *smörgåsbord*. The image of a rotund 'Skåning' tucking into mountainous portions and pausing only to sing jovial songs in praise of food and drink may be a little exaggerated, but it explains why Skåne is sometimes dubbed the 'Kingdom of Food' (Madariket in local dialect). The fertile farmlands traditionally ensured that there was plenty on the dinner table such as roast goose with prunes and apples, boiled ham or locally smoked fish.

From Höör take route 23 south across a peninsula of land stretching out into Ringsjön. On the left is the **Bosjökloster**, an eleventh-century Benedictine convent and once the richest in the whole of Denmark. But the Reformation changed all that and it became the home of a succession of aristocratic families. The current incumbent has popularised the white painted manor by holding regular exhibitions and shows. There is a small museum, a restaurant, golf, boating and fishing. Visitors can also wander around grounds where llamas and miniature ponies roam free past a huge hollow-stemmed oak tree known as the 1,000-year oak.

Continue south on the 23 joining the E22 for the final 20km (12 miles) to **Lund**. Having successfully negotiated the ring road and modern suburbs, motorists would be well advised to park in one of the quiet streets or squares around the edge of the centre. As in many old university towns, pedestrians and cycles rule supreme and anyone who does not get the message will probably find themselves facing down a ticket warden or circling endlessly in pursuit of ever more confusing road signs. Lund is one of Sweden's great seats of learning with some 25,000 students and a major teaching hospital. It was founded in the tenth century and owes much of its early development to the legendary King Canute of Denmark who spotted its potential as an important commercial and cultural centre. The rather grim looking grey cathedral was built some 100 years later in 1145 and is a good starting point for a walk around the heart of the old town. The tourist office is conveniently located diagonally across the road from the church with the Lundagård Konditori, once a famous student watering hole, a little further up the road. Lund's Domkyrka (Cathedral), said to be the finest Romanesque building in Scandinavia, was also the seat of its first archbishopric. The two chunky towers are visible from all around and are affectionately known as Lundapågarna meaning the Lund Lads. But the cathedral's most prized possession is the complex astronomical clock that can be found to the left of the main entrance. It was originally built around 1380 and was referred to by awed contemporaries as *horolgium mirabile Lundense*, the 'wonderful Lund clock'. The relationships between hands showing the sun, moon and stars are linked to phases of the moon, the signs of the zodiac, sun-up, sunset and so on. The clock provides additional entertainment value twice a day when, at the stroke of 12noon and 2pm (1pm and 3pm on Sundays) tiny trumpeters blow a fanfare, a door opens and three mechanical wise men slide slowly past a Madonna and Child. Two knights on horseback bearing the colours of the old adversaries, Denmark and Sweden clash on top of the clock as it strikes.

The cathedral has a fine fourteenth-century altarpiece and carved choir stalls originally built for monks at an associated monastery. All sorts of legends and fables have been told about the two strange stone figures that cling to pillars in the catherdral crypt. The taller figure is said to be 'Finn the Giant' who was immensely strong, although if he ever was a giant he must have shrunk. Legend has it that the other figure is his wife with a child. Less fanciful church literature however suggests the carving is really of Samson as he is about to demolish the temple in Gaza.

The small leafy area next to the cathedral is the Lundagård Park and beyond is the university quadrangle with grand latin-inscribed academic buildings set around a large fountain. The Lund University was founded in 1666 but the oldest of the buildings, a red brick construction with a round tower called Lundagården or 'The King's House' predates it by some 100 years and originally belonged to King Fredrik II of Denmark. It is still in use as, among other things, the department of philosophy. There is a group of six rune stones in one corner of the quadrangle with 1,000-year-old texts recording messages from the Vikings who once inhabited surrounding villages. All the stones have been moved to their current location. Beyond the quadrangle along Sandgatan is the Students Union building and the university library, the largest research library in the country with some 100km (62 miles) of shelves. The Skissernas Museum (Museum of Sketches) at the intersection of Sölvgatan and Finngatan contains an interesting display of 'roughs' illustrating how artists turn their ideas into reality. It houses sketches and sculptures by Nordic and foreign artists including Leger and Matisse. Also on Sölvgatan is the Antikmuseum (Museum of Classical Antiquity) with ceramics, classical sculpture and coins. Adelgatan, one of the city's most attractive streets, heads back toward the cathedral and one of Lund's most popular attractions, Kulturen (the Lund Cultural-Historical Museum). The large and fascinating collection, which was incidentally started by university students, includes a conventional museum covering just about every apsect of life in and around Lund through the centuries and a collecton of rune stones by the entrance. But just when you think you have seen all there is to see, a back door leads out into a sort of village within a town with more than thirty historic buildings ranging from an eighteenth-century vicarage to farms, houses, animal pens and a complete manor. Visitors can step inside most of the buildings and some have their own exhibitions. The houses have been painstakingly moved to their present location from surrounding towns and villages. Kulturen is just a couple of minutes walk from the cathedral.

Lund is a commercial as well as an academic centre with busy pedes-

The 1,000-year-old oak tree at Bosjökloster

trian shopping streets, chic boutiques, arcades and a regular market at Mårtens Torg. The presence of so many students ensures a better than average choice of cafeterias and restaurants.

✳   Sweden's third city **Malmö** is less than 20km (12 miles) from Lund down the main E22 and not much further from Copenhagen on the other side of Öresund. A little of the Danish capital's cosmopolitan street-life has therefore rubbed off on the town and its 250,000 strong population. Regular high speed, low cost passenger boats bridge the gap between the two cities in 45 minutes turning Copenhagen into an obvious target for a day out or a night on the tiles. Services with names like 'The Shopping Line' and 'The Arrow' (Pilen) ply to and fro from Skeppsbron near the central station. These ferries could soon face fierce competition if plans to build a 16km (10 mile) bridge and tunnel across Öresund go ahead. The road and rail link is the subject of much controversy because of its impli-cations for the local environment, but supporters of the scheme are con-fident that they will be able to drive to Copenhagen by the end of the twentieth century. Malmö of course can not really match the excitement of its colourful Danish neighbour and the weekend traffic is mostly in one direction, but it would be unfair to write it off as just another port.

Although the wide-stretched suburbs and motorway network point to a large industrial city, Malmö's centre is surprisingly compact. Like any sizeable town however it can look confusing to the uninitiated so a good way to get a feel for it is to join either the daily guided walking tour of the city or the twice-daily bus tour. Both leave, summertime only, from Malmö Tourist Centre opposite the main station. Alternatively the Rundan sightseeing boats make roundtrips on the canals that encircle the centre. They leave every half hour, May to August from the quay opposite the station and tickets can be bought from the kiosk there. Anyone planning to spend a day or more in the city may well find it worthwhile to buy a Malmö Card which entitles the holder to a number of privileges such as free museum entrance, free bus rides and parking on local authority meters, discount theatre tickets and a complimentary guided tour. The cards, available from the Tourist Centre and hotels are valid for 1 to 3 days

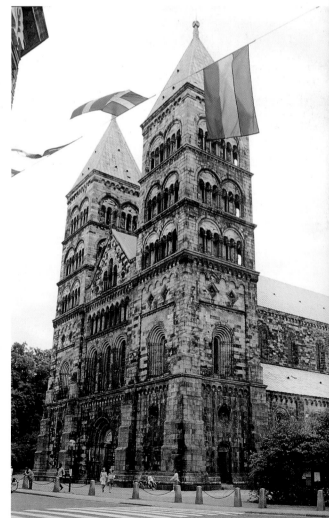

Lund Cathedral is said to be the finest Romanesque building in Scandinavia

with half-price for children. A good place to start any sightseeing tour is the main square, Stor Torget. This was once one of Scandinavia's biggest market squares and it still holds its own with a large equestrian statue of King Karl X Gustav, the man who finally winkled the province of Skåne from the Danes, as its centrepiece. Part of the square is now a parking area. The Town Hall foundations date from the 1500s but the Dutch style façade was extensively renovated during the nineteenth century. The smaller elegant white painted house also bordering the square is the provincial governor's residence. Apoteket Lejonet on one corner is worth a mention because it is the oldest chemist shop in Sweden with a mass of dark wood panelling and dusty old glass flasks — hopefully for display only! The konditori next door has a good selection of *spettkakor*. Diagonally across the square is Jörgen Kock's house, once a medieval merchant's dwelling now a fashionable restaurant. Malmö's most attractive church, St Petri dating from the fourteenth century lies just behind the Town Hall. Unfortunately the rich frescoes that once covered the interior were whitewashed over in the 1500s and most vanished completely during a nineteenth-century restoration.

Malmö's main shopping street Södergatan starts at Stortorget. It is a bustling pedestrian thoroughfare with pavement cafés that lend it a continental flavour. Another pedestrian street to the right reaches Lilla Torg (Little Square), a peaceful cobbled backwater surrounded by seventeenth- and eighteenth-century houses. The square once housed Malmö's leading craftsmen and one of the oldest properties, Hedmanska Gården, now contains a hyper-modern Swedish design centre. Södergatan ends at Gustav Adolfs Torg, a good place to pick up a taxi or bus, but the shops continue on the other side of the square along Södra Tullgatan and Södra Förstadsgatan to Triangeln. Further south in the old working class district is Möllevångstorget, the best and most colourful of Malmö's outdoor markets.

Malmö, once an insignificant farming village was first mentioned as a town in 1250. It remained a Danish city until 1658 but was constantly in the firing line as the Danes and Swedes fought over Skåne. Sixteenth-century Malmöhus Slott (castle) is a legacy of those days. It lies surrounded by a moat and parkland on the western edge of the city centre facing a distinctly twentieth-century container terminal. No-one could describe the plain façade as beautiful but it has been put to good use as the home of five museums including, Stadsmuseet (the City Museum), Konst Museet (the Art Museum) Naturmuseet (the Natural History Museum) the Akvarium and a Tropikarium. Several rooms in the oldest part of the castle have been furnished in period style. In one of them hangs a painting of Mary Stewart whose third husband the Earl of Bothwell was imprisoned here. He is said to have learnt fluent Danish during his 6-year incarceration — quite an achievement. The castle incorporates parts of a medieval mint and fortification from the 1400s.

There are two more museums on the other side of the main road.

Kommendanthuset (the Governor's House) occupies a seventeenth-century arsenal and tells the story of the Scanian wars and Sjöfartsmuseet (the Maritime Museum) has a complete submarine as its star attraction. In summer a 1920s museum tram rattles round the edge of the parkland starting at Banerskajen diagonally across from the castle and ending at the city library with several stops in between. Banerskajen is also known for its lopsided line of matchbox-sized fishermen's houses called 'Hoddarna'.

Malmö's centre is clearly defined by the canal that lines it on three sides. It breaks into an irregular pattern as it runs through the castle park with bridges, paths and ponds providing a pleasant place for a stroll. The main container terminal and harbour area is just to the north while to the south the suburbs stretch on toward a second harbour at Limhamn from where regular services operate to Dragör near Copenhagen airport (Malmö also has scheduled connections with Travemünde and Lübeck in Germany). The city is well endowed with parks and the largest of them, Pildammsparken, stretches several kilometres south from near the City Theatre. There are good sandy beaches less than 30 minutes walk from the centre of town at Ribersborgstranden, a coastal strip and pier that has somewhat hopefully been described as 'Malmö's Copocabana'. Malmö is known in Sweden for its long equestrian traditions and has one of its most famous race courses, Jägersro. It is the only one in the country that holds both traditional trotting competitions in which the jockey sits astride a two-wheel chariot and more familiar racing. During the Horse Sports Week held each summer Stor Torget in the centre of town becomes a scenic venue for show jumping and other equestrian events.

Follow the E6 south from Malmö. The landscape becomes flatter and northerners would say with distaste that the local dialect, always a subject of some amusement further up country, grows even more pronounced. In good weather a detour to Sweden's most south-westerly point is well worthwhile. Millions of birds think so too and this has become one of the best places in Scandinavia to view migrating flocks. Every autumn 100,000's of birds pass over **Nabben**, the most southerly point and experts say that on a good day between August and October you can spot more than fifty different breeds. Turn off the motorway at Vellinge and head for Skanör and Falsterbo, twin communities on a narrow tongue of sand and marsh separated by canal from the mainland. The birds unfortunately are not alone in choosing this landmark for a rest during their migration south. Its fine white sandy beaches and clear water also attract thousands of non-feathered summer visitors creating a potentially tricky mix for the conservationists. The shifting sands at Nabben are therefore protected from human invaders between the end of March and October.

The two neighbouring communities of **Skanör** and **Falsterbo** date back to the the 1100s although devastating fires have changed their character over the years. The long, one-storey houses are typical of fishing villages in southern Sweden but all that remains of Skanör's old fortress is a sorry

A colourful outdoor market stall in Malmö

The Dutch style façade of Malmö Town Hall

looking mound behind the church — its stones were unceremoniously removed in the seventeenth century to pave local roads. Today Skanör and Falsterbo effectively merge and it is difficult to see when you are leaving one and entering the other. Falsterbo lighthouse was built in 1796 to help shipping avoid the dangerously shifting sand banks and now looks out over a smart golfcourse. Low white dunes along this part of the coast flank what must be one of the finest beaches in Sweden. It is popular both with holidaymakers and with beachcombers looking for amber. Sufficient quantities are found for it to support a local amber polishing and jewellery cottage industry.

Return to the mainland and follow the coast road toward **Trelleborg** passing, at Maglarp, a strangely incongruous 90m (295ft) tall wind-powered electricity generator. It is said to be the second largest of its kind in the world but that does not impress the locals who view their high-tech neighbour with ill-disguised loathing. A golf course between the main road and the sea gives way to an Iron Age burial field, one of relatively few in the flat agricultural lands of the south. Practical farmers, understandably more concerned with crop yield than with ancient stones, used to plough up these relics and remove such unwanted obstructions from their land.

Trelleborg, now visibile across the bay, is a small ferry port with services to Travemünde and Sassnitz in Germany. It was so successful as a trading centre during the 1500s that neighbouring towns complained to the Danish king that it was pinching their business. For some reason he

The attractive Lilla Torg in Malmö surrounded by seventeenth- and eighteenth-century buildings

was persuaded to remove Trelleborg's town status in 1619 and it took nearly 50 years before it was returned. The town is particularly proud of its avenue of date palms which it claims are the most northerly date palms in the world, not surprisingly they spend winter in a greenhouse. The road to the east passes typical Skåne farms and villages as it heads toward the attractive old town of Ystad via Smygehuk, Sweden's southernmost tip. The little harbour at Smygehamn sports a signpost telling travellers that they are 1,581km (980 miles) from the country's most northerly tip 'Treriksröset' while London is a mere 989km (613 miles) away. The old lighthouse has been replaced by more modern technology and its buildings are now a youth hostel. A mine and other World War II paraphernalia are displayed nearby as a reminder that Sweden, although neutral, was not immune to the conflict on its doorstep.

While cows, pigs and sheep have their role to play, plump white geese dominate the farmyards of this part of Sweden. There are flocks of them everywhere, blissfully unaware that many will end up trussed and roasted for the traditional 'Mårtens Gås' goose dinner in November. The writer Selma Lagerlöf elevated the Skåne goose to legendary status when she put her young hero Nils Holgerson on the back of one for his 'wonderful voyage through Sweden'. The importance of this fairy story to Swedish culture is even recognised in the stuffy corridors of the national mint which produced new 20kr notes illustrating Nils flying over the fields of Skåne on the back of a goose. The village of Abbekås may look insignificant but is known throughout the nation as the home of 'Joachim the goose', feathered hero of a popular folk song.

✳   **Ystad** is one of Sweden's best preserved medieval towns with a complement of some 300 half-timbered houses. The oldest of them, Pilgrändshuset, dates back to the 1400s and the tourist office proudly points out that so little has changed you can still navigate around the centre with a map from 1753. The narrow streets have curious names like Sladdergränden meaning 'Tell-Tale Lane' and Supgränd, 'Booze Lane' while the spendid Gråbrödraklostret (Greyfriars Monastery) from 1267 is one of Sweden's best preserved monasteries from the period. The unfortunate monks were driven out during the Reformation and the monastery was both a poor house and a state distillery before it was finally restored at the beginning of the 1900s. Ystad has largely escaped the notorious fires that devastated so many of Sweden's old timber-built town centres. One of the reasons may have been the watchman who still symbolically guards over the town from the tower of thirteenth-century Maria Kyrkan (St Mary's Church). Every 15 minutes from 9.15pm to 3am he blows his horn to the north, south, east and west signalling that all is well and that the citizens, presumably immune to the nightly hooting, can sleep safely in their beds. The church has an attractive painted interior and pews beside the entrance once reserved for women waiting to be received back into the church after childbirth.

Ystad is a small town and it is a short step from the past into the present.

Just down the road is a busy rail and ferry terminal linking Sweden with Poland and the Danish island of Bornholm. There are good beaches with camping, a resort hotel and a youth hostel along the coast road heading east. About 10km (6 miles) after Ystad, turn right off the main road (Route 9) following signs for **Kåseberga**. One of Skånes' most mysterious monu- Π ments, Ales Stenar (Ales Stones) can be found here on a windswept down above the sea. The fifty-seven stone blocks set in an oblong shape known as a 'ship formation' have been rightly or wrongly described as Sweden's answer to Britain's Stonehenge. This is the biggest stone ring in Sweden and is said to date from the Iron Age. The stones are thought to have been carried some 20km (12 miles) to the spot, but no one knows how. Visitors can park at Kåseberga harbour from where there are steps up the side of the coastal escarpment and a 500m (1,640ft) trail to the stones. It is an eerie spectacle and well worth the effort.

Just a few kilometres east of Ales Stenar is **Backåkra**, once home to Dag Hammarsjöld, a well-respected UN Secretary General who was killed in a plane crash in the 1960s. His old farmhouse hidden away down a pot-holed dirt track is now a museum devoted to his life and work. 🏠

Water sports enthusiasts may choose to continue along the coast to Sandhammaren Nature Reserve where white sand dunes tail off onto an arc of bathing beaches. Otherwise turn inland through fields and past prosperous looking farms, then right onto the main Simrishamn road. The spooky medieval fortress of **Glimmingehus** is well signposted and al- 🏰 though not big, its red-roof and stepped gable stand out clearly against the flat surroundings. The commanding views were all part of the defensive design which includes an archers' gallery, walls 2½m (8ft) thick and the country's first central heating system. In fact these elaborate measures proved unnecessary as Glimmingehus was never attacked. Work on the fortress started in 1499 and it has been the subject of many legends and ghost stories. On bleak evenings it is said that you can see ethereal ladies in white gliding across the cobbled courtyard. In daylight the local cafeteria and museum look rather more welcoming.

Turn right from Glimmingehus following signs for the colourful little fishing port of **Simrishamn** on Skåne's east coast. Two things have helped shape this pleasant seaside town — the Danes and the local herring. It is still an important fishing port with narrow streets edging down toward the harbour from the grandly named but in reality tiny Stortorget, the 'Big Square'. It is worth taking time to explore some of them. Picturesque cobbled roads such as Stora Norregatan and Stora Rådmansgatan are lined with idyllic one-storey red-roofed houses dating from the 1700s and 1800s and painted in a rainbow of pastel colours. The old fishermen's homes are now much in demand and thus immaculately tended with roses and geraniums at the door and discreet double glazing. St Nicolai ⛪ Church behind Stortorget at the top of the town is thought originally to have been a fishermen's chapel dating from the 1200s. Two ship models presented by fishermen last century confirm its links with the sea. This

The prehistoric Kungsgraven (King's Grave) in the small village of Kivik

The elegant Renaissance castle of Vittskövle, near Åhus

part of Skåne is called Österlen and just round the corner from the church is Österlens Museum with an interesting collection of local folk costume and regional artefacts.

Head north along the main coast road (route number 9) signposted Kristianstad passing small fishing villages, low white painted farms and orchards full of apple trees. There is an 18-hole golf course at Vik and, 6km (4 miles) off the main road to the left, one of Skåne's most beautifully decorated churches, St Olof. The interior has wonderful carved and coloured reliefs from the 1400s and 1500s including one of St Olof carrying a detachable axe. The axe was said to have healing powers and became a point of pilgrimage for the sick. **Stenshuvud** signposted a few kilometres off the main road to the right is Sweden's most recently declared national park — a 120m (394ft) high wooded headland with a network of marked walking paths and nature trails, a good parking area and a popular beach. Just north of Stenshuvud is the small village of **Kivik** which boasts three separate claims to fame. Best known among Swedes is perhaps the annual Kivik's market, a huge commercial free-for-all that attracts some 300,000 visitors each July bringing total chaos to this otherwise peaceful backwater. The second is 'Kungsgraven' (King's Grave), on the southern edge of the community. The 3,000-year-old burial mound must have been built for a local dignitary of considerable standing as it measures 75m (246ft) across and is made up of thousands of stones. A path through the middle

Brightly painted houses in the pleasant seaside town of Simrishamn

ends in a chamber with a prehistoric tomb comprising eight decorated stone slabs. Experts have established that the decorations are strangely similar to ones found in burial chambers both in the orient and on continental Europe. The mound itself may once once have been even higher but has suffered centuries of indiscriminate stone quarrying. Local farmers discovered the tomb in the eighteenth century while taking building materials from the cairn and thinking there might be hidden treasure, investigated further. Unfortunately for them they found only some bones and pieces of bronze. There is a burial field with a number of raised stones across the road and a small cafeteria next to the grave.

Kivik's final claim to fame comes from the cider and sparkling wine produced by Kivik's Musteri (Apple Press) 3km (2 miles) down the road. Apples from the countless local orchards end up here, as does imported grape juice used to make Sweden's only commercially marketed grape wine. Alas the factory shop is not allowed to sell its own wine products because under Swedish law there is too much alcohol in them and they can only be stocked by the Systembolag (State Liquor Store).

Continue north on Route 9 passing signs for **Haväng**, an attractive piece of coastline with a small sandy estuary and another prehistoric stone monument. Haväng's youth hostel housed in a lovely old half-timbered farmhouse not far from the beach must be one of the most picturesque in Sweden. The main road contines through an area of undulating steep-sided hills used mainly as grazing grounds. Brösarps Backar as they are called come alive with wild flowers in spring. Turn right at Brösarp onto the busier Route 19 and head north through flatter countryside either directly to Kristianstad some 40km (25 miles) away or taking the alternative 118 via one of Skåne's most popular seaside resorts, **Åhus**. The elegant Renaissance castle of Vittskövle is just off to the left and to the right is the long flat sandy coastline that attracts thousands of summer visitors. Tourism may be important but Åhus residents joke that their local economy is really founded on three sinful luxuries — snuff, vodka and eels. Unfortunately snuff production has now ceased but the Absolut Vodka factory is in fine fettle churning out what has become an important Swedish export. Such is the local love of eel that it has given rise to a custom called *ålagille* or 'eel fancy' parties where seven different eel dishes are traditionally served. Freshly smoked eel can be bought direct from local smoke houses. In summer Åhus resident population of around 7,000 is multiplied many times over as the holidaymakers arrive. There is a large seaside campsite just north of the centre and an estimated 3,000 holiday cottages for rent. The area around the Åhus old town square has however managed to retain a quiet old world charm with a number of picturesque half-timbered houses and a museum about local fishing and maritime history.

Continue north on route 118 from Åhus to Kristianstad. **Trolle Ljungby** castle some 10km (6 miles) off the road to the east is worth a mention because of the strange legend that surrounds a horn and pipe kept permanently on display in a window overlooking the courtyard. It is said the two items were stolen from the trolls one Christmas night by a castle servant. The family that owned the castle refused to give them back and was subsequently dogged by bad luck.

Kristianstad, a sizeable town and the administrative centre for north- eastern Skåne was founded in the seventeenth century by the Danish king Christian IV as a frontline defence against the Swedes to the north. It therefore bears his name although it is actually pronounced 'Krischanstad'. The centre comprises a typical grid pattern of pedestrian shopping streets brightened up with interesting little sculptures and huge flower displays in summer. Traffic is largely contained on busy thoroughares beyond. The pattern is broken by the Lilla Torg (Little Square) and Stora Torg (Big Square) with the seventeenth-century Holy Trinity church in one corner and the Léns Museum (County Museum) at the other end. A local Film Museum recalls the heady days when Kristianstad, somewhat hopefully dubbed 'Sweden's Hollywood' was the cradle of the nation's early film industry.

Head north from Kristianstad on Route 19 and later the 23 gradually leaving behind the flat farmlands of Skåne and entering the huge forests that dominate the neighbouring province, Småland. This area is known as Göinge and was during the 1600s the scene of fierce battles and guerilla warfare between the Swedes and the Danes. Local farmers and peasants scored some notable successes, most famously at Loshult when they robbed a military transport and made off with most of the Swedish king's war coffer. Unpatriotic Swedish peasants north of the border then helped themselves to what was left. The road crosses into Småland just after Loshult. Turn left after a few kilometres following signs for route 120 and **Älmhult**, an unassuming little community that would probably have been condemned to obscurity had it not been for an enterprising local entrepreneur called Ingvar Kamprad. He founded the worldwide furniture chain Ikea — the name is made up of his own initials and those of his home villages. Älmhult remains Ikea's headquarters and main depot employing some 1,000 local people and still has the very first Ikea store.

Route 23 continues north from Älmhult to Växjö and the famous glass manufacturing district of Småland — refer to Chapter 3. To continue this itinerary follow the 120 for some 26km (16 miles) to Traryd then turn right onto the busy but fast E4 trunk road heading north. Laganland, 10km (6 miles) beyond Ljungby has a motel with tourist information and car museum as well as a commercial exhibition area. Directly to the west is Lake Bolmen, the biggest lake in southern Sweden. The largest of its many islands, Bolmsö, can be reached by bridge or a free ferry and in summer the boat *M/S Kavaljeren* operates regular cruises from Sunnaryd. Leave the E4 at Värnamo and take route 151 in the direction of Hillerstorp, Gnosjö and **Store Mosse** (Big Moss) **National Park**. After a few kilometres the forests, farms and small undulating fields are transformed into a wide expanse of flat marsh and fenland known for its rich birdlife. The road

runs straight across the marsh and has a parking area with local information about ornithological observation towers and walking trails.

Hillerstorp, a quiet community just the other side has an unlikely
neighbour in the form of a Wild West theme park complete with saloons,
mock gunfights, train robbers and a Hollywood-style western town. The
High Chaparral 9km (6 miles) south-west of Hillerstorp is the work of a
 larger-than-life cowboy fan who calls himself 'Big Bengt' and whose
frontier fantasies include a mock fort, 'Indian village', stunt shows and
horse riding. Visitors can stay in the 'Big Bengt Hotel' and there is an
eccentric 'Big Bengt Museum' housing an unbelievable hotchpotch of
memorabilia ranging from typewriters to steam engines.

Stay on route 151 crossing the River Nissan at Nissafors then turn left
onto route 26 and after about 8km (5 miles) turn right along the 27
signposted Borås. The road crosses from Småland into the province of
Västergötland passing forests and small farms. **Mossebo** has an attractive
country church and further on, 11km (7 miles) from the road, is the
 medieval fortress Torpa Stenhus where King Gustav Vasa married his
third wife. Ghost stories abound; the 'grey lady' is said to glide through
its corridors and one tale tells of a nobleman who plastered his daughter
into the wall and left her there to die. **Borås**, set in hilly wooded countryside at the junction of five major roads looks like any other sizeable
modern Swedish town with the usual pedestrian shopping malls and a
pleasant if unremarkable square. But it does have one great crowd-
pulling asset — it is the centre of the country's flourishing mail order
business. Most of the large mail order firms have bargain shops which sell
direct to the public in an area of the city known as Knalleland. They have
in their turn attracted other cut-price wholesalers to the region and bargain hunting has grown into a local sport. Coach tours with nick-names
like the 'Housewives Rally' take shoppers on day-trips to the cheapest
stores and the Borås tourist office can supply lists of likley targets for
independent minded shoppers. The emphasis is usually on clothing and
textiles.

The local retail mania dates back to the days when peddlers from the
area known as *knallar* wandered around the country selling their wares.
They began to settle in Borås which developed an important textile
industry. The district still accounts for half of Sweden's textile manufacture and a museum housed in a former cotton mill in the centre of town
traces its history. The Textil Museet (the Museum of Textiles) contains
300,000 cloth samples and some 2,500 garments. Borås other main attraction is its excellent Djurpark (Zoo) in pleasant wooded surroundings just
north of Knalleland. Both are well signposted from the centre.

Join the fast trunk road 40 heading for Göteborg, 60km (37 miles) to the
west. It cuts a broad swathe through hilly forest-clad countryside before
reaching Landvetter international airport and its final descent toward the
coast and the rocky suburbs of Sweden's second city. Refer to Chapter 1
for a guide to Göteborg and then, for the final stretch of this southern

The imposing Town Hall and square at Borås

Borås Zoo is a great attraction for young children

itinerary, take E6 motorway heading south.

Göteborg owed much to the enterprising foreign industrialists who settled in the city during the nineteenth century. They in turn made their fortunes there and one of them, the wealthy Scottish merchant James Dickson, decided to use some of his money to build an Elizabethan style mansion some 40km (25 miles) south of the city. He probably never imagined that the distinctly un-Swedish looking **Tjolöholm Manor**, signposted from the E6, would soon be attracting scores of day-trippers. In fact he died of blood poisoning and did not even live to see the completion of his Tudor dream home — that was left to his wife Blanche who reportedly had endless disagreements with the bemused Swedish architect before it was finally ready in 1904. Despite its sixteenth-century exterior the house was given the latest in turn-of-the-century 'mod-cons' including bathrooms with showers and a one ton vacuum cleaner which was so heavy it had to be pulled by horse (the horse thankfully remained outside while hoses were pushed through windows). It can still be seen in Tjolöholm's coach museum. The manor has extensive grounds with pleasant lawns stretching down toward Kungsbacka Fjord and a tiny beach. Part of the area is a nature reserve.

While the E6 takes the direct route south there is a good coast road allowing for a more leisurely pace. It is dotted with small holiday cottages and the rocky outcrops and sandy coves provide plenty of bathing possibilities. This is where the cliffs of Bohuslän Province in the north give way to the open beaches of Halland in the south. The campsites and recreation signs bear witness to its popularity as a local holiday destination. The little island of Getterön just north of Varberg is an important bird sanctuary complete with observation towers and a few prehistoric stone piles for good measure. More than 100 species of bird nest here in summer including rare types of mallard, the water rail and the ruff. The island witnessed a different sort of aerial display 3 days before the end of World War II when a British Mosquito aircraft crashed following an offshore dogfight. The pilot was killed, but his companion was taken to hospital and then, according to contemporary newspaper reports, accommodated in some style at Varberg's best hotel until he could be returned to Britain.

Varberg is a pleasant enough place with cobbled streets flanked by a mix of ageing wooden houses and modern office buildings. It was a popular resort and spa as far back as the early nineteenth century when those who could afford it came to enjoy the latest in bathing facilities, mud and seaweed treatment. Not every visitor appreciated the town's qualities however. Bishop Esaias Tegner who stayed there in the 1820s told a friend that it was the ugliest place in Sweden but that in common with ugly women he assumed it would be good for the health! It is still wellpatronised by holidaymakers and there is a fading grandeur in its wooden 'society house'. But Varberg's most famous attraction is undoubtedly its fortress (Fästning) parts of which date back to the thirteenth century. The fortress overlooks the sea and is one of a string of fortifications which remain along the west coast as evidence of its turbulent history and the constant skirmishing between the Danes, Swedes and Norwegians. At the beginning of the seventeenth century it was regarded as one of Europe's most modern fortifications. It is now a museum with pride of place going to the so-called Bocksten Find, said to be Europe's only completely pre-served medieval costume. The clothing was found on a body that had lain undisturbed in a local peat bog for hundreds of years. It was in such good condition that the farmer who made the gruesome discovery called the police and reported a murder. Tests showed however that the victim met his fate 600 years ago and that his killers had staked him to the ground to prevent his spirit from taking revenge. Another prized museum artefact, although of dubious pedigree, is a bullet-button which according to folklore was used to kill Sweden's 'Warrior King' Karl XII in 1718. The legend feeds on the then widely held belief that you had to employ magic to fell an important person who was of course protected by supernatural forces. The lead-filled brass button from the king's own uniform could have done the trick, but the evidence is circumstantial to say the least. Whatever the truth, the museum does a roaring trade in replica button key rings. A cobbled road leads to the fortress from the harbour. Along the way are well-preserved stone and wooden houses from the 1600s includ-ing a pleasantly located youth hostel.

The ever present E6 sweeps past Varberg and on to Falkenberg, its route marked by numerous campsites and seaside recreation areas. **Falkenberg** is a small town with a modern centre that looks just like any other provincial Swedish community. But hidden behind the obligatory pedes-trian shopping street and apartment blocks is a picturesque 'old town' with low pastel-coloured wooden houses and cobbled streets surround-ing the pretty fourteenth-century St Laurentii Church. The walls of the church were built 1m (3ft) thick so that the local population could use it as an ecclesiastical 'bunker' in wartime. The interior artwork has been restored after being painted over in the nineteenth century when it was deemed to offend the sensitive tastes of the period. Next to the old town is Tullbron (the Customs Bridge), a 200-year-old stone bridge which spans the River Ätran. It used to cost one *öre* to cross and the gatekeeper apparently did pretty well for himself.

His income was boosted during the 1800s with the arrival of scores of amateur fishermen eager to try their luck in one of Sweden's greatest salmon rivers. Many were attracted by accounts like those of nineteenth-century British angler and author W.M.Wilkinson who wrote; 'Fishing like this cannot be seen in any river that I have heard of, neither in Norway nor in Canada.' It is not difficult to understand why he was hooked. He is said to have caught a total of 2,834 salmon in 298 fishing days! The local tourist office would have had something to say about that today as there are strict limits on the size and number of fish that can be caught. But well organised conservation work means that Ätran is still self-sufficient in salmon with a season that lasts from March to September. Fishing is permitted right in the middle of the town, next to the old customs bridge and licences can be bought through the local tourist office. Although Ätran is the most famous location there is fine salmon fishing in no less than twelve rivers in Halland Province — a local industry that was in medieval times the exclusive right of the church.

Falkenberg caters for other watersports too and has good sandy beaches within walking distance of the centre. Tiny seaside cottages that sleep up to four can usually be rented from the tourist office. The Swedes take their sun-bathing very seriously and invariably manage to sport a healthy looking tan no matter how fair skinned they are. It could be because they also seem prepared to go bikini and goose-pimple clad on the beach in temperatures that send feeble foreigners in search of their sweaters. The whole coast of Halland Province is dotted with beaches, most of them offering good facilities such as cafeterias, snackbars, showers, changing rooms and first aid. But they can get crowded on hot summer weekends. Anyone looking for solitude may find one of the many inland lakes a better bet.

The E6 speeds on past Falkenberg, but a few miles south of the town a winding, pleasantly hilly coast road follows a more scenic route toward the next major town, Halmstad. On the way, at **Ugglarp**, is a strangely rural Vintage Car and Aircraft Museum with some 30 veteran planes and more than 100 cars while further south an area of wild coastal heather, scattered rocks and windswept shrubbery has been turned into a nature reserve. The best known beach on the west coast is at Tylösand, just north-west of Halmstad. Here, on a warm summer weekend you could even be forgiven for imagining yourself on a Spanish *playa* along with a few charter flights full of holidaymakers. With the beach comes all the usual seaside paraphernalia including summer cottage developments, hotels, camping and caravan sites. Local attractions also include two top-rate 18-hole golf courses, tennis courts, discotheques and several restaurants. Conference facilities and residential housing for Halmstad's overspill however ensure that there is life at Tylösand even out of season.

The city of **Halmstad** just a few kilometres away was Danish until 1645 but is now the administrative centre for the province of Halland. Its most enduring symbol is the statue of *Europa and the Bull* by Carl Milles set in the huge central square, Stora Torg. Although Halmstad dates back to the 1300s, much of it was destroyed by fire in the seventeenth century. Construction mania in the mid-twentieth century finished off many other fine old buildings and the result is an uncompromising mix of styles. Halmstad Slott (Castle), now restored, is one of the few remaining structures from before the fire. It stands in a solitary position by the River Nissan and is the elegant residence of the provincial governor. The most enduring of Halmstad's old properties is perhaps the half-timbered 'Three Hearts' building on the main square which has managed to hold its own against encroaching office developments and now houses a popular restaurant. The town gate, Norre Port, also remains as one of Sweden's few surviving city gates while St Nikolai Church dates from the fourteenth century.

Coffee and cakes are a Swedish national pastime — being enjoyed here at Flickorna Lundgren's picturesque konditori *near Jonstorp, Skåne*

Flowers thrive in the mild climate of Arild, Skåne

Halmstad is a sizeable town by Swedish standards and a good place for some leisurely shopping. Apart from the usual chain stores which have a habit of making urban centres look identical, the traffic-free streets behind the main square have a liberal smattering of small shops and boutiques. Local culture is on show at Museet i Halmstad (the Hälmstad Museum) near the banks of River Nissan just north of the centre. The collection of local folklore paintings is particularly prized. These so called Bonadsmålningar were used as Christmas decorations and were painted on bits of cloth or paper, whatever came to hand or the household could spare. The town also has the obligatory open-air museum, Hallandsgården with among other exhibits, old farmhouses from the region and a school museum. Do not forget to look out for the local salmon here too — it is even honoured in statue form near the river not far from a work by Picasso entitled *Man and Woman*.

The E6 sweeps south across flat, increasingly agricultural land toward Hallandsåsen, a wild forested fell which marks the boundary between the province of Halland and that of Skåne in the south. In the past bands of robbers used to hide here and travellers were considered lucky to make it across without incident. The safest way to journey over the fell was in convoy. But before joining the modern equivalent, a trail of heavy goods vehicles straining up the steep motorway incline, call in at **Båstad**, the home of Swedish tennis. Bjorn Borg served up his first triumphs in this exclusive little seaside resort which plays host to the annual Swedish Open. There are some thirty outdoor tennis courts here and almost as many expensive boutiques and restaurants. In the 1930s the late King Gustav V, would often call in for a game while a new generation of stars now go on from here to be feted at tournaments around the world.

Just along the coast from Båstad lie Trädgårdar (Norrvikens Gardens), a series of formal gardens laid out in various styles ranging from Baroque to Renaissance and from modern to medieval. There is a Japanese garden, a water garden and a forest plantation called Thor's Park which uses species common to Scandinavia thousands of years ago. Behind the gardens a steep road known as the Italian Way rises high above sea level toward Kattvik and **Hovs Hallar** one of the wildest parts of southern Sweden's coastline with steep cliffs and free-standing pinnacles of hard rock. There are plenty of well-marked trails and numerous warnings not to stray from them. The main road leads through an area rich in ancient history to the fishing village and summer resort of **Torekov** with an imaginative little Sjöfartsmuseum (Maritime Museum) ingeniously housed in the stern of an old sailing ship. Boats make excursions from Torekov to the uninhabited island of Hallands Väderö where a seal colony has added an extra dimension to the local bird and plant life.

Follow the minor road south-west from Torekov to Ängelholm. Alternatively the direct motorway route from Båstad crosses the Hallandsås fell passing a large service area and restaurant near the top. On the south side lies the Magaretetorp Inn, an integral part of the local landscape for hundreds of years with roots believed to go back to the thirteenth century. Queen Kristina is said to have rested here during her journey to Rome — reportedly changing into men's clothing so that she would not be recognised. The inn is believed to have been named after another strong-willed queen called Margarete who earned the nickname 'King Trouserless' after reigning supreme over Sweden, Norway and Denmark in the fourteenth century. Margaretetorp lay at the beginning or end of many perilous convoys across bandit country. Travellers still head there in great numbers today because of its pleasant atmosphere and good food.

Helsingborg, the starting point for this chapter, is now little more than 30km (19 miles) away down the E6. But if time allows take route 112 just south of Ängelholm toward Jonstorp and Mölle for a brief detour to the Kullaberg peninsula. Turn off at Jonstorp following the winding country road along its northern edge and look out for a copper kettle hanging by the road just after Svanshall. The idyllic *konditori* known as Flickorna Lundgren (meaning the Lundgren Girls) is one of southern Sweden's most popular 'watering holes', and is famous for its homemade cakes and its coffee served in traditional copper pots. Tables and chairs are scattered among the perennial borders of a cottage garden and do not be surprised to find the odd chicken begging for crumbs. The business was started in the 1930s by some of the Lundgren family's seven daughters who hit on the idea of serving refreshments at their 200-year-old thatched cottage. It was a great success and before long their patrons included the late King Gustav VI Adolf of Sweden who used to pop in while staying at nearby Sofiero Castle. His favourite cakes, shortcrust hearts filled with vanilla cream, are now called Kings Hearts.

A little further along the road lies twelfth-century Brunnby Church with frescoes from the 1500s and, to the right, the picturesque village of **Arild**. The old fishermen's homes that edge their way down the hillside to the harbour have now been largely taken over by summer visitors and commuters. The comparatively mild climate supports lush gardens and even the odd mulberry tree or fig. The narrow road comes to an abrupt end a few kilometres later at **Kullen** where farmland gives way to a rocky promontory crowned by deciduous woods, a large parking area and a lighthouse. It is a favourite place for weekend walks although unpredictable currents can make swimming dangerous. Cliffs rise some 70m (230ft) above the sea in places and there is plenty of evidence of prehistoric settlement including the aptly named but not all that interesting Kullaman's Grave. Not quite prehistoric but considered distinctly primitive by some, is the driftwood sculpture *Nimis* created by a local artist on an isolated pebble shore. The huge structure with rickety walkways and platforms looks like a cross between a child's tree house and a crazed attempt at scaffolding. It has been under threat of demolition from the local authority many times but has so far survived both the council and the elements. To get there go to Himmelstorp and follow the yellow marked path. But wear flat shoes and be prepared for a steep climb down to the shoreline.

The leafy deciduous woods which lead to the peninsula conceal a tricky golf course and several walking trails. Next to Kullen is the old seaside resort of **Mölle**, once regarded as a shameless place because it was among the first to allow mixed bathing. But 'Sinful Mölle' as it became known predictably attracted hoards of daring young things and a fair smattering of voyeurs who came to watch the scandalous goings on. Those days may have gone, but Mölle remains popular and the large vaguely spooky looking Grand Hotel perched above the village is still going strong. There are plenty of cheaper guest houses too and a bizarre model railway emporium called Konstnärsgården where guests can drink coffee in the garden as trains chug around them.

The main road back to Helsingborg passes sixteenth-century **Krapperup** castle; the seven stars on its façade symbolising the crest of the aristocratic Gyllenstierna (literally Gilded Star) family which still owns the castle. Parts of the park are open to the public and in summer there may well be an art exhibition in the 'pig sty' and music in the 'cowshed'.

Höganäs to the south is Sweden's premier pottery town. Rustic dark brown Höganäs pots used to be essential in every Swedish kitchen, not least to keep salt herring and preserves. Today the stoneware pots are just as popular as decorative items and are probably more likely to contain dried flowers than fish. The Höganäs Keramik factory on the outskirts of the town has a factory shop and the area has a concentration of potters and ceramics artists.

There are several windmills in southern Sweden — this one is in the middle of the old village of Viken

Before reaching Helsingborg the route passes the fishing villages of Viken and Domsten which, like so many of their kind, have become distinctly gentrified in recent years. Old **Viken**, with its winding roads, ☀ windmill and long, low fishermen's houses, is particularly worth a visit. The influence of the well-heeled commuter influx (and a few local celebrities) can be seen in the pristine houses and gardens with barely a bolt or a blade of grass out of place. It is somehow rather difficult to imagine the noise and smell of a working fishing community pervading this genteel atmosphere. Todays Viken wife is probably also a business executive and is more likely to get her fish frozen from a Helsingborg supermarket shelf.

Additional Information

Places to Visit

Backåkra (Dag Hammarskjöld's Home)
Löderup
☎ 0411 26010
Open: weekends early May to mid-September 12noon-5pm and daily mid-June to mid-August.

Båstad
Norrvikens Trädgårdar (Norrvikens Gardens)
☎ 0431 71070
Open: May to end September daily 10am-6pm.

Borås
Zoo (Djurpark)
3km (2 miles) from centre on Trollhättan road
☎ 033 138075
Open: daily June to mid-September 10am-4pm or later depending on date. Also open weekends in April, September, October and daily 10am-3pm during schools winter sport fortnight in early February.

Textil Museet (Museum of Textiles)
Druveforsvägen 8
☎ 033 168950
Open: Tuesday and Thursday 12noon-8pm, Wednesdays, Friday to Sunday 12noon-4pm. Closed Mondays.

Bosjökloster
Ringsjöarna (Between the Ring Lakes)
☎ 0413 25048
Park open: daily May to September 10am-6pm.

Fjärås
Tjolöholm Manor and Carriage Museum
☎ 0300 44200
Open: weekends 11am-4pm April, May, September, October and daily June to August.

Glimmingehus
Fortress
South-west of Simrishman
☎ 0414 32039
Open: April to September 9am-5pm, June, July and August 10am-6pm.

Halmstad
Museet i Halmstad (Halmstad Museum)
Tollsgatan
☎ 053 109480
Open: Monday to Friday 10am-4pm (Wednesday also 7-9pm). Saturday and Sunday 12noon-4pm.

Open-Air Museum (Hallandsgården)
Galgberget — near the E6
Buildings open: early June to mid-August 9am-6pm.

Helsingborg
Kärnan (Medieval Keep)
Stortorget
☎ 042 105991
Open: daily April to May 9am-4pm, June to August 10am-5pm, September to March 10am-2pm.

Stadsmuseet (Helsingborg Municipal Museum)
Södra Storgatan 31
☎ 042 105950
Open: Tuesday to Sunday 12noon-5pm.

Frediksdals Park, Theatre and Open-Air
   Museum
Hävertgatan
☎ as above
Open: May to September 10am-6pm (15
June to August 15 10am-7pm).

Hillerstorp
30km/19 miles north-west of Värnamo
High Chaparral Wild West Theme Park
☎ 0370 82220
Open: daily 10am-6pm early June to
mid-August. Weekends only in May
and end August.

Höganäs
Museum
Polhemsgatan
☎ 042 341335
Open: March to December daily 1-5pm.
Closed Monday.

Höganäs Pottery (Factory Shop)
Just north of town centre (route 111)
☎ 042 332075
Open: May to August weekdays 9-
10am, Saturday and Sunday 10am-5pm.

Höör
Djurpark (Skåne's Zoo)
☎ 0413 53203
Open: June to August 9am-5pm, September to May 9am-4pm.

Kivik
Kungagraven (The Kings' Grave)
Grave chamber open: May to September
10am-6pm and during school holidays.

Kristianstad
County Museum (Läns Museum)
Stora Torg
☎ 044 135245
Open: all year.

Film Museum
Östra Storgatan 53
Kristianstad
☎ 044 135729
Open: Tuesday to Saturday 1-4pm.

Landskrona
The Citadel (Citadellet)
Open: daily June to mid-August 11am-4pm.
☎ 0418 25838

Landksrona Museum
Slottsgatan
☎ 0418 79532
Open: Monday to Wednesday and Friday
12noon-4pm, Thursday 12noon-9pm,
Saturday and Sunday 12noon-5pm.

Lund
Kulturen (Lund Cultural-Historical Museum)
Karlins Plats
☎ 046 150480
Open: daily May to September 11am-
5pm, October to April 12noon-4pm.

Skissernas Museum (The Museum of Sketches)
Finngatan 2
☎ 046 107283
Open: Tuesday to Saturday 12noon-
4pm, Sunday 1-5pm. Wednesdays also
6.30-8.30pm.

Antikmuseum (Museum of Classical Antiquity)
Sölvegatan 2
Open: Monday to Friday 9am-1pm.

Medicinhistoriska Museet (Museum of
   Medical History)
St Lars Hospital
☎ 046 172290
Open: Tuesday to Friday 11am-4pm,
Sunday 12noon-4pm except June, July
and August.

Malmö
Form/Design Centre
Lilla Torg
☎ 040 103610
Open: Tuesday to Friday 11am-5pm
(Thursday to 8pm) Saturday 10am-4pm,
Sunday 12noon-4pm.

Malmöhus Castle with Museums of Art,
   Natural History, Municipal History, the
   Aquarium and Tropical House
☎ 040 344437
Open: Tuesday to Saturday 12noon-
4pm. Sunday 12noon-4.30pm. June to
August also Monday 12noon-4pm.

Sjöfartsmuseet (Maritime and Technology
   Museum)
Malmöhusvägen (diagonally opposite
the castle)
☎ 040 344438
Opening times as above.

Kommendanthuset *(Military Museum)*
Opposite the castle
☎ 040 344439
Open: as above May to September.

Vagnmuseet (The Carriage Museum)
Drottningtorget
☎ 040 344459
Open: Friday 9am-4pm.

Konstall (Malmö Contemporary Art Gallery)
St Johannesgatan 7
☎ 040 341293
Open: daily 11am-5pm, Tuesday and
Thursday to 8pm, Wednesday to 9pm.

Råå
Fishery and Marine Museum
Råå harbour
☎ 042 260468
Open: May to September, Wednesday
6-9pm, Saturday and Sunday 2-5pm.
July also Monday, Tuesday, Thursday
and Friday 6-9pm.

Simrishamn
Österlens Museum
Storgatan 24
☎ 0414 13650
Open: daily 1-4pm mid-April to end
September. Longer hours June and July.

Sofiero
Former Royal Summer Residence
Slottsvägen, 10km (6 miles) north of
Helsingborg
☎ 042 140440
Open: May to mid-September.

Torekov
Sjöfartsmuseet (Maritime Museum)
Torekov
☎ 0431 63180
Open: daily throughout summer.

Torpa Stenhus
☎ 033 167087
By Lake Åsunden (follow signs from
Dannike)
Open: May to August Saturday to
Thursday 11am-5pm (daily mid-June to
mid-August).

Trolle Ljungby
Castle
14km (9 miles) east of Kristianstad
☎ 044 55042

Park and courtyard open: on Wednesdays and Saturdays June to August
9am-5pm.

Trolleholm
Castle
8km (5 miles) north-west of Eslöv
Park open: daily until sunset.

Trollenäs
Castle
5km (3 miles) west of Eslöv
☎ 0413 45100/45050.
Castle open: May to September for pre-
booked groups only. Park open daily.

Ugglarp
Vintage Car and Aircraft Museum
Slöinge
☎ 0346 63180
Open: mid-June to mid-August daily
10am-7pm. (10am-5pm to 31 August).

Varberg
Varbergs Fästning (Museum)
Located in Varberg Fortress
☎ 0340 18520
Open: weekdays 10am-4pm, Saturday
and Sunday 12noon-4pm (mid-June to
mid-August 10am-7pm daily).

Ven
Tycho Brahe Museum
Open: 28 June to 15 September.
☎ 0418 169810

Useful Information: Malmö

ACCOMMODATION
Hotels
Anglais City Hotel
Stortorget 15
☎ (040) 71450

Hotel Astoria
Gråbrödersgatan 7
☎ (040) 78660

Garden Hotel
Baltzarsgatan 20
☎ (040) 104000

Mäster Johan
Mäster Johansgatan 13
☎ (040) 71560

Hotel Plaza
S. Förstadsgatan 30
☎ (040) 77100

Hotel Royal
Norra Vallgatan 62
☎ (040) 976303

SAS Royal Hotel
Östergatan 10
☎ (040) 239200

Scandic Crown
Amiralsgatan 19
☎ (040) 100730

Sheraton Malmö
Triangeln 2
☎ (040) 74000

St Jörgen Hotel
St Nygatan 35
☎ (040) 77300

Strand Hotel HB
Strandgatan 50
☎ (040) 162030

Youth Hostel
STF's Vandrarhem 'Södergarden'
Backavägen 18
☎ (0400 82220

Camping
Sibbarps Camping (open all year)
Strandgatan 101
☎ (040) 155165/342650

BANKS
Open: Monday to Friday 9.30am-3pm.
Main offices stay open until 5.30pm some evenings. Foreign exchange is available after banking hours at Forex offices: Norra Vallgatan 60 Open daily 8am-9pm and Gustav Adolfs Torg 12. Open daily 9am-6pm.
The Hydrofoil Terminal, Skeppsbron 4 Open daily 7.30am-7pm.
The Main Post Office, Skeppsbron 1 Open Monday to Friday 8am-6pm, Saturday 9.30am-1pm.

CAR HIRE
Avis
Stortorget 9
☎ 040 77830

Hertz
Skeppsbron 3
☎ (040) 74955

Inter Rent/Europacar
Mäster Nilsgatan 22
☎ (040) 380240

FERRIES
Flygbåtarna (to Copenhagen)
☎ (040) 103930
Pilen (to Copenhagen)
☎ (040) 234411
SAS Svävare (hovercraft to Copenhagen Airport)
☎ (040) 357151
Scand Lines (to Dragör, Denmark)
☎ (040) 103010
Scandinavian Seaways (Helsingborg to Oslo)
☎ (040) 103010
Euroway (to Germany)
☎ (040) 200800
Nordö Link
☎ (040) 111670
TR Line (from Trelleborg)
☎ (0410) 56200
Pol-Line (from Ystad to Poland)
☎ (0411) 16010

SIGHTSEEING
Boat *Rundan*
Departs hourly from opposite Central Station May to August.
☎ 040 117488

MEDICAL HELP
Urgent cases are treated at Malmö Allmänna Sjukus
Södra Förstadsgatan 101
☎ (040) 333685/331180
Doctor on call can be contacted on (040) 331000 7am-10pm then on 331000.
Chemist, City Apoteket Lejonet
Stortorget 8
☎ (040) 71235
Open Monday to Friday 8am-6pm, Saturday 9am-2pm.

Dentist
For urgent treatment ☎ (040) 331000

Emergencies
Ambulance, police, firebrigade ☎ 90000

TAXIS
City Cab ☎ (040) 71000
Malmo Taxi (040) 979797
Taxicentralen (040) 70000

TOURIST INFORMATION CENTRE
Skeppsbron 1
☎ 040 341270

TRAVEL
Air
Sturup Airport (domestic and international flights)
☎ (040) 501101
Airport bus service ☎ (040) 72055

Rail
Central Station ☎ (040) 202100
local services ☎ (040) 236338

Bus Information
☎ (040) 72055

Tourist Information Centres

Borås
Hallbergsgatan 14
☎ 033 167090/167087

Falkenberg
Holgersgatan 22
☎ 0346 17410

Halmstad
Lilla Torg
☎ 035 109345

Helsingborg
Knutpunkten, Järnvägsgatan
☎ 042 120310

Kristianstad
Stora Torg
☎ 044 121988

Landskrona
Rådhusgatan 3
☎ 0418 16980

Lund
Kyrkogatan 11 (opposite cathedral)
☎ 046 355040

Simrishamn
Tullhusgatan 2
☎ 0414 10666

Trelleborg
Hamngatan 4
☎ 0410 53322

Varberg
Brunnsparken
☎ 0340 88770

Ven
25 minutes by boat from Landskrona (summer only)
Landsvägen, St Ibb
☎ 0418 72420

Ystad
St Knuts Torg
☎ 0411 77279

Åhus
Köpmannagatan 2
☎ 044 240106

3
THE SOUTH-EAST

If you ever wondered where those strange hairy Nordic creatures known as troll come from, try peering into a forest in the province of Småland for inspiration. The tall dark pines, mossy boulders, weirdly-shaped roots and shadows would seem the perfect habitat. It has also proved an ideal environment for one of Sweden's most prestigious industries, the design and production of quality crystal and glassware. The so-called 'Kingdom of Crystal' is a central part of this itinerary which starts in the busy town of Jönköping before heading south through the vast Småland forests to the sea. It then turns north along the so-called Blue Coast archipelago, finally completing the circuit via the culturally rich eastern shore of Lake Vättern.

❋ The first port of call, **Jönköping**, has lain at the crossroads for more than 700 years drawing together transport routes from the four points of the compass. These days the main E4 motorway skirts the town on its way north to Stockholm, route 40 beats a direct path west to Göteborg, while two other busy roads link it with the Baltic coast. The town's prime location at the southern tip of Sweden's second largest lake, Vättern, historically gave it an additional maritime link. But what really put Jönköping on the map was a bright idea in the mid-1800s which became known around the world as the safety match. The Jönköping match was the first really effective lighting device that did not threaten to ignite the eyebrows or blow up in the face when struck. It became an instant success and won a medal at the 1855 World Exhibition in Paris spawning a boom in Swedish match production. Jönköping became known as 'The Match-stick Town', a name that has stuck even though not a single match is produced there any longer. The old industrial quarter known as the Tändsticksområdet (Matchstick Precinct) and situated a few minutes from the tourist office off Västra Storgatan has been preserved. It now houses trendy new enterprises and predictably a Tändsticksmuseum (Matchstick Museum) with tableaux showing how matches were made before mechanisation. It was a manual process well into the machine age with men traditionally making the sticks and dipping the heads while women and children filled the boxes. Safety matches were so called because unlike their phosphorus predecessors they had to be ignited against a special friction surface making the ubiquitous matchbox the oldest form of packaging still in use. In Jönköping even the local theatre is called 'The Stick'.

The long-stretched but narrow town centre is effectively divided into east and west by a small channel of water linking Munksjö lake with Vättern. The eastern side still has a pleasant mix of old wooden buildings and pedestrian shopping streets. Take a stroll along Smedjegatan to Östra Torget (East Square) where the elegant old Town Hall from 1699 still has pride of place. Just behind the square is the Länsmuseet (County Museum) with a collection of works by artist and illustrator John Bauer. Bauer was a local man whose evocative pictures of troll and golden-haired princesses, elk and dark dank forests summed up Nordic fairy stories at a brushstroke. Unfortunately his career ended abruptly in 1918 when, at the age of 36 he, his wife and child drowned in a storm on Lake Vättern. The museum also has a representative collection of other Swedish, especially Småland, artists. A couple of short bridges link the two sides of the town at what is effectively its centre. The current Town Hall, a gracious cream-coloured building, stands in its own small but immaculate park nearby. Jönköping's tourist office can be found at Djurläkaretorget, a small indoor shopping centre off Västra Storgatan on the western side of the town with a covered walkway to the railway station. Further to the west is the Stadsparken (Municipal Park) with a collection of historic wooden buildings, animal compounds housing goats, sheep and deer and a bird museum said to have Scandinavia's largest collection of stuffed birds. It is a popular spot for a Sunday stroll with refreshsments in summer at Värdshuset Stugan and regular dances in the park's 'dance rotunda' — do not expect to find a trendy disco. Boat excursions on Vättern usually depart from Jönköping harbour in summer although the times and programmes vary. They may include evening trips with a dinner dance or day sightseeing tours with light refreshments. The best bet is to check with the local tourist office.

Some 19km (12 miles) north of Jönköping is **Habo** church, one of Sweden's most remarkable and beautiful churches and well worth a visit if time allows. To get there follow route 47/48 toward Falköping and Hjo. About 7km (4 miles) after it has parted company from the 195 turn right following the signs for Habo church. The plain looking red wooden façade conceals an incredible painted interior in which the two Jönköping artists commissioned to decorate it have left hardly a centimetre of bare wood. What makes it even more remarkable is that this is no tiny country church but has room for 600 people.

It was built in 1723 with seating that followed the strict pecking order of the day. The six boxes both sides of the altar were for the local landed gentry, ordinary farmers had to make do with pews in the centre while humble crofters were put at the back. The interior was painted in the 1740s

THE SOUTH-EAST

with the Ten Commandments depicted along the side walls, the Creed or Articles of Faith on the ceiling underneath the galleries and the Lord's Prayer on the walls above the galleries. The main ceiling paintings show the Baptism, the Confession and Absolution, the Holy Communion and the Blessing. According to legend one of the artists was portraying the Devil in the picture of 'Deliver us from Evil' when the subject himself came into the church. The Devil is said to have climbed up the ladder and told the hapless artist; 'I am ugly, but not as ugly as you have painted me....and now I will make you even uglier'. With that the painter fell off his perch and scarred his face. Habo church was once the centre of the local community with no less than seven approach roads, but these days the village itself lies some 4km (2 miles) away.

There are a number of other local excursion possibilities from Jönköping. The neighbouring town of **Huskvarna** is known for its kitchen

Market day in Växjö

One of the many surrealistic sculptures by the artist Calle Örnemark, Riddersberg

appliances these days, but it was originally a centre for weapons manufacture. The trade thrived on Sweden's wars and border skirmishes during the seventeenth and eighteenth centuries and some of the homes and smithies built to house local gunsmiths can still be seen in Smedbyn (Smithy Village). Many have been turned into trendy arts and crafts studios but one or two, like Appelbladska Smedjan (Appelblad Smithy) have been preserved with their original contents intact. Huskvarna is also the unlikley setting for a Swedish version of 'Madame Tussaud's' known as Dr Skoras Vaxkabinett (Wax Cabinet) with a collection of famous people from the past and present. The emphasis is predictably on Swedish characters. It can be found just off the E4 north of the centre. The E6 motorway between Jönköping and Huskvarna however has the real crowd puller — a modern shopping centre called the A6 which is said to be the largest of its kind in Sweden. It straddles the road and has a 'Tropical House' with various parrots, reptiles and animals as an added attraction.

Anyone with a taste for the bizarre may enjoy an outing to **Riddersberg** 10km (6 miles) south of Jönköping where a crumbling life-size effigy of *The Bounty* lies marooned on dry land. The strange surrealistic ship is one of a number of odd wooden sculptures by artist Calle Örnemark scattered around the grounds of his former home. Any suggestion that small is beautiful seems to have passed Örnemark by in this creative period of his life although his first statue is said to have been just 10cm tall. Not far from *The Bounty* is a 103m (332ft) high pillar of scrap timber called *The Indian Rope Trick* and a huge grumpy looking giant. Other smaller works, all made of scrap timber and other unlikely accessories dot the grounds while the manor itself houses contemporary art exhibitions and a small shop. To get to Riddersberg take route 33/31 from Jönköping toward Nässjö, it is signposted from the road.

One of Örnemark's monumental works, the *Giant Vist*, has escaped from the park and can be seen by the E4 near Huskvarna. According to legend Vist was going to cross Lake Vättern with one stride and to help his wife over he threw a sod of earth into the middle as a stepping stone. The sod became Visingsö Island.

From Jönköping follow the E4 southward in the direction of Värnamo passing Taberg, a 350m (1,142ft) high hill and viewing point some 5km (3 miles) to the right, then take route 30 toward Växjö. Hok Manor is a renowned hotel and conference centre with an 18-hole golfcourse and Vrigstad is known for its twice-yearly fairs held every May and August.

Växjö — it looks unpronounceable but sounds rather like 'Veksher' — is the bright, well-kept capital of Kronoborg's Län, the second of Småland's two counties. Hidden away among the expansive forests, it has all the status of a large urban centre but the feel of a small town. The imposing governor's residence looks out over the congenial cobbled Stortorget (Market Square) where stall holders and shoppers all seem to know one another. Depending on the time of year you can choose from crates full of funghi, cranberries and bilberries freshly gathered from the surrounding area as well as local vegetables and flowers. There is a good central parking area on the other side of the square with the tourist office just across the road. The main pedestrian shopping street, Storgatan, runs from the square and has a couple of offshoots heading down towards the railway station. They include the usual chain stores and boutiques and a local handicraft shop on Kungsgatan. Towering above the low rise buildings are the oddly shaped twin spires of Växjö Cathedral. The building lost its characteristic profile in the 1600s when the spires were damaged by fire and had to wait until the 1950s before they were finally restored. The cathedral itself is from the twelfth century although the interior looks surprisingly modern.

But Växjö's main appeal to overseas visitors is as the jumping off point for Småland's renowned glass district and for its associations with the mass emigration of the late 1800s. Between 1850 and 1930 no less than 1.3 million impoverished Swedes left their homes to start a new life in America. Many never saw Sweden again although descendants have since returned in their thousands to trace their ancestry. Most head for Utvandrarnas Hus (House of the Emigrants) which has Europe's largest collection of books and documents on emigratrion history including old church registers and inventories. There is also an informative exhibition about the exodus with contemporary photographs, letters and documents to show how the population explosion of the nineteenth century strained peasant life to the limits. With a basic diet of potato, soured milk and cranberry it was hardly surprising that so many Småland peasants packed their bags and headed overseas. A fortunate few struck it rich. The museum devotes one display to a man who became known as 'Lucky Swede' after making millions in the Klondike gold fields. He married a dancehall girl and lived in great luxury until finally his luck ran out and he went bankrupt. For most immigrants life in America was rather more mundane as the displays and tableaux show. Apparently Swedish girls were renowned for hard work and cleanliness and were much in demand as house servants, often commanding higher salaries than their menfolk.

The Emigrants House is a few minutes walk from the town centre and well signposted. It also has a small cafeteria. Next to it is the Smålands Museum with a glassware section containing examples of local design and workmanship. The museum has displays ranging from archaeological finds to forestry and gives pride of place to emerald jewellery that once belonged to Växjö's most famous daughter, the nineteenth-century opera singer Kristina Nilsson. The jewellery caused a stir in 1986 when it was stolen from the National Museum in Stockholm and sold quite openly at auction. Växjö's best known contemporary protégé is of the tennis star Mats Wilander.

Five kilometres (3 miles) north of the town are the ruins of Kronoborg Castle, the scene of an annual folklore pageant and many a summer picnic. There is not much left of what was once a powerful Vasa fortress, but the

The Glass Trail

Glass has been made in Sweden since the 1400s. The first customers were the churches followed by discerning members of the aristocracy who quickly latched onto this continental fashion accessory. As demand grew so did the need for skilled craftsmen and for huge amounts of fuel to fire the furnaces. Småland's long iron working tradition and vast forests made it the ideal choice and in 1742 the Kosta glassworks was founded there. Others followed — there are now fifteen works within an 80km (50 mile) wide area. All are marked on a special *Kingdom of Crystal* map available from local tourist offices. Note that the word *bruk* in Swedish means 'works' or factory.

Orrefors, Kosta and Boda are the most famous and although part of the same manufacturing group the factories have maintained their distinct style. The other glassworks, arranged alphabetically, include:

Åfors Glasbruk; also part of Kosta Boda and known for its avant garde design, often in the form of one-off pieces.

Älghult Glasbruk; another part of the large group, makes restaurant and other table glasses.

Bergdala Glasbruk; best known for its simple blue-rimmed bowls.

Gullaskruf Glasatelje; the smallest of the works, unlike many others it smelts its own colours.

Johansfors Glasbruk; part of the Kosta Boda concern, makes mainly table glasses.

Lindshammar Glasbruk; famous for its coloured glass.

Målerås Glasbruk; known for its crystal reliefs depicting animals.

Nybro Glasbruk; specialises in pressed ornamental glass and has produced items for two successive Winter Olympics.

Rosdala Glasbruk; makes glass for lamps.

Sandvik; specialises mainly in 'stemware' table glasses.

SEA Glasbruk; part of Kosta Boda producing mainly ornamental glass and giftware including 'frosted' designs.

Skruf Glasbruk; a small manufacturer whose speciality is a water barometer based on an eighteenth-century design.

All have factory shops which are, as a general rule, open between 10am and

location on an islet in Lake Helgasjön is pleasant and summer visitors can indulge in homemade waffles with conserve and cream at the old grass-roofed homestead called Ryttmästargården. The veteran steamboat *Thor* makes regular excursions from a jetty near the ruins in summer. Kronoberg dates back to the 1300s but came into its own as a royal fortress in the sixteenth century. Its best known occupant was however peasant leader and rebel rouser Nils Dacke who managed to take it over and 'drink Christmas away' there in 1542. A few kilometres to the east is a popular beach, campsite and recreation area with canoe hire. Teleborg Castle, 3km (2 miles) south of Växjö is comparatively new even though it looks like something out of *Sleeping Beauty*. It is open to the public in summer. Just down the road is a bizarre local diversion known as *echo tempel*. The old water tower — described as an 'anchovy tin on stilts' — became so popular that the council had to lay on parking facilities. To get the best

4pm although it may be later (shorter hours at weekends). Most allow visitors into the works to watch the manufacturing process. The exceptions are SEA and Målerås, but times vary according to day or season. Växjö tourist office should have a precise list. As a rough guide, production is usually in full swing at most works between 10am and 3pm.

It would be wrong to complete this section without a brief word about the product itself. Glass must have at least 24 per cent lead in it to be called crystal. Other ingredients include sand (54 per cent), potash and arsenic all of which are heated to 2,600°F, (1,420°C) before they melt. Until fairly recently the furnaces were fuelled by enormous quantities of wood, but electricity and oil have now taken over. The moulten material has the consistency of syrup and to produce handmade glass craftsmen still use relatively simple tools such as a $1\frac{1}{2}$m (5ft) long blowing pipe, a mould for the rough shape, scissors and tongs. It takes 10 long years of training to become a 'master glass blower'.

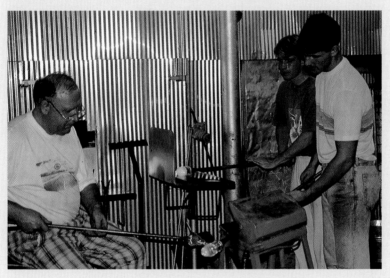

echo (15 to 20 repeats, they say) stand under the middle of it.

Växjö is the starting point for a privately owned narrow gauge railway that rattles at a leisurely pace along 187km (116 miles) of track to the east coast town of Västervik. This is not the transport for people in a hurry, but a relaxing way to see more of the countryside. It runs only in summer using orange coloured 'rail buses' from the 1950s and the occasional steam engine. Tickets are available from the station an hour before departure.

Växjö sometimes calls itself the 'capital' of the Kingdom of Crystal, but to see the great manufacturers at work you have to take route 25 (or the train) in the direction of Kalmar. There are some 13 major glass works scattered among the dense forests between the two towns plus another three or four further north. Among them are internationally famous names such as Kosta/Boda and Orrefors — now part of the same group — whose products have become synonymous with Scandinavian design and quality. Most of the glassworks allow visitors to watch the manufacturing process and they all have low-price factory shops selling seconds that look like 'firsts' to untrained eyes. Tax free shopping, packaging and shipping are usually readily available. The main text of this chapter will deal with three manufacturers covered in the itinerary.

Information boards and maps along route 25 leave motorists in no doubt that they are entering *glasriket* — the glass kingdom. The first factory known as *glasbruk* in Swedish is **Sandvik** while on the left the road passes Strömbergshyttan, an important retail outlet for some of the big names with its own Tourist Information Centre. Continue along route 25 to the village of **Lessebo**, famous not for glass but for high quality handmade paper. The tradition has passed from father to son for 300 years and has managed to survive even though today's machines can turn out in half a minute what Lessebo produces in a whole day. The factory has guided tours in summer.

Turn left at Lessebo following signs for Kosta and Orrefors along a typical forest road where the tall pines are broken only here and there by the odd red-painted cottage. There is a small glassworks called SEA on the left just before the road enters **Kosta** and signposts 'Kosta Glasbruk'. The size of the parking area leaves little doubt about the popularity of this venue and in summer the number of languages there can equal any UN conference. Inside the factory compound is a glass museum, shop and cafeteria as well as the workshop where visitors are allowed to wander freely as long as they keep a safe distance from the dangerously hot moulten glass. With incredible skill the craftsmen scoop shapeless bits of red hot 'syrup' onto the end of long metal pipes, blow briefly at the other end, then twirl it in an apparently arbitrary way until suddenly there is a wine glass or a vase hanging there. They do not seem the least put off by all the attention and whirring video cameras but then it takes 10 years to train craftsmen in the art of making handblown glass. They nearly always work together in teams which include the master, the blower and the stem maker.

Kosta, founded in 1742, is the oldest glassworks in the area and one of the best known names. The shop is huge and factory discounts normally put prices 40 per cent or more below those you would expect to pay in the high street. There are guided tours in English all year round.

If time allows, leave the village of Kosta and turn left for the 22km (14 miles) drive to **Orrefors**, another of the great names in glass blowing. The road unexpectedly transforms into a 'secret' runway in the middle of the forest and finally emerges at the small Orranäs lake with swimming and camping. Orrefors Glasbruk is signposted to the right. The label has won acclaim for its golden stemmed 'Nobel' glassware now used at the annual prize-giving dinner in Stockholm and its factory museum has a wonderful collection of engraved artefacts from the 1920s and 30s. At Orrefors visitors watch from a viewing gallery above the workshop floor which gives a birds-eye view of the process from beginning to end. Anyone who wants to see the engraving process should telephone in advance. Orrefors is traditionally famous for its heavy cut crystal vases, bowls and tableware, but has a wide range of modern designs too. The shop sells the entire production range at the customary 40 per cent or more off normal retail price.

Two glassworks may well be enough for most visitors although the next part of the route skirts another four before heading through 'emigrant country' to the coast. The itinerary can be cut short by taking trunk road 31/25 from Orrefors direct to Kalmar.

To continue however, follow trunk road 31 in the opposite direction and turn left for **Boda**, another glassworks community 18km (11 miles) away. The Boda label is famous for its design and the factory shop, although smaller than Orrefors, is worth a visit. There is a greater emphasis on avant garde design here with coloured bowls and serving plates adding an extra dimension to the more conventional glassware. Boda Nova sells tableware and other household items just down the road but despite the name it is no longer part of the Kosta/Boda concern.

Join the main route 25 heading west to Algutsboda and from there take the minor country road on the left passing glassworks communities at Johansfors and Skruf to Akerby in the parish of **Ljuder**. The name will be familiar to anyone who has read Wilhelm Moberg's moving novel, *The Emigrants* as the home of his two main characters, Karl Oskar and Kristina, whose fictional journey to the new world has come to represent the real-life exodus of hundreds of thousands of people. The crossroads at Åkerby was once a meeting place for families setting out on their long journey west and a commemorative stone bears an inscription about those who left. A few kilometres to the right is Ljuder church, built in 1843 with considerable sacrifices from the impoverished parishioners. Visitors there have sometimes found it hard to separate fact from fiction. One local clergyman was apparently asked if the church still had 'the wedding crown' presented to it by a local good-time-girl when she became a posh pastor's wife in America. Neither the donor nor the crown ever existed outside of Moberg's books.

About a kilometre the other side of the Åkerby crossroads is a tiny red cottage signposted 'Korpamoen', the name Moberg gave to Karl Oskar and Kristina's home but in reality an old peasant dwelling that has been moved to more or less the right 'fictional' location. It is open at limited times in summer but there is not much to see inside or out. All around though the small timber houses and pocket-sized fields wrested from stoney clearings show how hard it must have been to eek out a living. These days many are just summer homes. Determined Moberg fans may want to carry on down winding unmetalled forest roads past Moshult to the isolated community of Mosuhultmåla (about 8km/5 miles from the main road) where an inscribed stone marks the author's birthplace.

Join route 120 signposted Emmaboda either from Mosult or by heading south along the Ljuder road to **Långasjö**. A 200-year-old peasant small-

Ronneby's pleasant town square

Old Ronneby has cobbled streets and immaculate pastel-coloured wooden houses

holding used in the film *The Emigrants* is now a local tourist attraction here. The village in general did rather well out of former emigrants who returned to set up businesses here and at least one local industry is said to have been founded on money from the Klondike gold rush.

Follow the fast 120 trunk road past Rävemåla turning left for Hallabro to join route 30 bound for Ronneby in the province of Blekinge. This south-eastern corner of the country is sometimes referred to as the 'Garden of Sweden' although initially it does not look much different to Småland. The land slopes imperceptibly down toward the sea in three bands. In the north the stoney soil supports mainly pines and birch, then, as cultivation increases, come oaks and maple trees. The milder coastal climate in the south allows chestnut and walnut trees to flourish before the land finally gives way to a ragged green archipelago. Blomstergården (the Flower Garden), is a kind of floral 'Never-Never Land' complete with a fairy-tale castle that defies the poor conditions in the north of the province. It has been re-opened after years of neglect and includes a cafeteria and souvenir shop. To get there turn left off the main road at Backaryd and continue toward Eringsboda.

All of Blekinge's towns lie by the coast. **Ronneby** like the rest of them, once belonged to Denmark and was an important merchant centre for international trade with Sweden. The Swedish monarchs apparently took a dim view of its prosperity and much of the town was destroyed in the mid-1500s in what became known as the 'Ronneby bloodbath'. The discovery of iron-rich spring water there in 1705 put the town and possibly those who believed in the water's beneficial properties back on their feet. It became a popular health spa favoured by high society from all over Sweden. The large Brunnsparken (Spa Park) with its grandiose Victorian villas and pavilions is a legacy of those days and now provides a pleasant place for an afternoon stroll. The old spa hotel has been transformed into one of Sweden's largest hotel and conference centres with a golf course next door. A market is still held in the park each July following in a tradition started by local farmers and peasants who used to sell their goods to the hotel's gentrified inhabitants.

Ronneby's compact centre lies the other side of the Ronneby river around a pleasant open square. The oldest part is up a steep hill next to the twelfth-century white stone Heliga Kors Kyrka (Holy Cross Church). The church, with perilously low hanging chandeliers and a solemn ticking clock has wall paintings from the fourteenth, fifteenth and sixteenth centuries and a marvellously ornate pulpit from 1620. It was the last refuge for Ronneby's townsfolk during the bloodbath and marks on one door along the north wall are said to have been made by axe and fire as the Swedes tried to winkle them out. The setting is rather more peaceful these days with quiet cobbled streets and immaculate pastel-coloured wooden houses. Some have been turned into craft workshops and boutiques. There is an old mill building at the highest point behind which water, now harnessed by hidden turbines, used to rush down the steep drop.

Ronneby's tourist information office is near the church in the Kulturhus, a local cultural centre housing a cafeteria and exhibition hall.

It is a few minutes drive along the Ronneby river to the sea. In summer a local ferry makes several trips an hour between the jetty at Ekenäs and Karön, the nearest offshore island and Ronneby's best bathing area. The island restaurant becomes a popular nightspot on balmy evenings. Regular archipelago boats also go from Ekenäs along the coast to Tjärö, an island nature reserve with deciduous woods, heathland, meadows and plenty of smooth rocks or sandy beaches to swim from. It also has a restaurant, youth hostel and rowing boat hire.

To continue the itinerary take the main route 22 in the direction of Karlskrona. The area around Hjortsberga and Johannishus just a few kilometres down the road is known for its ancient burial grounds and monuments. One of the most remarkable is Björketorpstenen (the Björketorp Stone), a rune which lives up to the popularly held — but generally unfounded — belief that runes carry terrible curses. To get to it turn left at the sign for Tving, there is a small parking area about not far down the road on the right. An information board with an English description explains the strange stone arrangements and translates the 1,300-year-old Norse runes highlighted in red on one of three tall upright stones. 'The secret of the mighty runes hid I here — powerful runes. Abiding wrath shall plague the man who desecrates this monument. Treacherous death shall be his. I spell his ruin,' it says menacingly.

No-one knows who was buried and protected by the Björketorp rune, but the threatened curse has obviously worked through the centuries because unlike many stones this one has been left in its original place. The other monuments on the site, including two rough stone circles, are older than the rune stone and date from between 0 and AD500. There is another Viking burial ground with 110 graves further down the road opposite twelfth-century Hjortsberga church. Neighbouring **Edestad** church, also from the Middle Ages, was built in an area of strong pagan beliefs and rituals. It had a sacrificial spring and even as late as the eighteenth century the sick would risk warnings of eternal damnation and go there hoping to be cured. Just a few kilometres away down quiet country roads is Blekinge's largest castle, Johannishus.

Karlskrona is 25km (15½ miles) from Ronneby but you have to turn off the main trunk road to see any of the ragged coastline with its small coves and harbours. There is yet another burial ground at Hjortahammar but unfortunately the pleasant little fishing community of Hasslö lies within a Military Protection Zone and is restricted for foreigners.

Karlskrona is Sweden's foremost naval town and roadsigns that welcome visitors claim it has 'wind in its sails'. In 1981 it also had a certain Russian submarine on its rocks. The town hit the international headlines when astonished defence chiefs were informed that a Russian 'Whisky class' submarine had gone aground well inside the Military Protection Zone that guards its sensitive naval installations. At first no-one believed a Russian vessel could get so close to the town and thought it was all part of a training exercise. But the 'Whisky on the Rocks' affair became the talking point not only of Karlskrona, but of defence ministries throughout the Western world. It spawned a whole decade of frantic submarine hunting by the Swedish Navy and a bevy of tongue-in-cheek 'hunt the sub' boardgames. Karlskrona's founder King Karl XI would probably not have been amused. He ordered the building of the town (the name means 'Karl's Crown') in 1680 at a time when Sweden was still a great Baltic power and Russia, a major threat. The Baltic fleet needed an ice-free harbour not only with an eye to Russia, but also to keep arch enemy number one, the Danes, at bay. The island of Trossö was judged the perfect spot and the nation's greatest architects were told to plan a town of broad avenues and grandiose squares suitable for military parades. The king then ordered reluctant inhabitants to move in from neighbouring towns.

There is even today a grandiose feel about Karlskrona that is out of all proportion to its true size. Karl XI's statue presides over Stortorget, a huge windswept main square on the island's highest point with two churches. The most attractive of them is the rounded Trefaldighets or Holy Trinity Church, designed by Nicodemus Tessin, completed in 1750 and largely paid for by the king himself. Unfortunately it was badly damaged by fire 40 years later and had to be almost completely rebuilt. Fredrikskyrkan, the other church, also had to be restored after the same devastating fire that also left 3,000 local inhabitants homeless. The main shopping area is to the north around Ronnebygatan while broad boulevards lead south to the old docks and the marine museum. The tourist information office is next to Trefaldighetskrykan.

Marinmuseet (the Maritime Museum) is one of Sweden's oldest museum's and is justly renowned for its collection of gigantic figureheads that tower over visitors. The first ones were painted in red or yellow ochre but Nelson's victory at Trafalgar ushered in a new fashion for white. Other parts of the collection include ship models and sections of weapons and ship building. There is an imaginative children's playroom on the top floor with rigging, rope swings, and a hammock. Diagonally across the green Admiralitets Torg in front of the museum is Vallgatan whose barracks buildings edge the old naval docks. Admiralskykan (the Admiralty Church) down a little road to the right has an unusual poor box outside — a stocky wooden figure with outstretched hand whose hat lifts revealing a moneybox. The figure, known as Rosenbom, has become one of the wealthiest poor boxes in Sweden since featuring in a popular fairy story by Nobel Prize winning novelist Selma Lagerlöf. Few Swedish visitors would leave Karlskrona without putting a coin under 'The old man Rosenbom's' heavy black hat. According to legend it is an effigy of former dockyard worker Matts Rosenbom who froze to death while out begging on New Years Eve, 1717. He was found by the church next morning with his hat pushed down over his head and his hand stretched out. The current statue is the second 'Rosenbom', the original eighteenth-

Karlskrona's tranquil harbour

Björketorp rune stone is said to carry terrible curses

'Old man Rosenbom' at Karlskrona has become one of the wealthiest poor boxes in Swedem

Galleon figureheads at the Maritime Museum, Karlskrona

century version is inside the church.

Vallgatan reaches the sea at Kungsbron, the old entrance to the town with a dockyard defence called Bastion Aurora to the right. The decommissioned minesweeper Bremön is usually moored nearby and is open for visits in summer. The old dockyard with Sweden's first dry dock was founded at the same time as the town but is not accessible to foreigners. Next to it is a busy modern naval complex that continues Karlskrona's maritime traditions to this day.

Karlskrona has an open-air museum at Vämöparken to the north of the town and, back near the centre, Länsmuseet (the Blekinge County Museum) occupies a grand sixteenth-century house by Fisketorget (the Fish Market). Collections include arts and crafts, porcelain and silver as well as reconstructed period rooms. Local ferry services leave from Fisektorget bound for the archipelago islands off Karlskrona, but unfortunately most of them lie within the sensitive offshore Military Protection Zone and are out of bounds for foreigners. Overseas tourists can however take the boat to Nättraby across the bay or the roundtrip onboard the unflatteringly named *Spättan* meaning 'Flounder'. The oldest residential part of Karlskrona is at Björkholmen on the western edge of the town where streets running north to south are named after ships and west to east after admirals. Bridges link the central district with two further islands, Saltö and Dragsö where there are swimming and recreation areas.

The mass of bays, peninsulas and islands around Karlskrona can be seen from the road linking the town with the E22. Rejoin the trunk route heading first east, then north toward Kalmar. You can get away from the bulk of the traffic by diverting to the right at Jämjö and joining a pleasant coastal road. It passes **Kristianopel**, a peaceful seaside village that may not seem to quite deserve its grand name. But things were not always so quiet here and the early seventeenth-century step-gabled church and crumbling defensive walls are legacies of its time as a Danish border stronghold. The fortress was overrun several times during the 1600s and finally became obsolete when the province of Blekinge fell into Swedish hands. These days Kristianopel is invaded by holidaymakers instead and there are camping facilities, holiday cottages and a youth hostel as well as an attractive old guest house and restaurant. Canoes, rowing boats, windsurfers and bikes can be hired in summer and there are plenty of places along the coast to swim.

The coast road heads north to **Bröms**, a name engraved in the memories of local schoolchidren because of a famous treaty signed here in 1645 between the warring Swedes and Danes. A small stream once marked the frontier between the two countries and the so-called 'peace of Brömsebro' was supposed to be eternal — it lasted just 12 years!

Rejoin the main E22 and continue north to **Kalmar**. The town is usually represented by its castle, Kalmar Slott which looks exactly as a castle should with thick stone walls and sturdy defensible towers. It lies on a small island 200m (656ft) across the water from the main community but can be easily reached on foot by way of two short bridges. Kalmar Castle started out as a defence tower in the 1100s and developed apace with the continual skirmishing between the Nordic countries. Attempts to bring Sweden, Denmark and Norway together at the so-called Kalmar Union of 1397 ultimately failed and the fortifications were needed as much as ever. The castle owes its current appearance to Gustav Vasa and his sons but eventually lost its strategic importance and was used as a distillery, a warehouse and a prison before being restored and opened to the public. The interior is disappointing when compared with the romantic looking exterior although a number of rooms on the ground floor have been furnished in period style with useful descriptions in English. Upstairs apartments stand virtually empty except for the odd picture or chunky oak cabinet. One exception is a tower room with a collection of maritime instruments and stone steps descending to what was once the prison below. There is also a fully equipped castle church.

Kalmar is one of Sweden's oldest towns and the centre retains its low-rise charm having somehow escaped the dulling effect of large concrete shopping malls and office blocks. Situated on a small island called Kvarnholmen and protected by sturdy city walls, it was once known as 'Sweden's lock and key'. Parts of the walls to the east, south and west of the town are still intact. The Domkyrka (Cathedral) which dominates the main square was built in the latter part of the 1600s in a grandiose style reflecting the ego of what was then a great Nordic power. It is said to have been modelled on St Peter's in Rome and has a pleasant light interior and an altar painting depicting the creation of the world, but no bishop. Kalmar's cobbled streets and squares have an air of quiet prosperity and there are plenty of interesting boutiques and shops around Kaggensgatan and Larmgatan. Kalmar County Museum (Länsmuseet) by the harbour is well worth a visit. Much of it is devoted to artefacts that have been retrieved from a seventeenth-century warship called *Kronan* which was found on the sea bed 6km (4 miles) from Öland. A large exhibition and audio visual show with commentary in English has been built up around the project. *Kronan*, one of the Swedish Navy's mightiest and most expensive ships was blown to bits during a sea battle — not, embarrassingly enough, by enemy fire but because her gunpowder supplies accidentally caught fire during a manoeuvre. Only 40 of the 800 man crew were rescued and the incident became a propaganda coup for the enemy. There is, not surprsingly, little left of *Kronan* herself but divers have recovered a wealth of everyday items that give a vivid picture of shipboard life. Displays include combs, belts, buckles, even seventeenth-century hooks-and-eyes as well as more substantial carvings, cannons and a sizeable hoard of gold coins. The floor above the *Kronan* exhibition is devoted to fairy tale illustrator Jenny Nyström.

Just north of Kalmar the 6km (4 mile) long Ölands Bridge, the longest bridge in Europe, links the finger-shaped island just off the coast with the mainland. Take route 137 from Kalmar following the signs for Öland.

✳ **Öland** is known locally as the island of sunshine and wind. It attracts thousands of summer visitors, including the Swedish royal family which has its holiday home here, while the latter accounts for the large number of rickety looking windmills. It is Sweden's smallest province measuring 140km (87 miles) from north to south but no more than 16km (10 miles) at its widest point. The rich farmlands around the coast give way in the centre to a strangely beautiful barren landscape known as Alvaret — a 40km (25 mile) long flat treeless plain covered in low shrubs. Further north there are lush deciduous woods and limestone cliffs and finally a storm-swept pine forest known as Trollskogen (the Forest of the Trolls). The southern tip with its distinctive lighthouse lies in the path of major bird migration routes and is therefore a popular spot for ornithologists from all over Europe. The best way to see the island is to take the road that circles it calling in first at the tourist information centre, Träffpunk Öland (Meeting Point Öland) on the main road just after the bridge. The Ölands Djurpark (Öland Zoo) with a mixture of exotic animals and fun rides can be found about 600m (1,968ft) from the bridge.

For a circuit of the island turn right onto the 136 toward Mörbylånga passing Färjestaden, the pre-bridge 'ferry town' and several of the creaking old windmills that have come to symbolise the island. There were once 2,000 of them and some 400 still remain, protected as national monuments and lovingly preserved by local folklore societies. In reality some of them look too fragile to survive more than a gentle breeze. It is not long before the vast flat expanse of Alvaret comes into view on the left with the road acting as a kind of barrier separating its harsh environment from the

The grand five-towered Kalmar Castle

gently sloping coastal farmlands. Parts of Öland may look bleak, but the island comes alive in spring with wild flowers. The yellow potentilla is the most common of them but there are rare lilies, violets, anemones, primulas and some thirty different species of orchid.

Small villages on the edge of the uninhabited Alvaret line the road. Man has evidently set store by this route for thousands of years. Öland's oldest rune stone Karlevistenen just north of Vickleby commemorates the death at sea of Danish viking Sibbe the Wise in the tenth century, Mysinge hög is a Bronze Age burial mound just south of Resmo church and further on are some 4,000-year-old Stone Age graves. Gettlinge Gravfält south of Smedby is one of the largest burial fields with an assortment of stone settings, circles and tombs from the Iron Age scattered around a local windmill. It is worth turning left off the main road at, for example Degerham, and crossing Alvaret to get a real feel for this very un-Swedish looking landscape. After rejoining the 136 on the other side of the island turn right and follow signs to the right for Eketorps Borg. There, in the middle of the inhospitable moorland is a reconstructed fortress from the fifth century complete with parking area and a kiosk selling tickets and refreshments. Archaeologists found the foundations of houses from the fifth century to the Middle Ages here and are currently restoring the fortress to its former glory. Chickens, pigs and goats roam freely among the reconstructed huts as they would have done 1,000 years ago although why anyone should have wanted to live in this bleak place is a matter for conjecture.

The windmills of Öland have become the very symbol of the island

Return to the main road after which keen bird watchers may enjoy a detour to the island's southernmost point by the **Långe Jan** (Long Jan) lighthouse. The road passes Karl X's wall which was built across the island in 1650 to contain the king's stags and fallow deer and a sizeable herd still remains. A nature reserve surrounds the parking area and bird observation station on the island's southern tip. Some 300 different species of migrating bird have been spotted at this point attracting amateur ornithologists from all over Europe. There is a small Bird Museum and a cafeteria nearby while the 42m (138ft) high lighthouse, built by Russian prisoners of war in 1785, has a public viewing balcony at the top.

Follow the coast road north along the eastern side of the island where flat stony meadows reach down to the sea. There are still more ancient remains at Sandby Church and Runsten. The latter has a rune with an unusual inscription refering to its subject being buried 'in the church' — the only Swedish rune stone to mention a church in its text. Lerkaka to the north has one of the island's finest rows of windmills with five of them in a line along the road although there are seven further on at Störlinge. Off the main road to the left is the local heritage museum at **Himmelsberga** comprising three furnished farms from the eighteenth and nineteenth centuries with refreshments on offer from the museum's own bakery. Gärdlösa church on the left hand side of the main road is regarded as Öland's finest medieval church. Turn left and head inland through green agricultural countryside and woodland following signs for the provincial capital, Borgholm. There is another patch of barren heathland just before the Borgholm Slottsruin (Borgholm Castle Ruins) come into view. Only a bleak looking shell remains of what was once an impressive and elegant castle occupying a strategic position to the south of Borgholm town. What is left of it is open to the public and there is a restaurant and parking area nearby and good walks and picnic spots all around. Past kings may have left Borgholm Castle to its fate, but the royals have not completely deserted Öland. Little more than 1km (½ mile) away and rather less ostentatious is the present royal family's summer holiday home, **Solliden**. The comparatively modest Italian-style villa is set in pleasant gardens which are open to visitors even when the family is in residence. To get to the entrance follow the narrow road past the castle ruins until it reaches a large parking area.

The town of **Borgholm** lies some 40m (131ft) below the castle ruins and can be reached on foot via the steep Garderobs-trappan — literally the Cloakroom Stairs. It is really little more than a large village but in summer its numbers are swelled by thousands of tourists and day trippers. Borgholm has regular summer ferry links with the Timmernabben peninsula on the mainland — the crossing lasts about an hour. There is really not a great deal to see in the town and most people spend only a few hours there before heading off on excursions or to a beach. Öland is a popular destination for ordinary Swedish holidaymakers as well as royal ones and apart from a new hotel and conference development near the harbour,

Borgholm has no less than six campsites within striking distance. Most of the popular holiday areas lie between the town and the island's northern tip, 70km (43 miles) away. The first of them, Köpingsvik is just a few minutes drive from the centre. Sandvik, further north, has a good beach and a large windmill now housing a restaurant and café. There are first rate beaches around Bödasand on the east coast while Trollskogen (the Troll Wood) at the extreme northern tip of the island is an area of twisted storm-swept coastal pines with a nature and information centre and walking trails. Northern Öland's beaches and nature attract an annual influx of tourists and the area has been described as one of Sweden's most popular holiday destinations.

Byxelkrok, a small fishing village on the west coast gets similar attention. There are beaches here too and during the season regular boat excursions run from the harbour to an island National Park called **Blå** **Jungfrun** (the Blue Maiden) just visible off the coast. Many legends have been spun around the 1km (½ mile) wide red granite outcrop. Witches were rumoured to meet there while superstitious sailors refused to use the prefix 'Blue' because they were convinced it would cause a storm. A strange stone labyrinth laid out on flat rock on the island's southern slope and first discovered in 1741 may well have fuelled such beliefs. Blå Jungfrun rises 87m (285ft) over the sea and was turned into a National Park because of its geology and flora which includes linden, maple, oak and ash as well as firs and pines. There are summer only car ferries from Byxelkrok to Oskarshamn although since the bridge was built their future has hung in the balance.

Whether by bridge or ferry, continue the itinerary by returning to the mainland and head north to **Oskarshamn**, a small east coast port with services to Öland, Blå Jungfrun and larger ferries to the more distant island of Gotland. It was also the home of one of Sweden's best loved artists, a woodcarver called Axel Petersson but generally known as 'Döderhultaren' after the parish in which he was born. For years he chiselled his perceptive, humorous caricature figures of farmers, peasants and people in authority using the knots and twists in the wood for additional effect. Local people regarded him as a moody sort and few realised that he was a talented artist. Now, some 70 years after his death, the sculptures fetch huge prices at auction. Many of them can be seen at the Döderhult Museum in Oskarshamn Culture Centre.

Oskarshamn is otherwise a typical provincial town with a pleasant but unremarkable central square and the usual high street shops. Its history goes back to the days of sail and a few old houses from that era still hug the slopes above the harbour. The town lies at the southern edge of the ragged and popular archipelago coastline known as Blå Kusten (the Blue Coast) with islands served by a confusing flotilla of ferries up and down the coast. Excursion boats usually operate in summer from Oskarsham to Västervik in the north although schedules vary and it is best to contact the local tourist office in the main square for details.

The Island of Gotland

Is Gotland really Swedish? Even tourist brochures about the Baltic island 90km (56 miles) from the mainland admit there is some justification for the tongue-in-cheek question. Gotland's history was effectively quite separate from that of Sweden until the seventeenth century and it still has an atmosphere all of its own. It does not look much like Sweden either with its weirdly-shaped limestone formations and *rauker*, free-standing pillars of rock carved out of the sea over thousands of years.

Gotland is the largest of the Baltic islands measuring 140km (87 miles) north to south and about 50km (31 miles) across. The permanent population of 60,000 is swelled in summer by more than 400,000 holidaymakers who go there to enjoy the sandy beaches and what is said to be the mildest climate in Sweden. When it comes to sightseeing the well preserved medieval city of **Visby** deservedly comes top of the list. It was once an important and powerful Hanseatic town; part of an association of merchant centres that dominated trade in the Baltic. The old core is still surrounded on three sides by an impressive 3½km (2 mile) long defensive wall with forty-four watchtowers called Ringmuren (the Ring Wall). It was built in the thirteenth century by Visby's wealthy burghers and merchants largely to keep out the uncouth and rebellious Gotland peasants. Unfortunately they picked on the wrong enemy. The town's legendary affluence was all too tempting and in 1361 the Danish King Valdemar Atterdag invaded Gotland. At first the townsfolk closed the gates and are even said to have cheered from behind their wall as the invading army crushed the islanders outside. But they were next on Atterdag's agenda. His army went on to take Visby, marching through a breach in the wall and helping itself to most of the town's treasures. Stories of carnage and atrocities have been substantiated by recent excavations which revealed the remains of thousands of people including many women and children. The Valdemar's Cross, a stone memorial outside the Ring Wall to the east of the Söderport (South Gate) marks the mass grave of some of those who perished.

The town has about 150 medieval houses in various states of repair but the St Maria Catherdral (1225) is the only one of seventeen churches from the period to have survived intact. The ruins of eleven others can still be seen including St Katarina, a thirteenth-century abbey church by the main square (Stora Torget) and St Nikolaus, another thirteenth-century ruin near the North Gate. The latter is the setting for an annual drama, *Petrus da Dacia* which runs for about 3 weeks from mid-July. Step-gabled houses from the 1200s such as Gamla Apoteket (the Old Pharmacy) can be found on Strandgatan. There are also several attractive buildings from Visby's second period of prosperity in the seventeenth century. One of them, Burmeisterska Huset near Donnersplats houses a Tourist Information Centre (see Additional Information at the end of this chapter) and local craft centre. Also on Strandgatan is Gotlands Fornsal, the Gotland Museum, which chronicles not only the events of the fourteenth century but delves deeper into Visby's Viking past with a collection of Viking treasure. There is a large collection of medieval art and sculpture. The old town is still Visby's commercial centre with shops and cafés around Adelsgatan and small, picturesque streets such as Mellangatan and Fiskagränd. There are strict traffic regulations in the centre and car access for non-residents is restricted at certain times. Not surprisingly Visby has a thriving bicycle hire business in summer.

Daily ferry services run all year from Oskarshamn and Nynäshamn on the mainland to Visby. The crossing takes 4 hours from Oskarshamn and 5 from Nynäshamen and the frequency of sailings depends on the time of year. Several internal airlines also operate flights to the island from a variety of Swedish cities.

About 40 per cent of Gotland is covered in grassy woodland and the island supports an enormous variety of wild flowers including thirty-five different species of orchid. But it is the unusual limestone relief that provides its most distinctive features. They include the so-called Hoburgsgubben (Hoburg Man), a natural rock formation shaped like a head at the southern tip of the island and $2\frac{1}{2}$km (1 mile) of limestone caves called Lummelundagrottorna north of Visby. Some of the most interesting rock formations, and the best beaches, are to be found on the island of Fårö just off the northern tip of Gotland. The Langhammars Rauker, oddly shaped free-standing pinnacles of rock, are among the most photographed but there are plenty more. This is an area of sand-blown pines, patches of moorland, dunes, and grazing land for Gotland sheep, one of the mainstays of the local economy. The name actually means Sheep Island. Note that the southern part of Fårö lies within a Military Protection Zone and is therefore out of bounds to foreigners. Visitors from abroad should not divert off the main route 148 between the village of Rute until they reach the other side of the zone on the island. There are information boards along the road. Gotland incidentally also has its own breed of horse, a sturdy little animal called a Gotlandsruss. The local dialect can apparently be quite a problem for holidaymakers from the mainland who descend on the area in their thousands.

Gotland's strategic position in the Baltic and its mild climate had attracted settlements long before the Hansa merchants appeared on the scene. The island therefore has a large number of Stone and Bronze Age remains and several monuments from the Viking period. There are, for example, 350 'ship formations' in which large stones are laid in the shape of a vessel. One of the best is at Gannarve near Fröjel on the west coast of Gotland others can be found at Gnisvärd, Boge, Klinte and Alskog. From the local church and tower at Fröjel there are views across the water to two small island nature reserves called Stora Karlsö and Lilla Karlsö. Both are famous for their rich bird life and visitors who want to go there have to join summer boat excursions from Klintehamn.

Note that ferries to Gotland can get crowded in peak summer and it is advisable to book well in advance.

The Göta Hotel, a picturesque berth for landlubbers by the Göta Kanal

The countryside becomes more rugged as the E22 heads north. The smart seaside town of **Västervik** lies at the heart of the Blue Coast and is definitely the place for the style-conscious amateur yachtsman. In summer its sheltered harbour is a mass of clinking, creaking rigging while outdoor cafés and a better than average selection of restaurants — it claims to have more per inhabitant than anywhere else in Sweden — give it a continental flavour. Västervik's maritime traditions go back long before the smart set arrived but it was destroyed by fire three times and little of the old town survives. The fifteenth-century St Gertruds Church a few streets back from the harbour on Östra Kyrkogatan is really the only building that is as old as the town itself. Next door is an eighteenth-century poorhouse built by charitable donation. It apparently prompted the uncharitable comment that, 'in Västervik the poor live better than the rich'. There are some neatly restored houses from the 1700s around Strömsgatan and Varvsgatan and a number of listed seamen's homes in Båtmansgatan that are available for rent.

The community straddles Gamlebyviken, a long gash in the coastline with a causeway and bridge joining the two sides. Västervik's tourist office is suitably grand occupying an early twentieth-century bathhouse near the causeway and just a few boat lengths away are the ruins of Stegeholm Fortress built in 1360 and burnt in 1677 by the Danes. The best view of the town is from Kullabacken on the other side of the causeway where there is a local museum.

Västervik is a gateway to the most popular part of the the Blue Coast which in itself is roughly divided into four archipelagos (*skärgård* in Swedish). Closest to the town is Tjust Skärgård, further north off Valdermarsvik is Gryt Skärgård then comes St Anna and finally Arkösund Skärgård. The islands tend to be green and forested near the coast and increasingly barren further out to sea. The local tourist office has up-to-date information on tours and excursions, ferries and even local post boats that take passengers. Motorists can get a landbased feel for the archipelago by exploring one of the many small roads that wind out along irregular peninsulas to villages on the coast. For a change from the main E22 try the country road from Västervik over the thin Norrlandet spit rejoining the main road near Gamleby. Road number 213 from the E66 to the village of Loftahammar is a well trodden tourist route which comes to an end when the land gives way to a frayed patchwork of wooded skerries. There are a number of places to stay including a couple of camping and recreation sites with beach and boat hire facilities around the bay. Using the main trunk road as a point of reference it is possible to make several detours. Further north **Valdemarsvik**, a few kilometres from the main road and situated at the end of a steep sided 'mini-fjord' is the local centre for Gryt Archipelago. It is about 19km (12 miles) from here to Fyrudden, a small community and harbour restaurant jutting out to meet the archipelago. Postboats from Fyrudden take a few paying passengers on their daily tour around nine different islands including Harstena one of the most popular and picturesque of them.

The E22 passes signs for the more northerly St Anna archipelago as it begins to head inland to the next sizeable community, **Söderköping**. This was once a leading hanseatic trading centre and an important spa town but is now only a pale shadow of its thriving neighbour, Norrköping. It still has a pleasant small-town atmosphere, enhanced in summer by the coming and going of boats along the Göta Kanal.

Norrköping just 17km (11 miles) away is currently Sweden's fourth largest city and, other than Göteborg, the only one that still has an extensive tram network. The clanking yellow carriages can be a menace or a delight depending on your persuasion — either way it is worth keeping a wary eye open for them when crossing a street or manoeuvring the car. The town is an important industrial centre and was once nick-named 'Sweden's Manchester' because of its 122 textile factories. It lies at the junction of five major roads. The E4 swishes past on its way to Stockholm linking with the E22 from the south-east in a mass of roundabouts and roadsigns on its outskirts. Other major routes head off to Örebro and Eskilstuna. Norrköping's sprawling industrial suburbs, it now produces pulp and paper, electronics plastics and rubber, leave visitors in no doubt that this is a metropolis by Swedish standards. It has also been called 'the workers' town' and still has in its centre a Victorian cultural landmark known as *industrilandskapet* or 'the industrial land-scape'.

The town is effectively squeezed between the navigable saltwater inlet Bråviken to the east and Glan lake to the west. The water course that links the two, Motala Ström, runs right through the centre of the city and holds the key to much of its past development. To the north of the 'Ström' the main railway station faces an elegant boulevard with hotels, local admin-istrative buildings and the Town Hall. The small green lozinge is called Karl Johans Park and is known locally for its summer display of 25,000 cactuses. Modern development along the water's edge has left space for some pleasant terraces and during the tourist season sightseeing boats run from near Saltängsbron, the most central of the bridges across Motala Ström. The bridge heads straight into the heart of Norrköping's compact shopping and commercial centre. The square Town Hall tower to the left has a public viewing platform from where visitors can look down on a cramped grid pattern of one-way streets. Trams rule supreme in busy Drottninggatan which is closed to private vehicles but there are plenty of parking areas dotted around parallel thoroughfares. The yellow painted bell tower a few blocks from the Town Hall belongs to eighteenth-century St Olai Church.

Norrköping's prestigious Konstmuseet (the Art Museum) is housed in a modern building on the southern end of Drottninggatan. It has a fine collection of Swedish nineteenth- and twentieth-century art and a spin-ning metal spiral sculpture outside that caused local consternation when it first appeared. It has now become something of a landmark. The large modern library lies on the other side of a leafy thoroughfare near the museum. Norrköping's proud industrial past is being preserved for the posterity in Industrilandskapet. The nineteenth-century industrial setting may seem familiar to anyone brought up among reminders of Britain's industrial revolution, but it was comparatively unusual in Sweden's predominantly agrarian society. In its heyday metal workers, wool and cotton weavers all crammed into the industrial buildings along the water. One of the most attractive properties known unflatteringly as 'the iron' has been completely restored and now houses Arbets Museet (the Museum of Work). The general area can be best seen from Gamla Torget but to get to the museum cross nearby Gammlebro and turn left by Holmgränden over a small wooden bridge. Many of the old factories and warehouses are being taken over by small businesses while others await their turn to be rescued from creeping dilapidation. Norrköping's Stadsmuseum (City Museum), also in the industrial area has exhibitions about local trades and crafts while Färgaregården (the Colouring Shed) in parkland on the outskirts of the centre traces the history of textile dyeing.

Craftsmen of a different type were at work thousands of years ago on a flat rock south-west of the town. The **Himmelstalund** rock carvings are between 2,500 and 3,500 years old and include primitive figures of men, wild animals, swords, boats and bear paw prints. There are more than fifty carvings comprising one of the biggest groups in Sweden and unlike some they are easy to reach. The area is signposted off the E4 heading south and a surfaced path leads from the parking lot to the rock. Although high-

A tiny summer cottage on the Blue Coast

lighted in red paint the figures are not large and can take a bit of finding among the splits and puddles in the rock. Unfortunately the heat from a glue factory once sited here has cracked some of the surface.

Anyone planning to stay a few days in Norrköping and visit the zoo and safari park at Kolmården will probably find it pays to buy a Kolmården-Norrköping Card. It is valid for 3 days but is only available in peak season (end June to mid-August). The card entitles holders to free boat excursions, free entrance to the animal park, rides on the historic trams that run in the town centre each summer, free bus travel and a number of other benefits. Archipelago cruises and excursions to various islands, including some along the 'Blue Coast', run regularly in summer from Norrköping. The local tourist office should have the latest schedule.

Kolmården diagonally across the Bråviken inlet is Sweden's most popular animal park and includes a spacious zoo, the country's only dolphinarium, a safari park and a neighbouring tropicarium. It lies in a dark, forested area that was once the haunt of robbers and cut-throats. Today's four-footed inhabitants are rather less menacing although the safari park's zebras and giraffes do look a bit odd grazing among the Nordic pines. To get to Kolmården follow the main E4 in the direction of Stockholm and after some 18km (11 miles) take the right-hand turn signposting the animal park and its neighbour, the Wilderness Hotel. A well beaten tourist road winds through forest and past umpteen cafeterias before reaching first the safari park and then a large parking area near the main entrance. Entrance fees can be quite expensive depending on the season and it is usually cheaper to buy a triple ticket covering the park, safari park and dolphinarium or a family ticket if the party includes two adults and two children. Visitors to the safari park can either take their own cars or join one of the daily bus tours. The main zoo has a separate entrance with a 3km (2 mile) long gondola cablecar circling the area. The animal enclosures occupy a large rambling pine-clad knoll with pleasant walking paths, and plenty of space for the four footed inmates. There are several cafeterias and imaginative children's play areas including a Viking camp and a gingerbread house. Distances can be considerable so the baggage trolleys for hire at the entrance are usually much in demand. At the far end is the dolphinarium with two shows a day or more. The Tropics House opposite the main zoo entrance has a collection of parrots, snakes and other reptiles and an aquarium.

The E4 continues north-east to Stockholm, but to complete this itinerary head back to Norrköping and continue south past the city. A few kilometres later the E4 passes elegant Löfstad Castle, a seventeenth-century manor complete with obligatory resident ghost. The phantom in question is apparently Countess Sophie Piper who never quite recovered from her brother's gruesome death in 1810 at the hands of a baying Stockholm mob. Her shock was understandable as he is said to have been literally torn to pieces in full public view. The victim, a local aristocrat called Axel von Fersen was once romantically linked with the ill-fated French Queen

Marie Antionette and tried unsuccessfully to get her and King Louis XVI out of France during the Revolution. Löfstad Castle lies in pleasant parkland about 1km (½ mile) from the main road. The main road once continued past Löfstad and on to Kimstad. From Norsholm a few kilometres to the south a narrow winding and at times unmade road follows the northern edge of Lake Roxen to Berg. Alternatively follow the E4 straight to the old university town of **Linköping**. The cathedral is the second largest in the country with a 105m (344ft) tall spire clearly visible kilometres away across the flat countryside. Its roots go back to the 1200s. Just behind the cathedral is Linköping's castle which has been changed dramatically over the years and is now the official residence of the provincial governor. But the town's most appealing, and photographed, attraction is the immaculately preserved quarter known as 'Old Linköping', an urban nostalgia with some 80 buildings from the 1600, 1700 and 1800s. They house among other things, an old fashioned general store, craft studios, and a school museum. The development is far from haphazard however and most of the timber houses have been moved to their current location west of the modern town centre from other parts of the community. Many hide up-to-date apartments behind their old world façades.

Linköping has two sizeable museums. Länsmuseet (the County Museum) contains an eclectic mix of local artefacts ranging from archaeological finds to artwork and a not-so-local Egyptian collection. Just outside the town at **Malmslätt** is the Swedish Flygvapenmuseet (Airforce Museum) with a collection of more than 50 aircraft and other pieces of military aviation history.

Head north-west either on the main route 36 or the smaller parallel road to **Berg**. The Göta Kanal meets Lake Roxen here in a series of six locks that look like a watery staircase leading down to the lakeshore followed by a further three just inland. Berg's Slussar is the most concentrated stretch of locks on the canal. It makes for slow progress among the boating fraternity but a good viewing and picnic spot for landlubbers. Also at Berg is the remains of Vreta Kloster, Sweden's first convent. The church, which remains intact, was once intended as a royal burial chapel but all that remains of the convent is a maze of low walls and walkways. Route 36 north-west to Motala crosses Göta Canal at leafy Borensberg near one of the most appealing of the canalside hotels.

The fortunes of the small lakeside town of **Motala** were inextricably linked with the building of the canal and its chief architect Baltzar von Platen. His mausoleum can be seen in a leafy spot on the canal bank at the edge of the community and his statue stands in the town square. Von Platen worked on the canal for 29 years and planned Motala's layout to fit the shape of the Vättern shoreline at the point where the waterway meets the lake. The town was a centre for early Swedish broadcasting and now has a Radio Museum at Bondebacka with refreshments available at the nearby Heritage Museum. There is a small museum about the canal near the harbour. The kilometre long sandy beach at Varamon just north of the town is said to be the best lakeside beach in Sweden.

For the final part of this itinerary follow Lake Vättern's shoreline to **Vadstena** 16km (10 miles) further south. Its narrow streets and pastel timber houses sum up what Swedes like to call 'small town idyll' — an idyll which tends to be broken on summer weekends as coaches and cars disgorge another batch of day trippers. One of the reasons is that Vadstena has a historical significance disproportionate to its size as the home and final resting place of St Bridget (St Birgitta), a revered Swedish saint. Bridgit, a local woman and mother of eight children founded an abbey and religious order here in the fourteenth century after experiencing a series of revelations. Unfortunately she died in Rome in 1371 before the work was completed and was canonised 18 years later after which her remains were returned to Vadstena. They now lie with those of her daugther Chatarina in a decorated velvet casket in the Kloster Kyrka (Abbey Church) also known as the Blue Church. The church was consecrated in 1430 and Vadstena became the focus of a new Birgittine Order throughout Europe. The little town prospered until the Reformation and even then Vadstena convent was one of the last to be closed because its sisters, it seems, had friends in high places.

The plain grey façade of the Abbey Church hides a cavernous interior with two intricate triptyches. The oldest, from 1459, shows St Bridget surrounded by spiritual and secular characters and is housed by the reliquary in the small Brothers Choir just behind the high altar. The second triptych is an elaborate sixteenth-century work from Brussels. The insignificant looking entrance to the right of the altar is known as 'the Door of Grace and Honour' through which a Birgittine nun would pass only twice in her lifetime; once when being admitted to the order and again when her coffin was carried into the church at her funeral. The small hatches in the Brother's Choir were confessionals where ordained monks could listen to a nun's confession through the barred openings. Other medieval convent buildings near the church have been converted into a luxury hotel with conference facilities. Guests tempted to quibble about the bill may care to peep into the dark 2m (7ft) wide reconstructed cells once used by nuns of the order and consider themselves lucky! The oldest of the buildings is a red stone manor house dating from the mid-thirteenth century.

Just the other side of the convent walls is the lopsided looking Mårten Skinnare's Hus (Mårten the Furrier's House) from 1520 complete with a secret hiding place for treasure. The owner was a rich merchant who dealt in pelts but later fell from royal favour. An eighteenth-century Hospital Museum next door was also known as 'the large madhouse' and was the first institution in Sweden specifically for the mentally ill.

While the Birgittine sisters went about their cloistered life at one end of the town, their chief protagonist, the Reformation King, Gustav Vasa was putting down roots at the other. The result was Vadstena Castle, an

The impregnable looking Vadstena Castle and yacht harbour

The main street, Brahegatan, in Gränna

impregnable looking place with thick grey stone walls and a moat that is now effectively part of Vadstena's yacht harbour. Work started in 1545 but was not completed until more than 60 years later. King Gustav Vasa celebrated his wedding here and later installed his son Duke Magnus in the castle. The duke who was mentally unstable was the only one of Gustav Vasa's four sons never to become king and it was probably just as well. According to one story he threw himself out of a castle window in pursuit of what he claimed was a beautiful mermaid who was calling him. His servants had to fish him out of the moat. The castle is open to the public but there is not all that much to see inside. A few rooms at the top contain period furniture and portraits while the larger reception areas house special exhibitions or concerts. Behind the castle is Vadstena's old station from where a museum railway operates in summer.

Follow route 50 south along the Vättern shore. Lake Tåkern on the left is renowned for its varied bird life. About 20km (12 miles) south of Vadstena the road passes **Omberg** Crown Park, a 3km (2 mile) wide forested hill which rises above the surrounding agricultural land before dropping sharply in cliff and cave formations down to the lake on the other side. Its rugged nature is a contrast to the cosy farmland all around and although only 263m (862ft) high, the top, known as Hjässan (Crown of the Head), offers panoramic views. You are supposed to be able to see thirty church towers from the observation platform which is reached by a fairly easy 500m (1,640ft) ramble from the nearest carpark. A network of walking trails and a narrow surfaced road circles the hill and there is a nature centre and youth hostel. Omberg owes its name to Omma, the Queen of the Mists and is known for its varied flora and fauna, not least the large number of orchids that grow wild there. The so-called Western Rock Walls are broken by caves that are accessible only by boat. According to legend they were used by monks during the Reformation to hide ecclesiastical treasures from the king.

Many of those treasures were said to have come from Alvastra Monastery, now just a ruin at the foot of the hill but once a great religious centre founded by Cistercians in 1143. At its height the monastery owned more than 400 farms and contained the grave of St Bridget's husband. But it was destroyed during the Reformation and its stones were unceremoniously carted off to build Vadstena Castle. You need a good bit of imagination there these days, but the crumbling walls and arches dotted with lavender and herbs have a sort of eerie calm.

Sweden's most famous rune stone the **Rök** Stenen lies in this part of Östergötland province and, thanks to the prodigious scribe who hacked his rambling message into the 4-ton granite block, is well worth a detour. Turn left off the main route number 50 in the direction of Broby and Rök — the turn is almost opposite the road that heads up Omberg. A country road winds for some 5km (3 miles) before reaching the stone which stands some 50m (164ft) from the verge next to Rök's white-painted church with an explanatory exhibition nearby. It was discovered in the seventeenth century baked into the wall of a church storehouse, but is now regarded as so important that it has its own little roof to protect it from the elements. It dates from around AD850 and like most rune stones was erected as a monument to a dead kinsman. In this case Varin remembers his late son Vaemod in a long, rambling and obscure text with allusions to heroic Viking legends and ancient stories. He had so much to say that his runes cover both sides of the stone and its edges totalling 800 characters in all — the longest runic message in the world. The script is in 'short twig runes', a particularly complex form of writing that must have left the scholars cooing with delight. Each line is translated and analysed in the neighbouring exhibition area.

From Rök it is only a short distance to the main E4 trunk road heading south toward Gränna, alternatively return to route 50 and turn left, the two roads now run parallel for much of the way. There are good views out across Lake Vättern towards the long flat island of Visingsö as they approach the town. On the way they cross from the province of Östergötland back into Småland. Mention **Gränna** to virtually any Swede and they will automatically think of red and white striped sticks of rock. Gränna 'Polkagrisar' — the name actually means polka-pig, but no-one knows where it came from — are a symbol of this lakeside community. The local industry was founded in the 1850s by an impoverished young widow called Amalia Eriksson who had to find a way to feed and clothe herself and her daughter. She heard of a striped peppermint flavoured confection that was a great succes abroad, got the recipe and started to make it herself. By the time she died at the age of 98 she was rich and Gränna was famous. The tradition continues with several local manufacturers vying for the lucrative tourist market and the main street is awash with red and white 'barber-style' poles denoting *polkagris* sales. Among the best is the Gränna Polkagriskokeri on Brahegatan where visitors can watch the sticks being made and choose from an assortment of flavours that would probably make the widow Eriksson turn in her grave.

 Gränna is a narrow but long-stretched town situated between a steep rocky ridge and the lake shore. The main street, Brahegatan, runs its full length and in the middle is a steeply sloping cobbled square with parking and the local tourist office. Next to the square, the Andrée Museum tells the dramatic story of Gränna's most famous protege, Salomon August Andrée whose ill-fated balloon expedition to the North Pole in 1897 captured the imagination of a generation. The balloon called *The Eagle* made a forced landing after only 3 days, but its occupants survived on the polar ice for another 3 months. They managed to reach a small arctic island before they finally succumbed to cold, hunger and probably the polar bears. No-one knew what had happened to them until their remains were found by accident in 1930 and brought home amid much pomp and circumstance to Sweden. Expedition notebooks, film and clothing had been preserved in the ice during the intervening 33 years and much of it is on display in the museum. Balloonists now meet at Gränna every year in honour of Andrée's audacious flight.

The town owes its lay-out and position to one of Sweden's first Counts, Per Brahe who had no less than three castles in the area. One of them, Brahehus, lies in ruins on a cliff above Gränna. As local governor in the sixteenth century Brahe apparently insisted that Gränna's streets should be planned in such a way that he would be able to see what was going on there from his lofty residence. The main thoroughfare is therefore comparatively broad for such a small community. Brahe had a second castle on the island of **Visingsö**, a half-hour ferry ride from the town's tiny harbour. The 14km (9 mile) long island is a popular summer destination, not least because of its traditional transport system using horses and multiple occupancy carts on which passengers sit back-to-back.

These so-called *remmalag* are usually on standby at the ferry quay during the holiday season but can be booked through the tourist office at other times. Some ferries take cars although the cost and limited use once there means that most visitors leave them on the mainland. Anyone taking a vehicle by ferry should book the passage in advance at the harbour office. Bicycles are probably a better bet for those who want to see the island independently, they can be hired in summer from the Visingsö tourist office by the harbour or arranged through the main Gränna tourist office out of season.

Visingsö, a mixture of agriculture and woodland has been inhabited for more than 6,000 years. Per Brahe's once splendid Visingsborg Castle comes into view as the ferry approaches the island but is just a ruin these days. The seventeenth-century Brahe church nearby is still going strong however and the local Strandgården restaurant serves dishes from the Brahe era with honey ice-cream as a house speciality. Örtagården 'The Herb Garden' also has its roots in the 1600s lying as it does on the site of the original castle plantation. A couple of kilometres to the south are three burial fields with a total of 800 graves and beyond them, at the southern end of the island is yet another castle ruin called Näs. It is 500 years older than Visingsborg and is mentioned in ancient Icelandic sagas as a powerful, strategic fortress. Visingsö's many fine oaks are not a fortunate accident of fate but the result of a philanthropic early nineteenth-century planting programme when quality timber was needed for shipbuilding.

The island has a number of small beaches and campsites and its own youth hostel. Back on the mainland an artificial sandy 'lagoon' has been created for bathers next to Gränna harbour although water temperatures can be bracing because Vättern is not only Sweden's second largest lake but also one of its deepest. Just south of Gränna the E4 passes a baronial style hotel and restaurant called Gyllene Uttern, which was created in the 1930s by an entrepreneurial couple whose stated aim was to put romance and fantasy into motoring holidays. The terrace has views along the lakeshore back towards Gränna. Right below it in a narrow green valley is picturesque Röttleby hamlet where a couple of mills that once worked for the powerful Brahe family can still put on a show for summer tourists. The E4 is at its most scenic from here as it skirts the lake back to Jönköping, the starting point for this itinerary.

Gränna is famous for its striped sticks of rock

Gyllene Uttern, a baronial style hotel and restaurant south of Gränna

Additional Information

Places to Visit

Blekinge
Blomstergården (Flower Garden)
Eringsboda
☎ 0455 72088
Open: daily 13 June to 6 September
10am-6pm.

Boda
Glassworks
360 65 Boda
☎ 0481 24030
Open: daily for sales, visits to workshop
weekdays only.

Borgholm
Slottsruin (Castle Ruins)
☎ 0485 10649
Open: 1 May to 31 August 10am-6pm.

Eketorp
Eketorps Borg (Fortress)
On southern Alvar
☎ 0485 39020/39000
Open: May to end August 9am-5pm,
September 10am-5pm. Guided tours.

Gränna
Andrée Museum
Brahegatan 38
☎ 0390 11015
Open: 15 May to 31 August daily 10am-
5pm, 1 September to 14 May daily
12noon-4pm.

Huskvarna
*Dr Skoras Vaxkabinett
(Dr Skoras Waxworks)*
Grännavägen 24
☎ 036 142080
Open: March, April, September, Octo-
ber, Tuesday to Sunday 11am-5pm.
May to August daily, 10am-7pm.

Jönköping
Tändsticksmuseum (Matchstick Museum)
Västra Storgatan 18A
Tändsticksområdet
☎ 036 105543
Open: 1 January to 9 June and 1 September to 31 December, Tuesday to Thursday 12noon-4pm. Saturday 11am-3pm.
10 June to 31 August, Monday to Friday
10am-5pm, Saturday and Sunday 10am-
3pm.

County Museum (Länsmuseet)
Dag Hammarskjölds Plats 1
☎ 036 301800
Open: Tuesday, Thursday, Friday
11am-6pm, Wednesdays 11am-8pm,
Saturday 11am-4pm, Sunday 11am-
5pm. Mondays closed.

Kalmar
Castle
Open: Monday to Saturday 10am-4pm,
Sunday 1-4pm.

Länsmuseet (Kalmar County Museum)
Skeppsbrogatan 51
☎ 0480 56300
Open: Tuesday to Friday 10am-4pm,
Saturday and Sunday 1-4pm, closed
Mondays.

Karlskrona
Marinmuseet (Maritime Museum)
Amiralstorget
☎ 0455 84000
Open: daily 12noon-4pm, June, August
10am-4pm, July 10am-6pm.

Länsmuseet (Blekinge County Museum)
Fisketorget 2
☎ 0455 80120
Open: May, June, September, October
9am-4pm (Wednesday 9am-8pm, Saturday and Sunday 11am-4pm). July and
August Monday to Friday 9am-7pm.

Kolmården
Djurpark (Animal and Safari Park)
☎ 011 95150
Open: 1 January to 20 March 10am-3pm,
21 March to 8 May 10am-4pm, 9 May to
19 June 10am-5pm, 20 June to 16 August
10am-6pm, 17 August to 27 September
10am-4pm, 28 September to 13 December 10am-3pm.
NB with the exception of some weekends, the Safari Park is closed 1 October
to 8 May.

Kosta
Glasbruk (Glassworks)
360 52 Kosta
☎ 0478 50300
Open: daily for sales and visits to
workshop.

Linköping
Östergötland County Museum
Raoul Wallenbergsplats
☎ 013 230300
Open: daily 12noon-4pm (later some
days). Mondays closed.

Slott (Löfstad Castle)
By E4, 10km (6 miles) south of
Norrköping
☎ 011 35067
Open: for guided tours May to August.

Malmslätt
*Flygvapenmuseet (Swedish Airforce
    Museum)*
Carl Cederströmsgatan
☎ 013 283567
Open: May to September 12noon-4pm,
October to April 12noon-3pm.

Motala
Radio Museum
Bondebacka
☎ 0141 14530
Open: daily 1 June to 31 August 11am-
4pm.

Norrköping
Konstmuseum (Art Museum)
Kristinaplatsen
☎ 011 152600
Open: daily 12noon-4pm (1 September
to 14 May also 7-9pm on Monday,
Tuesday, Wednesday, Thursday).

Arbetsmuseet (Museum of Work)
Industrilandskapet
☎ 011 189800

Stadsmuseum (City Museum)
Västgötegatan 19-21
☎ 011 152620
Open: Monday to Friday 10am-4pm,
Saturday and Sunday 12noon-4pm.

Colouring Shed (Färgaregården)
St Persgatan 3
☎ 011 152640
Open: 1 May to 11 September 12noon-4pm.

Orrefors
Glassworks
380 40 Orrefors
☎ 0481 34000
Open: daily for sales and visits to
workshop.

Oskarshamn
Döderhult Museum
Kultur Centrum, Hantverksgatan
☎ 0491 11725
Open: 11 June to 1 September 9am-6pm
(Wednesdays 11am-4pm). 1 September
to 31 May Tuesday to Thursday
12noon-6pm, Saturday 11am-3pm,
Friday to Sunday 12noon-4pm.

Riddersberg
Riddersberg Manor
Rogberga
☎ 036 93210
Open: 15 June to 15 August daily 11am-
7pm. Other times daily 11am-6pm.

Solliden
Just outside Borgholm
Park open: 1 June to 31 August 11am-
5pm.

Teleborg
Castle
Open: for guided tours 17 June to 12
August. Contact Växjö tourist office.

Vadstena
Slott (Castle)
Open: May to September.

Mårten Skinnares Hus/Hospital Museum
Next to convent
Open: for guided tours June to August.
Contact tourist office.

Växjö
Utvandrarnas Hus (House of the Emigrants)
Museiparken
☎ 0470 20120
Open: weekdays daily 9am-4pm. 1 June
to 31 August 9am-5pm, Saturday 11am-
3pm, Sunday 1-5pm.

Smålands Museum
Museiparken
☎ 0470 45245
Open: weekdays 9am-4pm, Saturday
11am-1pm, Sunday 1-5pm.

Visby
Gotlands Fornsal (The Gotland Museum)
Strandgatan 14
☎ 0498 47010
Open: Tuesday to Sunday 12noon-4pm
all year. Daily 11am-6pm from mid-
May to September.

Öland
Djurpark (Zoo)
On route 137
Open: May to September.
☎ 0485 30873

Tourist Information Centres

Gränna
Torget
☎ 0390 11010

Jönköping
Djurlekartorget
☎ 036 105050

Kalmar
Larmgatan 6
☎ 0480 15350

Karlskrona
Stadsbiblioteket
Stortorget 15-17
☎ 0455 83490

Linköping
Agatan 39
☎ 013 206835

Motala
Repslagaregatan 1
☎ 0141 25254

Norrköping
Destination Norrköping (Tourist Office)
Drottninggatan 11
☎ 011 150000

Ronneby
Kultur Centrum
Kallingevägen 3
☎ 0457 17650

Strömbergshyttan
Hovmantorp
☎ 0478 11731/10610

Vadstena
Uddjönssons Hus
☎ 0143 15125

Västervik
Strömsholmen
☎ 0490 88700

Växjö
Kronobergsgatan 8
☎ 0470 41410/41000

Visby
Burmeisterska Huset
Box 1081 S621 02 Visby
☎ 0498 2100982
Open: April to September.
At other times of the year contact:
Gotlands Turistförening
Box 2081
S-621 02 Visby
☎ 0498 247065

Visingsö
By the harbour (open summer only)
☎ 0390 40193

Öland
Träffpunkt Öland
On route 137 near bridge
☎ 0485 39060

Borgholm office (In public library)
☎ 0485 89000

4
STOCKHOLM AND LAKE MÄLAREN

✳ It has been variously described as the 'Venice of the North', 'beauty on water' and the loveliest city in Scandinavia — locals would probably add 'the world'. They may sound like cliches, but **Stockholm**, Sweden's elegant, cosmopolitan and squeaky clean capital is a clear contender for all three accolades. It straddles no less than fourteen islands on the threshold between Lake Mälaren and the Baltic Sea, an eclectic combination of narrow cobbled streets, modern shopping malls, medieval buildings, high tech design and more than fifty museums. Beyond the city lies what local tourist brochures like to call its 'pearl necklace', a string of 24,000 islands forming a lush green archipelago.

The fact that Stockholm has evolved across such a geographical patchwork of land can also make it a distinctly confusing place to get around. Visiting motorists are all too easily swept across the wrong bridge to the wrong island where they find themselves on a one-way road to the wrong place. Even walkers, and by far the best way to see the inner city is on foot, will probably turn the street map upside down a few times before working out which bridge to cross. Fortunately most Stockholmers speak English and will be happy to point out the right direction. The capital also boasts an excellent public transport system with an underground which, centrally at least, is a tourist attraction in its own right and a flotilla of small white ferries linking the city islands with more distant ones in the lake or the Baltic, known locally as the Salt Sea. It is worth taking at least one ferry ride, not just as a means of transport but to help get acquainted with Stockholm's many waterways.

Although the capital has direct ferry links with Finland and the Baltic States most foreign visitors arrive either at its international airport Arlanda some 45km (28 miles) to the north, by train to the Central Station or by road through the sprawling modern suburbs. It is undeniably the most international of Sweden's cities and its bustling street-life, 700-plus restaurants (said to equal Paris in number) and thriving café society can make a welcome change after miles of forest and quiet 'early to bed' provincial towns. In the evening Stockholmers make the most of their

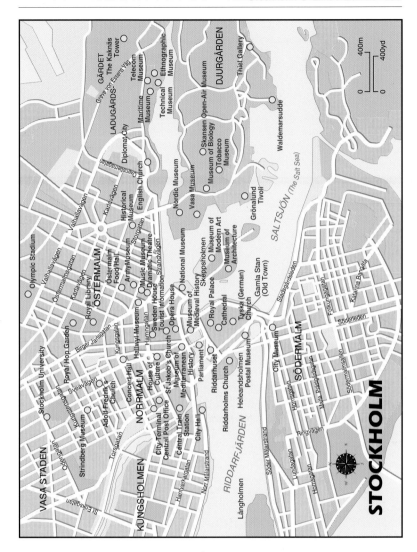

forty theatres and glitzy nightclubs while window shopping is a serious pastime during the day. Smart shopping malls like Gallerian at Stureplan vie for business with established department stores and designer boutiques. Stockholmers are also keen to point out that a third of their city is parkland and that its water is not only clean enough for swimming and even for the notoriously fastidious salmon. The right to fish in the centre of town, a privilege that dates back to Queen Kristina in the 1600s, is still enthusiastically exercised by amateur anglers today.

Although the Mälare Valley has been inhabited since the Stone Age, Stockholm's history really began with the growth of trade and the establishment of trading sites in the ninth and tenth centuries. In the twelfth century a defensive round tower was built on a small island where Lake Mälaren rushed to meet the sea and a community of merchants and craftsmen gradually established itself there. The **Gamla Stan** (Old Town) grew on the island which, together with two smaller ones, **Riddarholmen** (Knights' Island) and **Helgeandsholmen** (Holy Ghost Island) now form the medieval heart of Stockholm. They house the Royal Palace, the Swedish parliament building and Stockholm's 'Great Church' or Cathedral. The old paths once tramped by merchants with their porters were transformed into the narrow cobbled streets that still remain today. Trade flourished during the Hanseatic period and the town expanded beyond its city walls. By the time Stockholm became the capital of Sweden in the sixteenth century development had begun to spread to the mainland and neighbouring islands. One of them, **Skeppsholmen**, just to the east of Gamla Stan has a former Naval headquarters, the Museum of Modern Art and two particularly well located youth hostels. To the north, connected by bridge to both Gamla Stan and Skeppsholmen is **Norrmalm** with its smart shops, offices, hotels and Stockholm's most famous and lively park, Kungstradgården, the Kings Garden — it actually was the palace vegetable plot once. Part of Norrmalm underwent dramatic changes in the 1960s leaving some fairly uninspiring modern architecture around the bleak looking Sergels Torg. The neighbouring district of **Östermalm** was where the royal household kept its farm animals. It underwent dramatic transformation at the turn of the century and the broad streets are now among the most fashionable places to live in Stockholm. The influx of well-helled residents attracted restaurants and bars and the sumptuous Östermalm Food Halls are well worth a visit.

Östermalm is linked by bridge to **Djurgården** (literally the Animal Yard), the former royal hunting ground, now an area of green fields and woodland which also lays claim to some of the city's most popular tourist attractions such as the Vasa Museum, Skansen Open-Air Museum and the Gröna Lund Tivoli amusement park. To the north on **Ladugårdsgärdet** the Kaknäs Tower offers panoramic views across Stockholm and perhaps a chance to sort out some of those confusing islands.

Travelling west, and separated by water from Norrmalm is the island of **Kungsholmen**, the King's Island. It was laid out in the late 1600s as a workers' quarter but is now a prosperous mix of residential and administrative accommodation with pride of place going to Stockholm's elegant City Hall, the police headquarters and the lawcourts. Kungsholmen has pleasant walks along the Mälare shores and even places to swim. The really energetic can join in free open-air gymnastics sessions performed to disco music. For a more leisurely activity try fishing — licences are not required in Stockholm waters as long as there is no commercial motive. While the lake yields salmon, pike and perch the Baltic is famous for its herring. The Marieberg area on the southern part of Kungsholmen is the home of Sweden's main newspapers.

A bridge links the island to its smaller neighbour **Långholmen**, the former Alcatraz of Stockholm where a once notorious prison has been transformed into an imaginative youth hostel and finally to **Södermalm**, the largest, most densely populated and least fashionable of the city islands. The preceding paragraphs serve only as the briefest orientation guide to the central districts and beyond lie many more islands, one or two of which will be dealt with in detail later in this chapter.

The best advice for anyone arriving in Stockholm is to call in at the Stockholm Information Service whose main centre is in Sverigehuset (Sweden House) on the corner of Kungsträdgården and the busy shopping street, Hamngatan. Staff there are a veritable mine of useful information and can provide free maps brochures and timetables. Remember to pick up a *Stockholm this Week* brochure which lists coming events along with details of museums, sightseeing and other handy tit-bits. Coach tours of the city and its surroundings leave regularly from outside.

Sverigehuset is also a good point from which to explore the inner city on foot — and why not start where Stockholm itself began, with **Gamla** **Stan**. Walking through Kungsträdgården today it is difficult to imagine that they once grew the royal potatoes here. Although officially a park it really feels more like a square with flowers and shrubs confined to small ornamental areas. But in summer this is definitely the place to be and be seen. A giant chess board has been a popular feature for years, there are live theatre performances, open-air music, dancing, and cafés. In winter a temporary ice rink offers alternative entertainment. Tucked away at the southern end of the park is the seventeenth-century St Jakob's Church whose little churchyard is a peaceful haven in an area very much preoccupied with more worldly pleasures.

Beyond the church with its back to the park lies **Operan** (the Opera House) which was founded by the arts and theatre-loving King Gustav III. He also met an untimely end there when, in 1792, he was shot and mortally wounded by the assassin Ankarström during a masquerade ball. The incident inspired Verdi to write his opera *Un Ballo In Maschera* (*The Masked Ball*). The original building was torn down and the present one dates from the 1890s. Operan is renowned not only for its fine opera and ballet but also for its gastronomic performances. The Operakällare (Opera Cellar) is one of the best and most expensive restaurants in Stockholm attracting an international clientele of bon-viveurs. As an alternative the budget might stretch to the less pricey but not exactly cheap Bakficka (Back-Pocket) restaurant while the art-nouveau Café Opera is a trendy discotheque at night with a seemingly perennial queue waiting outside whatever the weather.

Turn right down Strömgatan to Gustav Adolfs Torg named after the statue of the king. Opposite the front entrance of the Opera House is the Crown Prince's Palace which now houses the Ministry of Foreign Affairs and just off the square lies the **Medelhavs Museum** (Museum of Mediterranean and Near Eastern Antiquities). Exhibits include objects from ancient civilisations around the Mediterranean with 2,500-year-old

A panoramic view of Stockholm's Old Town as seen from the City Hall

Shopping is something of a national sport in Sweden — a busy street scene, Stockholm

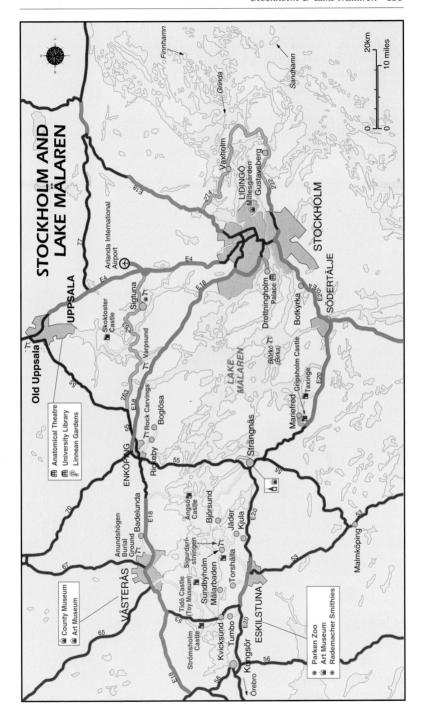

STOCKHOLM AND
LAKE MÄLAREN

20km
10 miles

Finnhamn
Grinda
Sandhamn

UPPSALA

Old Uppsala

⊞ Anatomical Theatre
⊞✳ University Library
Linnean Gardens

Arlanda International
Airport

Skokloster
Castle
Sigtuna
Varpsund
Rock Carvings
Boglösa
Rickeby

ENKÖPING

Växholm
LIDINGÖ
Millesgården
Gustavsberg

STOCKHOLM

Drottningholm
Palace ⊞
Björkö
(Birka)
Botkyrka
Mariefred Gripsholm Castle
Taxinge

SÖDERTÄLJE

LAKE
MÄLAREN

Strängnäs

County Museum
Art Museum

VÄSTERÅS

Anundshögen
Burial
Ground Badelunda
Sigurds-
ristningen
Tidö Castle
(Toy Museum)
Sundbyholm
Strömsholm
Castle
Kvicksund
Tumbo
Kungsör

Ängsö
Castle
Björsund
Jäder
Kjula
Torshälla
Mälarbaden

ESKILSTUNA

Malmköping

Parken Zoo
Art Museum
Rademacher Smithies

Örebro

terracotta figures, Greco-Roman collections and Egyptian mummies. There is also a display of Islamic art and culture. Turn left and cross the Norrbro Bridge to **Helgeandsholmen** (Holy Ghost Island). The columned **Riksdagshuset** (parliament building) with its symbolic statue of *Moder Svea* (Mother Sweden) is now on the right. Its first foundation stone was laid by King Oscar II in 1897 with the comment, 'Let wise discussion take place in this parliament building'. Looking at the rise in Swedish living standards during the twentieth century it probably did. The parliament is in fact two buildings connected by walkways, with most of the business of the day being conducted in the semi-circular back half. The building was recently refurbished and to everyone's surprise excavations for an underground garage revealed relics from medieval Stockholm. So, instead of just a parking lot a **Medeltidsmuseum** (Museum of Medieval History) took shape (the entrance is below the level of the road at Strömparterren). It is an award winning museum which cleverly uses its underground site to recreate the atmosphere of early Stockholm with everything from reconstructed dwellings to the piped cry of seagulls and is well worth a visit.

Ahead now lies the slightly austere but imposing façade of **Kungliga Slottet** (the Royal Palace), the largest royal residence in the world. It was designed by the architect Nicodemus Tessin as a replacement for the previous castle that burned down in 1697. It took more than 50 years to build and its 608 rooms were not ready to receive their royal occupants until the 1750s. The palace is based on a simple but elegant quadrangle with a large rather bleak cobbled courtyard in the centre. Two additional wings jut out toward Norrström and there is a semi-circular outer courtyard at the opposite end. Sweden's present King Carl Gustav and Queen Silvia still have offices here but decided some years ago to move the family to Drottningholm Palace in the leafy outskirts of Stockholm. Although the palace is used regularly for state occasions several parts are open to the public. Among the most interesting is Skattkammaren (the Treasury) where the Swedish crown jewels lie in glittering splendour. They include Gustav Vasa's swords of State, Erik XIV's Coronation crown and bejewelled regalia and small children's crowns demonstrating that even young princes and princesses had to look regal. Visningsvåningarna (the Royal Apartments) comprise the Bernadotte, State and Guest apartments with their creaking polished floors, enormous chandeliers and sumptuous furniture. King Oscar II who died in 1907 was the last monarch to live here and his writing room has been left completely intact, as has the small breakfast room presented to him and his wife Sofia by the royal household. Livsrustkammaren (the Royal Armoury) contains an assortment of coaches, Coronation clothes, armour and hunting weapons. The costume worn by the ill-fated Gustav III at the masked ball is a star attraction as is Streiff, King Gustav II Adolf's favourite horse which has been stuffed and put on display along with the garments the king wore on the day he was killed at the Battle of Lutzen, 1632.

Also open to the public are Slottsmuseet (the Palace Museum) with 🏛 remnants of the old Three Crowns Palace, the Hall of State where the king used to read his 'State of the Nation' address, Slottskyrkan (the Palace Church) dating from the eighteenth century and still in use and Gustav III's Anitkmuseum (Gustav III's Museum of Antiquities), housing the 🏛 result of his collectors' mania. His royal status evidently failed to protect him from the odd cheat as some of the works on display are fakes. Souvenir hunters are catered for in the palace shop (Slottsboden) strategically placed by the outer courtyard and selling a range of generally tasteful but expensive souvenirs. There is a ceremonial changing of the guard at 12noon on weekdays — 1.10pm on Sundays and Bank Holidays so as not to clash with the service in the neighbouring cathedral.

The Royal Palace occupies a huge rectangular area in the northern corner of Gamla Stan, to reach the main entrance turn left from Norrbro onto Slottskajen and follow the road along the water to Slottsbacken. The cobbled rise also leads to **Stor Krykan**, meaning the Great Church, Stock- ⛪ holm's cathedral. The church with its Baroque façade in burnt sienna and green copper roof stands conveniently shoulder to shoulder with the Royal Palace and is the traditional setting for royal Coronations and weddings. It was first mentioned in 1279 although scholars believe it to be older than that. Most of what you see dates from the 1700s although brickwork in the west wall has survived more than 700 years of fires, invasions and renovations. Inside, the beautifully detailed fifteenth-century wooden sculpture of *St George and the Dragon* by Bernt Notkes is regarded as one of the best of its kind in northern Europe. The cathedral also houses the oldest known painting of Stockholm dating from 1535 and showing the fledgling city under a solar halo.

The front of the cathedral is crammed in among the seventeenth-century houses and meandering streets of the old town. Not long ago this area was a slum, but fortunately plans to demolish large parts of it were never carried out and Gamla Stan is now a major tourist attraction and one of the best addresses in town. The narrow lanes and tightly packed buildings seem a million miles from modern Sweden with its ubiquitous shopping malls and office blocks. A leisurely stroll is the best way to explore the hidden nooks and crannies, tiny stepped passages, elegant merchants houses and the burgeoning boutiques, antique shops, bars and restaurants. Although the majority of buildings date from the prosperous seventeenth century there are reminders of earlier times too. Turn left out of Storkyrkan along Trångsund and left again into **Stortorget**, the main ☀ square at the heart of the old city. This was once the local execution site where, in the sixteenth century, King Christian of Denmark beheaded over eighty Swedish noblemen in what became known as the 'Stockholm bloodbath'. The old red house facing the square has as many white stones as there were victims. Börsen (the Stock Exchange) was built in the 1700s on the remains of the old City Hall and also houses the meeting rooms of the Swedish Academy. Continue down Köpmangatan with its antique shops and a bronze copy of the cathedral's *St George and the Dragon* and turn right into Österlångatan where parts of the Blackfriars Monastery date from 1300. The nearby restaurant Den Gyllene Freden (The Golden Peace) was established in 1772 and is the oldest in Stockholm. Another right turn across the tiny Järn Torget (Iron Square) leads to the Old Town's main tourist trail, Västra Långgatan with its mix of designer boutiques, restaurants and cafés. Try a quick stroll along Mårten Trotzig's Lane immediately to the right — but perhaps not after a good dinner because it is just 90cm wide in places! The tall tower belongs to the sixteenth-century German church (Tyska Kyrkan), once owned by wealthy German merchants whose guilds met there.

Turn left down Ignatigränden and continue to where a busy thorough-fare flanking the Riddarholms Canal channels traffic around the edge of

Stockholm's waterfront bathed in the light of the setting sun

A public walkway through the parliament building, Stockholm

Stockholm is famous for the beauty of its setting

the old town.   A few paces to the left, at Lilla Nygatan 6 lies Stockholm's rebuilt **Postmuseum** (Postal Museum) containing just about everything there is to know about the history of Swedish stamps and a fair number of foreign collections too. A small bridge takes pedestrians across the three-lane 'Centralbron' highway as it swishes past the island, skimming the water on low stilts. The tiny adjacent islet of Riddarholmen is dominated by the thirteenth-century **Riddarholms Church** with its distinctive cast-iron spire. It is one of the oldest buildings in Stockholm and was for centuries the traditional mausoleum of Swedish monarchs. The tombs of Gustav II Adolf and Gustav III are among those found here. The Wrangel family palace nearby was once a gift from Queen Kristina to Field Marshal Carl-Gustaf for his management of the Thirty Years War. There are good views across the Riddarfjärd to Stockholm's distinctive City Hall surmounted by its three gilded crowns.

Return across the same small bridge. Ahead lies one of Stockholm's most beautiful buildings, **Riddarhuset** (the House of Nobility) where the aristocrats met regularly as one of the Four Estates that governed the country. Their 2,325 coats of arms are on display along with heraldic china and other aristocratic memorabilia. Myntgatan continues towards the back of the parliament building. MPs chambers are accommodated at number 18 and a covered causeway enables them to get to the parliament without having to brave the vagaries of the weather. Turn left across the 'Stable Bridge' which connects the old town with Helgeandsholmen and continue between the two halves of the parliament before crossing Bishops Bridge back onto the mainland. Ahead lies Drottninggatan, one of Stockholm's busiest shopping streets and a favourite with illegal street hawkers who disappear as if by magic at the sight of a policeman. But to return to Sverigehuset and the starting point of the walk, turn right along Strömgatan and past the Opera House to Kungsträdgården.

Gamla Stan effectively holds the key to the door of Lake Mälaren with complex locks regulating a 40cm difference in water levels between the lake and the sea. The neighbouring island of **Skeppsholmen** (within easy walking distance of Kungsträdgården) lies on the seaward side of the lock and was of strategic importance from the 1600s as a naval base. Stockholmers have found new uses for the old maritime buildings and the island now houses **Moderna Museet** (the Museum of Modern Art) and two popular youth hostels which easily challenge the nearby Grand Hotel for some of the best views in the city. The one is housed on board the nineteenth-century sailing boat *AF Chapman*, itself a local tourist attraction.

You cannot miss the museum because of the weird assortment of sculpture in bright primary colours nearby. It has a wide-ranging collection of twentieth-century works including Dali's famous *Enigma of William Tell*, a goat stuck in a car tyre and a pair of shoes trussed up to look like the Sunday roast. One room is devoted to a surrealistic boxing ring with sound recordings of a fight but for more conventional modernists

there are works by Picasso, Matisse and Modigliani. The **Arkitektur**
Museet (the Museum of Architecture) and the **Ostasiatiska Museum**
(Museum of Far Eastern Antiquities) with the largest collection of Stone
Age ceramics outside China are also on Skeppsholmen. Anyone feeling
energetic can then continue across a bridge to the microscopic
Kastellholmen islet which still has remnants of its naval past including the
cannons that are traditionally fired to mark the birth of Royal babies.

Back on the mainland and with a splendid waterfront position is **Na-**
tional Museet (the National Museum) housing the nation's greatest
paintings as well as an interesting selection of applied arts. Sweden was
a wealthy and powerful nation from the sixteenth to the eighteenth
centuries and large quantities of art were bought or simply taken as spoils
of war. Unfortunately some of the collection went up in smoke in 1697
when the Royal Palace burned to the ground and no-one knows exactly
what was lost. The second floor of the museum is nevertheless crammed
with great works including Rembrandt's monumental *Batavians Oath Of*
Allegiance which was originally painted to decorate the new Amsterdam
City Hall but for some unknown reason later taken down and reworked.
The collection includes several other Rembrandts and is generally well
endowed with seventeenth-century Dutch and eighteenth-century
French paintings. Swedish artist Anders Zorn sparked off an early interest
in the Impressionists when he donated Manet's *Young Man Peeling A Pear*
and the museum went on to acquire a healthy collection which includes
Renoir, Degas and Gaugin. But take time to look at works by the great
Swedish artists too, some of them may seem familiar. They are dominated
by Anders Zorn with his Impressionist portraits and buxom nudes, Bruno
Liljefors with evocative animal portraits and Carl Larsson whose family
scenes from the book *A Home* have been reproduced all over the world.
Larsson also painted the huge murals in the entrance hall culminating in
The Entry of Gustaf Vasa into Stockholm opposite the staircase on the upper
hall. Sadly his final mural, *Midwinter Sacrifice* which he hoped would
decorate the western section of the wall was refused by the museum and
ended up in Japan.

The National Museum and its elegant neighbour, the Grand Hotel lie on
a small peninsula opposite the Royal Palace. Look to the east across the
Nybroviken bay and you can just see the Vasa Museum where an
embarassing episode in Sweden's history has been turned into one of its
most famous tourist attractions. The Vasa, the Skansen open-air museum,
the Nordic Museum and Gröna Lund amusement park all lie within
walking distance of each other on the leafy island of **Djurgården**. To get
there you can take a ferry from Nybroviken or Skeppsbron in Gamla Stan
or walk along Strandvägen crossing the short bridge. Alternatively there
is a nostalgic tram line — one of the few left in Sweden — that runs in
summer from Nybroplan onto the island. The old trams have proved
popular since being reintroduced a few years ago. Local buses will also
take you directly there. On the way is Stockholm's **Dramatiska Teater** (the
Dramatic Theatre) which boasts Ingmar Bergman as its director and

beyond lie the elegant façades of Strandvägen, one of the city's most fashionable boulevards.

The **Vasa Museet** is at the end of a short slip road almost immediately after the bridge onto Djurgården. It is difficult not to be impressed by the spectacular seventeenth-century warship which was raised from the seabed in 1961, more than three centuries after she sank. Years of painstaking restoration and preservation followed and she now rests serenely in a museum especially designed so that visitors can view her from various heights and angles. Unfortunately the *Vasa's* maritime history was far from glorious or serene. Some 1,000 oak trees were felled to construct what was to have been Sweden's greatest ship. She was ready in 1628 — the pride of the royal fleet and looking all the more fearsome because of an extra row of cannons that had been added at the king's request. The result may have been awe-inspiring, but it was also distinctly unstable. The captain obviously had some inkling of that because he ordered his men to run to and fro across the decks to see how much she rocked. The result was alarming, but with the king and dignitaries there to give her a royal send-off no-one dared dispute her seaworthiness. The *Vasa* never got out of Stockholm harbour — she capsized and sank 15 minutes after setting sail. Most of her sixty-four brass cannons were retrieved from the seabed in the late 1600s and sold to Germany where, according to one rumour at least, they were turned into church bells. The rest of the 62m (203ft) long ship is on display, her ornate decorative carvings restored to their former glory and her dark oak beams preserved

The unusual assortment of sculptures at the Museum of Modern Art, Stockholm

Waterside apartment blocks in central Stockholm

for posterity. She is an impressive sight and one that should not be missed. The hangar-like building also houses several exhibitions about life on board, a cinema showing videos about the *Vasa's* history and a set of high tech computer screens providing yet more information. Literally round the corner from the Vasa Museum on the main road is **Nordiska Museet** (the Nordic Museum) with a giant sculpture of the ship's namesake, *King Gustav Vasa* by Swedish sculptor Carl Milles in the entrance hall. The museum traces the cultural history of Sweden over the past 500 years with a special exhibition on more modern developments.

On the other side of the main Djurgårdsvägen lies **Biologiska Museet** (the Museum of Biology) with displays of Nordic animals against a backdrop of paintings by Bruno Liljefors. Two of Djurgården's main attractions can be found a few hundred metres further on. They are **Gröna Lund Tivoli**, Stockholm's venerable old amusement park dating from 1883 but now with a range of modern fun rides, dancing and a variety of entertainment. Even more popular however is **Skansen**, Stockholm's unsurpassed open-air heritage museum and one of the first such museums in the world. Its extensive grounds include more than 150 historically significant buildings brought together from all over Sweden and reconstructed here as a permanent record of how people lived. There is a town street, a manor house, windmills and numerous farmhouses representing different building techniques and life styles. All are furnished in the appropriate style and usually come complete with daytime occupants who are dressed to fit the province and period. Many are craftsmen and women who demonstrate traditional skills as well as being mines of information about the particular property and lifestyle. All the houses are open to visitors in summer and a selection are open in winter with more at the weekends than during the week. Some of the farms have paddocks for cattle, sheep and goats beyond which lies a small animal park housing Nordic species such as brown bear and elk. There are plenty of restaurants and refreshment stalls. Skansen is all about Swedish cultural history so its aquarium with crocodile pool, snakes and monkeys may seem a little incongruous, but no less interesting for that.

Djurgården island has two unusual art museums which are well worth a visit if time allows. At the far eastern end of the island (bus 69 from the centre) is **Thielska Galleriet** (the Thiel Gallery). It was once the private home of wealthy Swedish banker Ernst Thiel and the meeting place of poets, artists and sculptors. But Thiel's business failed, he was declared bankrupt and his house and contents were bought by the State. They were opened to the public in 1926. Paintings include Edvard Munch's marvellous *On the Bridge* and *The Sick Child* as well as works by Carl Larsson, Anders Zorn and Impressionist masters Toulouse Lautrec and Edouard Vuillard. A large sentimental painting called *The Knight And The Maiden* by Richard Berg is particularly well-known in Sweden and has a sad history. Berg's wife was to have been the model, but she died so he painted their young daughter in his wife's dress, putting her on a concealed chair to give her more height. Further to the west is another grand private home

turned art gallery. **Waldemarsudde** (bus 47 or tram) belonged to King Gustav V's talented younger brother Prince Eugen the 'Painter Prince' whose works are ranked along with the best in Scandinavia. He was of course hardly a struggling artist and his villa is set in parkland with views across the water to Stockholm harbour. It houses a large collection of Nordic art from 1880 to 1940 as well as temporary exhibitions. The main rooms are permanently decorated with fresh flowers just as they were in the prince's day and his custom of keeping twelve flowering plants in memory of his mother, Queen Sophia under her portrait by Zorn continues today.

The island of Djurgården was once the royal hunting park and as the land is still owned by the king even the grandest properties stand on rented ground. To the north of Djurgården is Ladugårds Gärdet, an area of flat open heathland that was once a military exercise field. The small pink house peering from among some trees is where the royal ladies gathered to discreetly observe the manoeuvres. Today the heath is used for other forms of exercise including horse riding and rock concerts. The

area is dominated by the 155m (508ft) tall **Kaknäs Tower** with a restaurant at the top and inevitable souvenir shop at the bottom. It is worth a visit, if for no other reason than to get your bearings and to view Stockholm's islands from a different angle. The nearest of the Baltic archipelago islands, Fjäderholmarna are clearly visible and can be reached in 25 minutes by ferry from the centre of town. Their old sea tavern, once a popular watering hole for sailors, has been eclipsed by a modern restaurant and an impressive **Baltic Aquarium** housed in a cavern blasted out of the rock. The aquarium specialises in local species including an entire shoal of Baltic herring.

Also visible from the tower is the Stockholm Globe Arena said to be the highest spherical construction in the world with space for 16,000 spectators and the capital's artificial ski slope somewhat unglamorously built up on an old garbage dump. Just beneath the tower lie a whole batch of museums including **Sjöhistoriska Museet** (the Maritime Museum), **Telemuseet** (the Telecommunications Museum), **Tekniska Museet** (the Technical Museum) and **Folkens Museum Etnokgrafiska** (the National Museum of World Ethnography).

The route across Ladugårds Gärdet back to the city centre passes a stone obelisk in the shape of a clenched fist — a reminder of the 1 May rallies traditionally held on Ladugårds Gärdet. Nearby, police patrols and high security fencing mark out the area of Stockholm known as **Diplomatstaden** (Diplomat City) because of its many embassies and official residences. The district also houses the main TV headquarters and the peaceful little English church which proves a pleasant contrast to the bristling technology and surveillance all around it. To the west lies the district of **Östermalm**, once a ramshackle collection of old huts and barns for housing livestock, now the height of fashion. The Östermalm Foodhall at Östermalm's Torg is a tempting diversion for gourmets and generally regarded as 'the' place to shop if you are planning a lavish dinner party. Local game, fresh and smoked reindeer meat, cured salmon and piles of shellfish vie for space with international delicacies and exotic vegetables not easily found in Sweden. Small bars and cafés inside the hall serve up-market snacks such as a plate of fresh prawns with a glass of chilled white wine and upstairs is a popular and reasonably priced Indian restaurant. The lively streets around the foodhalls also have a good choice of both ethnic and international restaurants.

There are several museums in Östermalm including **Musik Museet** (the Music Museum) housed in a former royal bakery and containing a collection of every imaginable instrument with a brave invitation to visitors to 'make their own music'. Almost next door in what was the home of the Royal Artillery is **Arme Museet** (the Army Museum) with assorted uniforms, documents and weapons. It is a reminder that soldiers were once quartered around here — conveniently close for manoeuvres on the Ladugårds Gärdet heath. The current Military Academy still lies on Valhallavägen close to the old red brick stadium that hosted the 1912 Stockholm Olympics. Finally there is **Historiska Museet** (the Historical Museum) with important collections from the Stone, Bronze and Iron Ages, a mock Viking dwelling and finds from the Viking town of Birka. A separate section houses one of northern Europe's finest collections of medieval wooden sculpture, silver and textiles and the Royal Coin Cabinet in the same building gives pride of place to the world's largest coin,

Getting About In Stockholm

Stockholm may look a bit confusing on a map, but fortunately it has first rate public transport network which includes buses, metro, ferries and a few trams. There is also a well organised Turistlinjen (Tourist Line) bus which stops close to all major attractions and from which for a fixed fee passengers can get on and off at will.

But travelling around and paying individual entrance fees for museums can be an expensive business. The best value for anyone wanting to make the most of their stay is Stockholmkortet (the Stockholm Card) which acts like a passport entitling the holder to free travel, parking, sightseeing and entrance fees to more than fifty attractions. It includes roundtrips on the Strömma Kanalbolag's sightseeing boats which leave regularly from Nybroplan for what is called the 'Cityring' hour-long tour on the Baltic side of the locks or from Slottet (the Royal Palace) and Stadshuskajen (the Town Hall Quay) for the 2 hour 'Big Stockholm Tour'. The Turistline buses are also free for cardholders. The price of the card depends on the number of hours for which it is valid, 48 hours and 72 hours are the most popular, and it comes complete with a handy little booklet which includes brief details about all the major sights.

Parking on marked spaces is free for cardholders, quite a bonus in any capital city. But a general word of warning may be appropriate here. Strict rules govern all parking in the city, backed up by a depressingly efficient band of traffic police and wardens. Park only

Busking in Stockholm's underground

where you see 'P' signs or where it specifically says you can. Do not assume that the absence of lines on the road or obvious restrictions makes the spot fair game and remember that parking restrictions can run until late in the evening, 9pm or 10pm in some cases.

Stockholm's underground system (free with the Stockholm card) is extensive and efficient stretching way out into the suburbs. Look for signs with a blue 'T' on a white background. Local artists were commissioned to design stations on the line from Kungsträdgården to Akalla and Hjulsta and the result is known as 'the world's longest art gallery'. It is well-worth taking a ride from Kungsträdgården station just to admire the cavernous platform and fake archaeological site complete with 'Roman' urns, plinths and chipped statues. The next station, T-Centralen is a large powder blue cave with painted silhouette figures while a giant boot hangs upside down on the ceiling of Rådhuset station.

Stockholm has literally thousands of buses and, as previously mentioned, some of its old trams have been brought out of retirement to run from Nybroviken past Skansen and Gröna Lund on Djurgården. Ferries also play an important part in the local transport system and services run all year round from Skeppsbron to Djurgården with a summer only service from Nybroviken. There are numerous waterborn sightseeing possibilities with boats running from Strömkajen, Nybroplan or, for Lake Mälaren, tours from the City Hall quay (Stadshusbron). Many of these include evening archipelago cruises with dinner and perhaps a concert or that very Swedish tradition, dancing on the jetty. Boats to Fjäderholmarna leave from Nybroplan.

The grave of the late Swedish Prime Minister Olof Palme, Adolf Fredrik's Church, Stockholm

which at 20 kilo, is not something to carry in your pocket with the loose change.

Between Östermalm and Stockholm's commercial centre, Norrmalm is the royal **Humlegården** park, literally the Royal Hops Garden which once ♣ provided the king's beer. It now houses the Royal Library and a statue of eighteenth-century botanist Linneaus who categorised all known plant species. Birger Jarlsgatan heads into a fashionable shopping area around Stureplan with small side streets flanked by elegant boutiques and restaurants and populated by shoppers who look as if they can afford the prices. Just around the corner in Hamngatan lies **Hallwylska Museet** (the Hallwyl Museum), formerly the home of Countess Wilhelmina von Hallwyl whose passion for collecting has turned it into a cornucopia of priceless paintings, glassware, tapestries and china. The countess faithfully catalogued everything she bought and by the time she died her collection filled seventy-eight volumes. The palace and its contents were donated to the Swedish State in 1920 and has been open to the public since 1938.

Hamngatan takes a direct route to modern Stockholm's commercial heart in **Norrmalm**. Here the small boutiques give way to department stores and ubiquitous pedestrian shopping malls — the elegant façades to faceless office blocks bearing all the hallmarks of vintage 1960s and 70s architecture. Few Swedes have much good to say about the bleak area around Sergels Torg which was a favourite spot for police baiting during the days of student demonstrations. The square is still a popular meeting place today although protests are likely to involve nothing more demonstrative than the signing of a petition. A draughty pedestrian underpass links the various corners as well as providing access to the metro and shops. At street level the square is dominated by a modern sculpture called *The Obelisk* and a large fountain, but do not be put off by the dull appearance of the Culture House which fronts one side. It is a lively place offering music, theatre, special exhibitions, a café as well as a library with books, records, magazines and every conceivable foreign newspaper.

There are a number of large department and chain stores in this area. Do not miss the excellent NK department store diagonally opposite Sverigehuset on Hamngatan. A Swedish arts and crafts shop can be found on Drottninggatan although thirsty foreigners may be disappointed to find that PUB a little further along is not an enormous drinking palace but another large shop. The busiest pedestrian shopping street, Sergelgatan leads northward under the shadow of five particularly ugly office blocks to **Hötorget** (the Hay Market). Here a noisy outdoor fruit and vegetable market is supplemented by a large and diverse food hall called Hötorgshallen which sells Swedish and ethnic edibles and contains several reasonably priced cafés.

Further north the shopping frenzy begins to abate as the big stores give way to smaller shops, offices and flats. Two blocks from Hötorget the grid pattern of streets crosses Olof Palmes Gata, named in honour of the late Swedish Prime Minister who was assassinated just around the corner
 from here as he walked home from the cinema. Palme's grave, marked by a simple stone with his signature etched on it, can be seen a block away at Adolf Fredrik's Church. Also in this part of Stockholm is **Strindberg Museet** (the Strindberg Museum) which is devoted to the memory of the great but gloomy author. It is located in Strindberg's last home, the so-called 'Blue Tower' where he lived between 1908 and 1912. His study and library can be seen as he left them.

Few areas of Stockholm have undergone as much change as Norrmalm and few areas of Norrmalm have suffered quite so much as the district around Klara. Once a Bohemian mix of pubs, cafés and grimy newspaper offices it had to make way in the 1960s and 70s for modern government buildings and plush hotels. Many of these now jostle around Stockholm's huge Central Station and Cityterminalen, the focal point for local road and rail transport in and around the capital. Just beyond the station on **Kungsholmen** island is however one of Stockholm's most abiding landmarks, **Stadshuset** (the City Hall). The building was Sweden's most lavish construction project when it was completed in 1923 and it is not difficult to see why. Some 19 million gilded mosaic tiles are said to have been used to decorate the 'Golden Hall' which plays host to visiting dignitaries and the annual Nobel Prize dinners. The Blue Hall is only slightly less grand while the three gold crowns above the tower represent the symbol of Sweden and a reminder of its former union with Norway and Denmark. Visiting monarchs and presidents often arrive at Stadshuset's own jetty by ceremonial launch, while tourists have to make do with guided tours.

Places To Visit Around Stockholm

The islands dealt with so far in this chapter comprise only the hub of the city whose modern suburbs reach out over the neighbouring archipelago and mainland. One of the biggest and most exclusive, **Lidingö** was also the home of Swedish sculptor Carl Milles whose work is represented in towns and cities around the country. He certainly picked a good spot to show off his creations. Precarious figures of gods and angels are perched on tall columns at the top of a cliff which in turn looks out across the water towards Stockholm. Passengers on the Silja Line boats to Finland get a good view of the strange assortment of plinths almost opposite the ferry terminal. The sculptor, whose work also sold well in the USA died a wealthy man in 1955 and Millesgården (the Milles House) with its spectacular terraces and southern European feel is now a popular museum.

On the opposite side of the city 11km (7 miles) from the centre lies **Drottningholm** palace, the permanent home of King Carl Gustav, Queen Silvia and their three children. Local tourist guides like to describe the elegant seventeenth-century residence as the 'Swedish Versailles' and although it is much smaller it owes much to the French architectural fashion of the time. It is easy to understand why the king chose to move his family from Stockholm Slott to this peaceful oasis on the island of Lovön. It is simple to drive there, but the most pleasant method is by ferry from Stadshusbron. The journey takes 50 minutes. Drottningholm was designed by the royal architect Nicodemus Tessin for the country's widowed Queen Hedvig Eleonora. Its gardens were laid out in French style and although outwardly Baroque much of the inside was later redecorated to suit the rococo tastes of the 1700s. Its library has been described as 'the most beautiful room in Sweden'. Some of the apartments are open to the public even though it is also a private home and the lovely eighteenth-century Drottningholm Theatre next door complete with 200-year-old stage machinery and special effects is well worth a visit. Regular performances and guided tours are held there in spring and summer.

Beyond the formal French gardens is Drottningholm's English park and hidden among the trees is an odd eighteenth-century Chinese pavilion built by King Adolf Frederick as a birthday surprise for his Queen at a time when chinoiserie was the height of fashion. They seem to have taken the oriental fad to extremes and an attempt to farm silkworms nearby failed when the specially imported creatures froze to death in the Nordic winter.

The island of **Björkö** may not look much, but it is one of the most important historical and archaeological sites in Sweden. It was once the location of a major eighth-century Viking town called *Birka* with a population of some 15,000 people and trading connections as far afield as the Black and Caspian Seas. Visitors these days need a bit of an imagination to picture how it must have looked, but the island continues to attract a steady trail of sightseers and school classes. Some 3,000 graves have been discovered along with evidence of the town's importance as a trading

Precarious figures sculptured by Carl Milles at Millesgården

The magnificent Gripsholm Castle at the lakeside town of Mariefred

The unusual canons known as the Boar and the Sow at Gripsholm Castle, Mariefred

post. The interesting finds have been carted off to the Museum of National Antiquities so there are few remaining bits of physical evidence on the island. Birka is thought to have been a claustrophobic jumble of houses protected by a rampart and pile barriers in the harbour to ensure that, heaven forbid, the Vikings were not looted themselves. Christian missionaries from Bremen are known to have come here in the ninth century but no-one knows why the settlement was later abandoned. Ferries to Björkö go from Stadshusbron (the City Hall quay) and the journey takes about 2 hours.

A rather longer excursion, but well worthwhile if you do not have time to take the 'Around Lake Mälaren' itinerary, goes to the idyllic lakeside town of **Mariefred** with its magnificent Gripsholm Castle. The name Mariefred comes from a fifteenth-century convent called Pax Mariae or Maria's Peace and it fits this tranquil spot perfectly. The streets are lined with well-kept eighteenth-century timber houses and a smattering of boutiques that survive on the annual influx of summer visitors. On the edge of the community is Gripsholm, a sturdy landmark with rounded towers and walls that are several metres thick in parts. It was built by King Gustav Vasa in the mid-1500s on the site of an earlier fortress belonging to a nobleman called 'Grip'. The king, a contemporary of England's Henry VIII, introduced hereditary monarchy and the reformation into Sweden and had little respect for the neighbouring convent. It was unceremoniously demolished and its stones were used as building materials for Gripsholm. Rumour has it that some of the treasures confiscated from the unfortunate nuns are still hidden in a secret chamber behind the castle walls.

If you have time to visit just one castle in Sweden then perhaps it should be this one with its dark evocative rooms, creaking floorboards and private eighteenth-century theatre. It has seen much of Sweden's history pass through its doors and now houses the national portrait collection — a permanent reminder of some of the powerful figures who once lived there. Not everyone appreciated their stay at the castle. Two of Gustav Vasa's sons were imprisoned here — each the other's jailer as they struggled for power. In the seventeenth century Queen Maria Eleonora, the devoted and probably deranged widow of Gustav II Adolfus was kept under guard too, but managed to escape taking with her the dead king's heart in a gold casket. Later, towards the end of the eighteenth century, Gustav III tried to turn Gripsholm into a new Versailles and installed a theatre in one of its towers. He then caused considerable amusement and general embarrassment when he insisted on directing and starring in his own plays.

π   With attention focused on the castle it is easy to miss the rune stones near the entrance, one of which carries a lengthy inscription about two brothers who vanquished their enemies in the east and travelled on to the land of the Saricens (probably Persia). The outer courtyard gives pride of place to two cannons known as the Boar and the Sow because of their animal-shaped muzzels. Both were captured as spoils of war during the 1500s. An inner porch leads to a dark cobbled courtyard with wooden steps rising to the main entrance. Once inside the first few rooms are dark and gloomy evoking the castle's sixteenth-century roots, but they give way to brighter seventeenth- and eighteenth-century accommodation and finally Gustav III's perfectly preserved theatre on the top floor. The portrait collection follows a similar chronology from Gustav Vasa and his daughter Kristina to recently commissioned paintings of politicians, writers and the present royal family. Gripsholm was not designed as an art gallery and on dark autumn days visitors are presented with torches to help them see paintings hung in particularly gloomy corners.

The nicest way to get to Gripsholm during the summer is on board the old steamer *Mariefred* which docks by Stockholm's City Hall and takes a leisurely 3½ hours. There are also faster boat services taking 1½ hours. Buses depart from Liljeholmens Subway Station or you can take the historic Mariefred railway. The town lies a few kilometres off the main E20 and is easily accessible by car, it can therefore be taken in as part of the round Mälaren itinerary.

Stockholm's Archipelago

No visit to Stockholm is really complete without a trip to at least one or two of the 24,000 offshore islands stretching from Arholma in the north to Nåtterö in the south. Local ferry companies offer a wide choice of roundtrips many of which include extras such as dinner onboard, a barbecue, fresh prawns and dancing. Alternatively you can do as the Stockholmers themselves and use the regular services that provide a daily lifeline for archipelago dwellers. The Båt Luffar Kort (Inter-Skerries Card) which gives unlimited travel on the inter-island ferries is ideal for anyone with more time to spend. The card is valid for 16 days and is best value between June and August because that is when the ferry services are at their most frequent. Passengers on the large Baltic ferries to Finland, Russia and Estonia on the other hand effectively get a free archipelago cruise as the giants manoeuvre through a seemingly impossible jigsaw of land and sea.

Stockholm is justifiably proud of its archipelago and in summer city dwellers head there en masse to swim, sail and relax. Many move the entire household to one of 35,000 island cottages for the season and commute by ferry to work. Some inner islands like Vaxholm can be reached by road and operate free car ferries to neighbouring communities, but most rely entirely on boat transport. They range from tiny outcrops with just one or two red painted houses and a makeshift jetty to whole communities with shops, hotels and restaurants. Several, such as Finnhamn have excellent youth hostels with self catering facilities or cottages for rent. Svenska Turistföreningen STF can give details about where to find the hostels while staff at Sverigehuset (Sweden House) in Stockholm should have information on holiday cottages and hotels. The larger islands also have Tourist Information Centres during the summer months.

It is impossible for a book like this to detail all the choices available as so much depends on the time of year, the weather and the time available. For a brief taste of the archipelago try **Vaxholm**, a sizeable community of old wooden houses (brick construction was forbidden here until 1912) with a sixteenth-century fortress some 35km (22 miles) north-east of Stockholm and accessible by car, bus or boat. Ferries run all year round from Strömkajen and the journey takes an hour. By car follow the distinctly unappealing E18 north and turn right along route 274 or, a little more complicated, take route 222 running east from Stockholm past the porcelain manufacturing community of Gustavsberg, then left onto the 274 crossing by car ferry to Rindö and a second ferry to Vaxholm. Buses go from Tekniska Högskolan at Valhallavägen and take about 45 minutes. Vaxholm is often referred to as the gateway to the archipelago. The village is predictably well endowed with hotels, pensions, shops and cafés and seems to hibernate through winter recharging its batteries ready for the influx of summer holidaymakers. If time allows you can continue by ferry

Old wooden houses in Vaxholm

past one skerry after another to the more distant island of Grinda with its clear water and excellent bathing and further on still to the sailors paradise at Sandhamn. In the old days this used to be a long and uncomfortable journey but today it is possible to get to Sandhamn and back in a day with regular summer ferry services from Stockholm or all year round by bus from Slussen to Stavsnäs and then ferry. The island also has two hotels, restaurants, shops and recreation facilities including boat hire.

About 150 of the archipelago islands are inhabited all year round. In general the inner islands tend to be larger and wooded while further out they become more sparsely scattered and barren. It is important to mention that Stockholm's archipelago does not have official camp sites although there is nothing to stop individuals pitching their tents in accordance with Sweden's liberal but strictly observed country code, Allemans Rätten. Remember to take a good supply of drinking water and note that the lighting of fires is forbidden in many places. Note also that the northern island of Arholma and Nåtterö in the south lie within Military Protection Zones and are out of bounds to foreigners.

Around Lake Mälaren

Lake Mälaren, Sweden's third largest lake stretches westward from Stockholm with its own archipelago of wooded islands. The countless bathing spots, sheltered harbours and accessibility make it a popular

Village mailboxes near Lake Mälaren

An unusual view of the Baroque Skokloster castle

venue for summer outings. Mälaren is also at the heart of an area rich in Swedish cultural history. Some of the earliest settlements and trading posts developed here, rune stones tell of Vikings who ventured off to trade or to torment their foes while a ring of castles and country estates testify to the prosperity of the region in more recent times.

First head north from Stockholm along the busy industrialised E4 towards Arlanda, Stockholm's international airport, but turn off just before you get there in the direction of **Sigtuna** some 14km (9 miles) away. It is rather ironic that one of Sweden's oldest and quaintest little towns should have the country's busiest airport within its community boundary. Fortunately Sigtuna's picturesque main street with its low wooden houses and eighteenth-century 'gingerbread house' Town Hall seems a million miles away from the roaring jumbo jets. The town was founded in AD970 by Sweden's first Christian king, Olof Skötkonung. Christianity seems to have taken quite a hold because Sigtuna has three church ruins all dating from the twelfth and thirteenth centuries and one that got away. Maria Kyrkan, with wall paintings from the fourteenth and fifteenth centuries, survived fire and the Reformation and is still standing. Take a stroll down Stora Gatan ('Big' Street) which is said to be the oldest shopping street in Sweden with a small community museum at one end and the tourist office at the other. Four rune stones at Prästgatan and Runestigen confirm the town's importance as a resting place for pilgrims on the road to Uppsala, the next major stop on this itinerary.

Uppsala, just north of Sigtuna is Scandinavia's oldest university town. By far the quickest way to get there is to head on up the dreary E4, but for a more interesting alternative continue through Sigtuna on the road past Billby, then left and finally right following the signs for a detour to **Skokloster**. The road passes rolling farm and woodland surrounded by water on three sides before descending gently to a fine Baroque castle. Skokloster, a rigidly rectangular affair with regimented rows windows and a turret in each corner is a treasure trove of seventeenth-century furniture, textiles, porcelain and glassware. Many items have barely been disturbed since they were put there by the original owner Field Marshall Carl Gustav Wrangel. The castle was opened to the public in the 1960s and its attractive lakeside setting is now a venue for summer weekend concerts. There is an incongruous looking Motor Museum across the road.

Return along the same route heading towards the E18 and the town of Enköping. On the way you pass four conical burial mounds dating from between AD800 and AD1000 and doubtless a real bane for the local farmer who has to plough around them. One has an oddly placed rune stone stuck on top. There are yet more runes at **Varpsund** where the tall inscribed stone is one of twenty so-called Ingvarstenar (Ingvar Stones) found in central Sweden all telling the story of an expedition to Russia led by a Viking chief called Ingvar in the eleventh century. The smaller road now joins the 263, turn right towards Enköping and about 10km (6 miles) further on, right again along route 55 to **Uppsala**. The tall twin spires of

Uppsala's monumental cathedral come into view first. They dominate the town and somehow even manage to make its pinkish coloured castle look a little insignificant. It was hardly surprising then that when he constructed the castle in the sixteenth century, King Gustav Vasa, never the greatest fan of church power, deliberately built a bastion overlooking the Bishop's residence to remind unruly clergy who was really in charge. The bastion is to this day called Styrbiskop meaning Rule Bishop.

Uppsala has been an archbishopric for more than 800 years and a revered centre of learning for five centuries. But it was once also a focus for pagan rites and sacrifices under the pre-Christian Svea kings. Three 1,500-year-old burial mounds marking the graves of these kings can still be seen at Gamla Uppsala 2km (1 mile) north of the present centre. A pagan temple is believed to have stood where the twelfth-century Old Uppsala church is now. Every ninth year great ceremonies were held in which people and animals were sacrificed to appease gods like Tor, Odin and Frö — their bodies strung up and left to decompose. In the nineteenth century a few sceptics claimed Uppsala's three 'piles', as they are called locally, were natural phenomenon and a dig was carried out to check the theory. They were however confirmed as being the burial mounds of kings or chieftain and today you can stroll over the grassy humps, visit the small museum and sample what is proudly claimed to be 'the drink of the Vikings', a local mead brewed to a fourteenth-century recipe.

Modern Uppsala is effectively divided by the River Fyrisån with the cathedral and the old part of town on one side and the modern shopping centre with its malls and chain stores on the other. The cathedral, built in red brick with bits added and taken away through the centuries may not be to everyone's taste. But the light, cavernous interior is worth a visit, not least because of its importance to Swedish history. It was founded at the end of the thirteenth century after the cathedral at Old Uppsala burned down and was itself severely damaged by fire in the 1700s leaving little to show for its medieval origins. The famous spires were added in the nineteenth century during major reconstruction work at which time the cathedral was also divested of the stone angels and gargoyles that threatened to fall on the heads of worshippers. A chapel behind the altar houses the tomb of King Gustav Vasa surrounded by colourful scenes from his equally colourful life — one of his sons, Johan III lies in another part of a church as do the tombs of botanist Carl von Linné and mystic Emanuel Swedenborg. But the most cherished relic is a gilded silver casket with the remains of Erik the Holy, Sweden's patron saint and twelfth-century king who helped spread Christianity before being killed while trying to fight off the Danes. His remains used to be carried over the fields each spring in the belief that they would bring a good harvest.

Uppsala's rather characterless castle can be found on a low ridge not far from the cathedral. It was originally built by Gustav Vasa in the mid-1500s as a fortress but turned out to be of more use as a royal residence for his sons. The coffers seem to have been somewhat stretched for this building project and when the archbishop asked his royal neighbour to help pay for a new church organ the king is said to have suggested that a street organ would do. Several leading members of the nobility were executed in the notorious castle dungeons and the state hall witnessed the abdication of Queen Kristina in 1564. It was largely rebuilt after a fire in the eighteenth century and now houses university offices and a castle museum.

Uppsala is often described as Sweden's Oxford (England) and in term time the 150,000 strong population is swelled by thousands of students. The town still has a lively café life but the days when students would discuss the state of the universe over a traditional glass of Swedish *punsch* liqueur and a coffee are gone — drink driving laws and liquor prices have seen to that. One tradition that has not disappeared is the Valpurgis Eve celebration. On 30 April each year virtually the entire university takes to the streets to 'chase winter away' and boisterously welcome spring. The students who don white caps for the event usually gather outside the University Library, the Carolina Rediviva. It is one of the largest in Scandinavia with over 2 million books and a manuscript collection which includes a lovely sixth-century 'silver Bible', a Mozart manuscript and the Edda of Snorre Sturlasson, one of the great Norse epics. The Gustavianum dating from 1625 and situated opposite the cathedral was originally the university's main building. Inside its cupola is a seventeenth-century anatomical theatre with sharply rising octagonal tiers from where students could peer down at gruesome dissections taking place on the slab below. By law only the bodies of executed criminals could be used so classes usually had to make do with dead animals. The main university building nearby was constructed in neo-Renaissance style at the end of the nineteenth century.

Among Uppsala university's famous scholars was botanist Carl von Linné and Anders Celsius who invented the temperature scale that bears his name. The Linnean Gardens across the river from the old town were restored by Linné while Professor of Medicine and Botany at the university. Among the 1,300 different species are a few that have survived from his day.

Leave Uppsala by retracing the itinerary south along route 55. Then turn right on the E18 to **Enköping**, a typical provincial Swedish town whose main claim to fame was once its excellent horseradish (it was known in the 1800s as the horseradish town). Just to the south however lies an area well-known for its concentration of rock carvings. The province of Uppland, in which both Uppsala and Enköping lie, has the largest number of ancient runes, carvings and grave monuments in Sweden, evidence of the early settlement in the area. But do not expect to get to see them all as there are about 150,000 in total. Some can be found in the **Rickeby** and **Boglösa** district, just south of Enköping where they are dotted about the countryside in such an arbitrary manner that even the most determined sightseer is reduced to a sort of treasure hunt in order to find them. Important locations are marked with the familiar 'Site of

Interest' sign along the road but often involve a short ramble across fields or scrub. The reward is usually a flat bit of rock with etched wheels, ships and other symbols highlighted in protective red paint that certainly was not there when they were etched about 3,000 years ago. There are some 800 rock carvings in the Enköping area, many are obscure and indistinct but the two most important ones are Brandskogsskeppet (the Brandforest Ship) marked to the left of the road shortly before Boglösa church and further north 'The Chair', a strange two-legged shape sharing a piece of rock with several smaller symbols near Rickeby. Whether the drawings were of magical or ceremonial significance can only be guessed at, what is known however is that they were once close to the water's edge and that the slow rise of the land, some 20m (66ft) in the past 3,000 years, has left the ancient ships and figures distinctly landlocked.

From Enköping route 55 uses two of Mälaren's many islands as stepping stones to cross the lake to Strangnäs on its southern shore. To complete the circuit however continue west towards Västerås, a regional industrial and commercial centre that describes itself as 'the city on Lake Mälaren'. Ängsö castle (sometimes spelt Engsö) a few kilometres off to the left of the E18 tempts visitors with a well-known local ghost story, the legend of the Ängsö Chain. The trinket, which is on display inside, is said to have been won from the Devil by a former resident, John Sparre, during a midnight game of dice. An old bill of sale notes the following spooky provenance; '...the gold chain which is one brought during the night and put on a table in the Ängsö stone house by a ghost.' The house (it is strictly speaking too small to be called a castle) lies on an unspoilt island nature reserve. It dates back to the 1200s but has been extensively restored over the years and is now a well-maintained example of the Swedish Rococo style.

Västerås, some 25km (15½ miles) from Ängsö may be Sweden's most bicycle-friendly town and have its largest inland harbour but it can hardly be described as a major tourist centre. The first impressions are indeed of dull modern suburbs and dubious 1960s architecture. Its industrial pedigree is based on huge concerns like Asea Brown Boveri who manufacture engines, machine robots and other sophisticated technical equipment here. The regional tax authorities also have their base at Västerås in a new building by the harbour appropriately dubbed 'the tax scraper'. But the modern industry conceals a pleasant older core and with the advantage of regular boat excursions from the harbour around Lake Mälaren Västerås warrants at least a brief stop.

In common with many Swedish towns there is an old and a new part — the two sides meeting uncomfortably in Stora Torget where traditional timber buildings around the tourist office on one side face the concrete edifice of the Domus department store on the other. The old town follows Svartån, the Black River through the centre of Västerås. At one end lies the grand looking Konst Museum (the Art Museum) which was sumptuously rehoused in the former nineteenth-century Town Hall when civic staff moved to a glass and concrete construction next door. The nearby castle is a functional looking affair completely lacking in towers and turrets but housing both the County Governor and the County Museum. Further north a picturesque row of wooden and half-timbered houses cling to the riverbank in an area where the small cobbled streets have kept encroaching development at bay. The city's thirteenth-century cathedral lies beyond Stora Torget next to another old part of the town. It is surprisingly light and airy inside and contains the marble sarcophagus of Gustav Vasa's son Erik XIV who was allegedly poisoned with an innocent looking bowl of pea soup. Near the cathedral is a grim reminder of what used to happen to badly behaved school pupils. 'Proban' is a gloomy underground punishment hole, the ultimate deterrent for anyone caught playing truant, fighting or otherwise misbehaving. Even the odd teacher is alleged to have ended up in there. Today's schoolchildren will be relieved to know that it has not been used since 1801.

Anyone who has not had enough of ancient relics can visit a sizeable burial mound called Anundshögen at **Badelunda** where according to tradition Bröt Anund is buried with his treasure of gold. The mound and two stone ship formations lie 6km (4 miles) from the city. Fifteen kilometres (9 miles) away to the south is **Tidö** castle, another lakeside castle and one of the most elegant of the grand houses in this region. It is open to the public in summer and has a popular Toy Museum with some 30,000 exhibits — among them King Karl XVI Gustav's cherished Austin Seven Racer pedal car which he was given as a child. Continuing over the peninsula the country road passes Rytterne and then joins the larger route 53 which crosses Mälaren at Kvicksund, its narrowest point. Off to the right is Strömsholm Castle and the 110km (68 mile) long Strömsholm Kanal which was once used to transport ore from the mining areas further north. In summer the *M/S Strömsholm* makes regular excursions through the twenty-six locks.

The village of **Tumbo** on the right just after Kvicksund boasts seven rune stones, including one unceremoniously stuck in the church wall next to a drainpipe. Medieval vandalism ensured that many such relics were used as building materials. Just along the coast is the small community of **Torshälla**, named after an ancient sacrificial site but now a tranquil village. **Mälarbaden** 4km (2 miles) to the north is a popular summer recreation centre with camping, swimming and golf. **Eskilstuna**, a modern town in the opposite direction has alternative entertainment in the form of Parken Zoo, a combined animal and amusement park. The park is best known locally for its white tigers. Eskilstuna was named after an eleventh-century English missionary called Eskil who became bishop of what was then known as Tuna. When he was martyred the place became known as Eskilstuna. It owes much of its development to immigrant craftsmen from Germany who taught people how to work local metals. Rademachersmedjorna (Rademacher's Smithies) have been carefully preserved since the seventeenth century and some still produce souvenir metal goods in copper, silver and gold although others are just as likely to sell crafted wood and textiles. The town's Art Museum has a good collection of works by Swedish artists.

The Mälare Valley is littered with runes and rock carvings, but one of the most famous is **Sigurdsristningen** (the Sigurd Carving) near the old castle of Sundbyholm. It is known not so much for its text as for its detailed images which tell the complicated saga of *Sigurd the Dragon Slayer*. These have been irreverently described as Sweden's first strip cartoon. To get there leave Eskilstuna on the E20 in the direction of Strängnäs turning left after a few kilometres to the village of Kjula. Small country roads wind their way through farm and woodland past other runes and remains to Sundbyholm. The Sigurd Carving lies in total obscurity down a narrow unmade road to the right, just before the main drive to Sundbyholm Castle. There is a small parking area and an ill defined track where people have scrambled up the tree-clad knoll to take a look. The carving is on a large smooth rock with the runic inscription; 'Sigrid, Alrik's mother, Orm's daughter, made this bridge for her husband Holmger's Sigröd's father's soul'. The water level has since dropped and there is no longer need for a bridge here—but 1,000 years ago Sigrid no doubt believed such a charitable act would send her husband to heaven, implying that she and her family were Christians.

Sundbyholm castle just down the road is worth a quick pause and perhaps a swim from one of the sandy beaches nearby. The surrounding parkland has a small yacht harbour, a golf course and marked walking trails. Sundbyholm, more of a simple seventeenth-century manor house than a castle, fell into disrepair after a fire but was immortalised in its dilapidated state by artist Prins Eugen whose much admired oil painting *The Old Castle* has been turned into a best selling print. It has now been fully restored and is open to the public in summer.

Return to the E20 which hugs the southern lake shore without ever managing to produce a good glimpse of it and head east for Strängräs. Alternatively you can follow the small country lanes through farmland and forest and cross the bridge at Björsundet onto the **Fogdö** peninsula which has a ruined Viking fort, the remains of a thirteenth-century convent at Vårfruberga and several attractive old village churches. The next stop on the route back towards Stockholm is the peaceful lakeside town of **Strängnäs**. It was not always so tranquil. This was another great pagan centre and the unfortunate Eskil was stoned to death here as he tried to introduce Christianity to its reluctant residents. As if to make up for all that Strängnäs now lies in the shadow of a large thirteenth-century cathedral. Narrow cobbled streets lined with small wooden houses rise up to the church in the old part of town. One of them, Gyllenhielmsgatan has even been called 'Sweden's loveliest'. The cathedral, whose mellow red-brick tower provides high-rise accommodation for hundreds of noisy crows, contains the tombs of King Karl IX and his family and that of his illegitimate son Karl Karlson Gyllenhielm. The leg irons nearby are a

The peaceful lakeside town of Strängnäs

Old world charm survives in Västerås — wooden houses on the banks of Svartån

Runes And Remains

The Vikings may have had a bad press but theirs is just one of many ancient cultures which have left an indelible mark on the Swedish countryside. Using its primeval rock as building blocks, generations have marked out their own beliefs, religion and burial rites in mysterious stone formations across the countryside. Some, like Ales Stenar in the province of Skåne or the rock carvings in Bohuslän are impressive sites requiring little imagination to appreciate the creative forces that put them there. Others, perhaps just an oddly shaped upright stone or a pile of smaller rocks call for a more finely honed interest in prehistoric relics.

Rune Stone at Gripsholm Castle, Mariefred

There are far too many such sites to detail and only the most important can be picked out in this book. Suffice to say that even lesser relics are marked with a 'sight of interest' sign and the travellers' individual schedule can be left to determine whether it warrants further investigation, which can mean a lengthy scramble across rough terrain.

As a brief guide, the main types of remains are:

1. Stone Age graves (up to about 1500BC): of which the most impressive consist of stone blocks placed on their sides with one on top as a roof or structures known as 'Gångriftor' where the large stones form a T-shape with an inner chamber containing the graves of generations of the same family.

2. Bronze Age graves (1500-500BC): stone cairns dating from this era cover several graves and are usually sited in a dominant position, on high ground for example. They can be found all over the country.

3. Early Iron Age (500BC-AD500): it now became usual to conduct burials within a burial field and graves are marked by cairns or stone formations. The so-called 'Bautastenar', individual raised stones without text, come from this period as do the 'ship formations', an oval ring in the vague form of a ship usually with taller stones at either end. Stone circles called 'Judgement Rings' in Sweden are also from the era. They are believed to have been graves which served a double purpose as meeting or *ting* sites.

4. Late Iron Age (AD500-AD1050): burial grounds are found in each village. Christianity had an influence towards the end of this period and bodies were no longer burned. Graves were marked by piles of stones or single monuments.

5. Rune Stones (mainly between AD800-AD10000: they are a form of personal memorial with a Norse reworking of ancient Greek or Latin script adapted for carving into stone or wood. The text often includes details of the person who raised the stone, the deceased and how they died. There may be either Christian and magical symbolism and, very occasionally, a curse as on the Björketorp Stone in Blekinge province (see Chapter 3, The South-East).

6. Rock Carvings or 'Hallristningar' (up to 1500BC): these symbolic drawings can be found on flat pieces of rock in several parts of Sweden. They include pictures of ships, people and animals and may have magical significance.

bizarre souvenir of 12 years imprisonment in Poland. Gyllenhielm may have been illegitimate (his mother was the daughter of a local priest) but his good work, including the establishment of Sweden's first State school, was not forgotten. Even Queen Kristina is said to have followed his funeral procession along the road that now bears his name.

The fifteenth-century building near the cathedral is called Roggeborgen, and is generally held to be where, on 6 June 1523, Gustav Vasa was officially elected king of Sweden. Another local landmark is the red painted windmill near the waters edge. Strängnäs like many other Mälare towns is the departure point for a variety of boat excursions and ferry services, including sightseeing tours, regular connections with Stockholm and day trips to neighbouring communities.

Follow the signs for the E20 and pick up the busy trunk road east of Strängnäs as it heads into prosperous Stockholm commuter country. The turn-off for Mariefred and Gripsholm is 17km (10½ miles) further on — details about them are found in the 'Places to Visit Around Stockholm' section at the end of this chapter. Across the little bay lies Taxinge, yet another of Mälaren's many grand houses with pleasant gardens, lovely views over the lake and islands and a restaurant in summer.

Stockholm commuter belt begins with a vengeance at Södertälje as the E20 meets the E4 motorway from the south in a mass of road signs and lane markings. Lurking behind the traffic is in fact one of Sweden's oldest towns although you would not know it today. The Russians burned **Södertälje** to the ground three times during the sixteenth and seventeenth centuries and there followed self-inflicted destruction in the 1960s when much of the old centre disappeared to make way for commercial develop-

ments. SAAB Scania now makes trucks and engines here. The twelfth-century St Ragnhilds Church has survived and a number of old buildings

including a photographic studio and a fire brigade museum have been assembled at Torekällbergets Museum on the edge of town.

Stockholm is now just 35km (22 miles) away and all that remains is to join the trail of commuters and commercial vehicles as the E20 motorway leaves the hilly wooded countryside behind and heads into the suburbs. The grey stone church at **Botkyrka**, visible on the left, contains the remains of Botvid, a twelfth-century Swedish saint and evidently a questionable judge of character. He was murdered with his own axe by a man he planned to turn into a missionary. The motorway continues towards inner Stockholm, turning into Essingleden as it crosses Lake Mälaren on a 1km (½ mile) long bridge. Traffic conditions rarely allow more than a fleeting glimpse of the pleasant views toward central Stockholm in the east and the islands of Lake Mälaren in the west.

Additional Information

Places to Visit in Stockholm

Arme Museet (Army Museum)
Riddargatan 13
☎ 08 661 7602
Open: Tuesday to Sunday 11am-4pm.
Closed Monday except June to August
when also 11am-4pm.

**Arkitektur Museet (Museum of
Architecture)**
Skeppsholmen
☎ 08 679 7510
Open: Tuesday 11am-9pm, Wednesday
to Sunday 11am-5pm. Mondays closed.

Baltic Aquarium
Fjäderholmarna (take the boat from
Strömkajen or Nybrokajen)
Open: daily 28 April to 20 June 11am-
6pm, 22 June to 5 August 11am-9pm,
6 August to 2 September 11am-8pm, 3
September to 30 September 11am-6pm.

Biologiska Museet (Museum of Biology)
Djurgården
☎ 08 661 1383
Open: daily 10am-3pm (April to September 10am-4pm).

**Folkens Museum Etnokgrafiska (National
Museum of World Ethnography)**
Djurgårdsbrunnsvägen 34
☎ 08 666 5000
Open: Tuesday to Friday 11am-4pm,
Saturday and Sunday 12noon-5pm.
Mondays closed.

Gröna Lund Tivoli
Djurgården
Open: end April to mid-September.
☎ 08 660 3000 for precise times.

Hallwylska Museet (Hallwyl Museum)
Hamngatan 4
☎ 08 666 4499
Open: Tuesday to Sunday 12noon-3pm,
July to August daily 11am-4pm.

**Historiska Museet (Historical Museum)
and the Royal Coin Cabinet**
Narvavägen 13-17
Open: Tuesday to Sunday 12noon-5pm.
Mondays closed.

Kaknäs Tornet (Kaknäs Tower)
Djurgården
☎ 08 789 2435
Open: daily January to March and
October to December 9am-6pm, April
and September 9am-10pm, May to
August 9am-12midnight.

Kungliga Slottet (the Royal Palace)
Skattkammaren (Royal Treasury)
Slottet
Södra Valvet
Open: Monday to Saturday 11am-3pm
(May to August to 4pm), Sunday
12noon-4pm.

Visningsvåningarna (Royal Apartments)
☎ 08 789 8500
Open: Tuesday to Sunday 12noon-3pm
(May to August 10am-3pm, Sunday
12noon-3pm). Mondays closed.

Livsrustkammaren (Royal Armoury)
Slottsbacken 3
☎ 08 666 4475
Open: Tuesday to Friday 10am-4pm,
Saturday and Sunday 11am-4pm. Also
open Mondays 10am-4pm during
period May to August.

Slottsmuseet (Palace Museum)
Open: May to September, Monday to
Sunday 12noon-3pm.

Slottskyrkan (Palace Church)
Open: May to September, Monday to
Sunday 12noon-3pm.

*Gustav III's Antikmuseet (Gustav III's
Museum of Antiquities)*
The Royal Palace
Lejonbacken
☎ 008 789 8500
Open: June to August, Monday to
Sunday 12noon-3pm.

Riksalen (Hall of State)
☎ 08 789 8500
Open: May to September, Monday to
Sunday 12noon-3pm.

**Medelhavs Museet (Museum of Mediter-
ranean and Near Eastern Antiquities)**
Fredsgatan 2
Open: Tuesday 11am-9pm, Wednesday
to Sunday 11am-4pm. Closed Mondays.

Medeltidsmuseet (Museum of Medieval History)
Strömparterren
Norrbro
☎ 08 206168
Open: Tuesday to Sunday 11am-5pm (Wednesday to 7pm). June to August, Tuesday and Thursday also open to 7pm.

Moderna Museet (Museum of Modern Art)
Skeppsholmen
☎ 08 666 4250
Open: Tuesday to Thursday 11am-9pm. Friday to Sunday 11am-6pm. Mondays closed.

Musik Museet (Museum of Music)
Sibyllegatan 2
☎ 08 666 4530
Open: Tuesday to Sunday 11am-4pm. Mondays closed.

National Museet (National Museum)
Blasieholmen
☎ 08 666 4250
Open: Tuesday to Sunday 10am-5pm (Tuesday and Thursday late opening), Mondays closed.

Nordiska Museet (Nordic Museum)
Djurgårdsbron
☎ 08 666 4750
Open: Tuesday to Friday 10am-4pm (Thursday 8pm), Weekends 11am-4pm. Mondays closed except June to August when open 10am-4pm.

Ostasiatiska Museet (Museum of Far Eastern Antiquities)
Skeppsholmen
☎ 08 666 4250
Open: Tuesday 11am-9pm, Wednesday to Sunday 11am-5pm. Mondays closed.

Postmuseum (Postal Museum)
Lilla Nygatan 6
☎ 08 781 1755
Open: Tuesday to Saturday 11am-3pm (Wednesday to 8pm). Sunday 11am-4pm. Mondays closed.

Riddarhuset (House of Nobility)
☎ 08 100857
Riddarhustorget 10
Open: all year Monday to Friday 11.30am-12.30pm.

Riksdagshuset (Parliament)
Helgeandsholmen
☎ 08 786 4000
Open: January to May, Saturday and Sunday 12noon-2pm, end June to early September Monday to Friday 12noon-3.30pm. Guided tours only.

Skansen (Open-Air Museum)
Djurgården
☎ 08 663 0500
Open: daily 9am-5pm (May to August 9am-10pm).

Sjöhistoriska Museet (Maritime Museum)
Djurgårdsbrovägen 24
☎ 08 666 4900
Open: daily 10am-5pm (Tuesday to 8.30pm in spring and autumn).

Stadshuset (City Hall)
Hantverkargatan 1
☎ 08 785 9000
Guided tours daily at 10am and 12noon. Tower open May to September 10am-4.30pm.

Strindberg Museet
Drottninggatan 85
☎ 08 113 789
Open: Tuesday to Friday 10am-4pm, Saturday and Sunday 12noon-4pm. Mondays closed.

Tekniska Museet (Technical Museum)
Museivägen 7
☎ 08 663 100085
Open: Monday to Friday 10am-4pm, Saturday and Sunday 12noon-4pm.

Telemuseet (Telecommunications Museum)
Museivägen 7
☎ 08 663 1085
Open: Monday to Friday 10am-4pm, Saturday and Sunday 12noon-4pm.

Thielska Galleriet (Thiel Gallery)
Sjötullsbacken 6-8
Djurgården
☎ 08 662 5884
Open: Monday to Saturday 12noon-4pm, Sunday 1-4pm.

Vasa Museet (Vasa Museum)
Galärvarvet, Djurgården
☎ 08 666 4800
Open: daily 10am-5pm (June to August
9.30am-7pm). September to June until
8pm on Wednesdays.

Waldemarsudde
Djurgården
☎ 08 662 1833
Open: Tuesday to Sunday 11am-4pm
(June to August 11am-5pm, Tuesday
and Thursday to 9pm) Mondays closed.

Stockholm: Useful Information

ACCOMMODATION

For hotel information and reservations
Hotellcentralen (accommodation
booking office and information)
Central Station
☎ (08) 240880 (Fax) 7918686
Postal address: Centralstationen
11120 Stockholm

**Hotellcentralen (accommodation
booking office and information)**
Central Station, ground floor
☎ 08 240880
Postal address: Centralstationen
111 20 Stockholm

For private room and guest house
information
Hotel Tjänsten
Vasagatan 15-17
☎ (08) 104437

For information about Youth Hostels in
the Stockholm area and on the islands
contact
STF (Svenska Turistföreningen)
Drottninggatan 31-33
☎ (08) 7903100

Hotels
Grand Hotel
Södra Blasieholmshamnen
☎ (08) 6793500

Diplomat Hotel
Strandvägen 7C
☎ (08) 6635800

Sheraton Stockholm Hotel and Towers
Tegelbacken 6
☎ (08) 142600

Sergel Plaza Hotel
Brunkebergstorg 9
☎ (08) 226600

Royal Viking Hotel, SAS
Vasagatan 1
☎ (08) 141000

Resman Hotel
Drottninggatan 77
☎ (08) 141395

Queen's Hotel
Drottninggatan 71A
☎ (08) 249460

Kung Carl Hotel
Birger Jarlsgatan 23
☎ (08) 6113110

KOM Hotel
Döbelnsgatan 17-19
☎ (08) 235630

Central Hotel
Vasagatan 38
☎ (08) 220840

Birger Jarl Hotel
Tulegatan 8
☎ (08) 151020

Örnskold Hotel
Nybrogatan 6
☎ (08) 6670285

Strand Hotel SAS
Nybrokajen 9
☎ (08) 678780

Stockholm Plaza Hotel
Birger Jarlsgatan 29
☎ (08) 145120

Lord Nelson Hotel
Västerlångatan 22
☎ (08) 232390

Youth Hostels
AF Chapman
Skeppsholmen
☎ (08) 6795015 (open April to December)

Hantverkshuset
Skeppsholmen
☎ (08) 6795017 (open all year except
Christmas)

Columbus Hotel and Vandrarhem
Tärhovsgatan 11
☎ (08) 6441717 (open all year except
Christmas)

Gustav af Klint
Stadsgårdskajen
☎ (08) 6404077 (open all year)

Långholmen
Kronohäktet
☎ (08) 6680510 (open all year)

Zinken
Zinkens väg 20
☎ (08) 6582900 (open all year)

Campsites
Farstanäsets Camping
Ågestavägen
123 52 Stockholm (open May to September)
☎ (08) 945765

Ängby Camping
16155 Bromma
☎ (08) 370420 (open all year)

Bredäng Camping
12731 Skärholmen
☎ (08) 977071 (open all year)

Rösjöbadets Camping
19156 Sollentuna
☎ (08) 962184

BANKS
Bank opening hours are Monday to Friday 9.30am-3pm. Some in the city centre stay open until 5.30pm.
The Forex currency exchange office in the Central Station is open Monday to Sunday 8am-9pm.
Forex, City Terminalen, Karabergsviadukten is open Monday to Friday 9am-7pm. Some post offices also have an exchange service.
There is a 7-day currency exchange service at Arlanda international airport.

CAR HIRE
Avis
Sveavägen 61
☎ (08) 349910

Budget
Sveavägen 153-155
☎ (08) 334383
Reservation Centre 020 787787

Hertz
Vasagatan 26
☎ (08) 240720
Reservation Service (08) 181315

Interrent
Hotel Sheraton
Tegelbacken 6
☎ (08) 210650

EMERGENCIES
For police, ambulance, firebrigade
☎ 90 000
Stockholm Police Headquarters
Agnegatan 33-37
☎ (08) 7693000
Local police stations at Bryggargatan 19 and Tuleg 4.

MEDICAL HELP
Emergency medical care is available from hospitals in each district. Call the local hospital or City Akuten ☎ (08) 117102. For doctor on duty out of hours call (08) 6449200.
24-hour Pharmacy
C.W. Scheele
Klarabergsgatan 64
☎ (08) 248280

Dentist
Emergency dental treatment is available at St Eriks Hospital, Fleminggatan 22 from 8am-7pm. Acute cases only after 7pm. Information 8am-9pm ☎ (08) 6541117. For emergencies after 9pm call (08) 6449200.

POST OFFICES
Post offices are usually open Monday to Friday 9.30am-6pm. Saturday 10am-1pm.
The main Stockholm post office at Vasagatan 28-34 ☎ (08) 7812000) opens 8am-6.30pm.
The Post Office at the Central Station opens Monday to Friday 7am-10pm, Saturday 10am-7pm, Sunday 12noon-7pm.

TAXIS
Taxi Stockholm ☎ (08) 150000
Taxi 1 ☎ (08) 6700000

TELEPHONE SERVICES
Telecom Centre, Central Station
Open: daily 8am-9pm.

TRAVEL

Air
Arlanda Airport (45km/28 miles north
of Stockholm)
☎ (08) 7976000
Airport buses leave every 10-15 minutes
from Cityterminalen
Klarabergsviadukten ☎ (08) 6736000

Road
Bus/local rail/underground
for information ☎ (08) 600100
Buses go from City terminalen

Rail
Stockholm's main station, Central
Stationen is the terminus for mainline
and local trains.
For information ☎ (020) 757575

Motoring Information
Motormännens Resebyrå
Sveagatan 22
☎ (08) 7822810

Local Ferry/Sightseeing Services
Strömma Kanalbolaget
Scheduled services and excursions from
Nybroviken ☎ (08) 233375

Waxholmsbolaget
Boats from Strömkajen, opposite Grand
Hotel
☎ (08) 6795830/140830

Stockholm Sightseeing Boats
From Strömkajen
☎ (08) 240470

International Ferry Services
Silja Line (to Finland)
Kungsgatan 2
☎ (08) 222140

Viking Line (to Finland)
Central Stationen
☎ (08) 7145600

**Baltic Express (to St Petersburg/Baltic
States)**
Vasagatan 4
☎ (020) 290029

SIGHTSEEING

Boats from Stömkajen
☎ 08 240470

Archipelago Visits and Excursions
The Excursion Shop, Sweden House for
information, timetables, tourist tickets
for boats, buses, excursions.
(Address and telephone same as the
main tourist centre).

TOURIST INFORMATION CENTRE

Sverigehuset (Sweden House)
Kungsträdgården
Postal address Box 7542
10393 Stockholm
☎ (08) 7892490

Places to Visit Around Stockholm

Drottningholm
*Drottningholms Slott (Drottningholm
Palace)*
☎ 08 759 0310
Open: daily May to August 11am-
4.30pm, September weekdays 1-3.30pm,
Saturday and Sunday 12noon-3.30pm.

Drottningholm Court Theatre
☎ 08 759 0406
Open: May to August Monday to
Saturday 12noon-4.30pm, Sunday 1-
4.30pm. September daily 1-3.30pm.

Lidingö
Millesgården (Milles House)
Carl Milles Väg 2
☎ 08 731 5060
Open: Tuesday to Sunday 11am-4pm,
May to September 10am-5pm including
Mondays.

Mariefred
Gripsholm Castle
☎ 0159 10194
Open: November to February weekends
12noon-3pm only. March, April, September and October Tuesday to Friday 10am-
3pm, Saturday and Sunday 12noon-3pm.
May to August daily 10am-4pm.

Places to Visit Around Lake Mälaren

Ängsö
Castle
On Ängsö peninsula east of Västerås
☎ 0171 44025/44020

Eskilstuna
Rademachersmedjorna (Rademacher Smithies)
Rademachergatan 42-50
Open: April to August daily 10am-4pm (June, July, August to 6pm) September to November Tuesday to Sunday 10am-4pm, December to March Tuesday to Saturday 10am-4pm.

Parken Zoo
Open: May to early September daily from 10am.

Konst Museet (Art Museum)
Kyrkogatan 9
☎ 016 101369
Open: Tuesday to Sunday 12noon-4pm. Mondays closed.

Strängnäs
Museum
☎ 0152 13400
Open: Tuesday to Friday 12noon-3pm, Saturday and Sunday 12noon-4pm. Also open Monday June to August.

Södertälje
Torekällbergets Museum (Open-Air museum)
☎ 0755 19044
Open: daily all year 11am-4pm.

Skokloster
Castle
Skohalvön
Open: May to September with guided tours every hour from 11am-4pm.

Skokloster Motor Museum
☎ 018 386100
Open: all year, summer 11am-5pm, winter 12noon-4pm.

Tidö
Castle and Toy Museum
15km (9 miles) south of Västerås
☎ 021 53042
Open: May and September, Saturday and Sunday only 12noon-5pm, June to August Tuesday to Sunday 12noon-5pm.

Uppsala
Carolina Rediviva (University Library)
Carolinabacken
☎ 018 182084
Open: Monday to Friday 9am-8.30pm, Saturday 9am-5.30pm (June to August, also Sunday 1-3.30pm).

Gustavianum (Anatomical Theatre)
Open: daily 10 June to 25 August 11am-3pm.

Linnean Gardens and Museum
Svartbäcksgatan 27
Open: May to August daily 9am-9pm, September daily 9am-7pm. Museum open mid-May to mid-September, Tuesday to Sunday 1-4pm.

Uppsala Castle
Open: April to September Monday to Saturday 11am-3pm, Sunday 11am-4pm (24 June to 20 August Monday to Friday 9am-7pm, Saturday and Sunday 10am-5pm).

Upplands Museum
St Eriks Torg 10
☎ 018 102290
Open: Monday to Friday 12noon-4pm, Saturday 11am-4pm, Sunday 12noon-5pm.

Västerås
Konst Museet (Art Museum)
Fiskartorget 3
Open: Tuesday to Saturday 11am-4pm, Sunday 12noon-4pm. Mondays closed.

Västmanland County Museum
Västerås Castle (by Svartån river)
Open: Tuesday to Sunday 12noon-4pm. Mondays closed.

Tourist Information Centres

Eskilstuna
Hamngatan 19
Rademachersmedjorna
☎ 016 114500

Sigtuna
Stora gatan 33
☎ 00760 51432

Södertälje
Gamla Centralstationen
☎ 0755 18899

Strängnäs
Järnvägsgatan 1
☎ 0152 18143

Uppsala
Fyris torg 6 and at the castle
☎ 018 117500/174800

Västerås
Stora Torget 5
☎ 021 161830

5
DALARNA - THE FOLKLORE DISTRICT

A sk any group of foreign tourists what they bought from Sweden and the chances are that a fair number will admit to having a wooden Dalecarlian horse tucked away in the luggage. Marketing men have tried to update Sweden's image with smart new logos and slick advertising executives have called for a change — but the stocky red horse just kicks back. The perennially popular 'Dala Häst' is, and looks set to remain, the most familiar international symbol of Sweden. It is no coincidence therefore that the horse bears the name of the province that more than any other has come to represent tradition and folklore. It originates from Dalarna and forms part of a local folk-art heritage which has for years attracted both Swedish and foreign visitors to the area. The influx of tourists has in turn helped to boost local interest in Dalecarlian traditions while also prompting criticism, mainly unfounded, that too many camp sites and plastic waterslides are springing up in the area.

The painting of Dalecarlian horses, to which we shall return later in this chapter, is one of many ways in which generations of talented and artistic Dalecarlians expressed themselves. Their regional costumes, now worn only at special celebrations such as Midsummer are among the most colourful and varied in Sweden. The local fiddle music lives on and naive Dala folk-art from the eighteenth and nineteenth centuries is coveted all over the country. Many of the pictures show biblical scenes, but here the familiar Old and New Testament subjects wear the yellow woollen breeches or striped aprons of Dalecarlian folk dress. Local artists who had no idea what Jerusalem looked like simply modelled it on their own communities and the people who lived there. Decorative panache and imagination provided the final touch and many painters not content with small works covered whole walls and ceilings with images and proverbs at a time when wallpaper was strictly for the wealthy. Wooden furniture was similarly decorated with stylised flowers and leaves and original pieces now sell for astronomic prices at auction.

But creative traditions in Dalarna went beyond simple folk art. Two of Sweden's most talented and internationally admired painters, Carl

Larsson and Anders Zorn also lived and worked in the province. Their homes are open to the public and it is significant that one room in Carl Larsson's homestead is covered from floor to ceiling in the naive Dalecarlian folk paintings that he also admired.

Summer in Dalarna is a time of festivals, open-air plays and a good humoured sporting event on Lake Siljan called 'Church Boat Races' in which decorated long boats once used to ferry the faithful become the focus of a more secular spectacle. The races begin after Midsummer, a time of year greeted with great celebrations everywhere in Sweden but most famously and boisterously in Dalarna. Here every village has its own Maypole around which festivities continue right through the year's shortest night. Locals who usually favour jeans and tee-shirts enjoy the opportunity to don otherwise impractical Dalecarlian costumes and maybe join a nostalgic folk dance. Nowadays they are likely to find themselves putting on the show for appreciative coachloads of 'southerners' from Göteborg or Malmö where such traditions are thin on the ground. Open-air theatre performances form part of the summer calendar too. The most famous of them, *Himmlaspelet* or *The Heaven Play* easily rivals Agatha Christie's *Mousetrap* in sheer staying power. For more than 50 years now 'Mats the Farmhand' has been entertaining audiences as he heads off to heaven to demand justice for his betrothed who suffered the misfortune of being burned at the stake as a witch. The play, set to look like one of those Dala folk paintings, is performed in Leksand throughout July.

Dalarna lies in the heart of Sweden in more ways than one. Although just 3 hours drive from Stockholm it is here that the northern fells meet the central lowlands. The meadows and farmland in the south-eastern corner give way to forested hills and dales and, in the north-west, to low mountains that stretch across the Norwegian border. Lake Siljan at the centre dominates a landscape said to have been shaped 360 million years ago when a huge meteor collided with the earth. The interesting geology of what is known as the 'Siljan Ring' has attracted oil exploration projects but would-be Swedish oil tycoons have so far had little to show for their efforts. While 'black gold' remains elusive, the bedrock in the south-eastern part of the province sustained not only the local economy but came to be known as Sweden's 'treasure chest'. Ores such as copper and zinc have been mined in the area for hundreds of years and, with local iron, played a major role in helping Sweden to flex its muscles as a wealthy and influential Nordic power during the seventeenth century. Right at the heart of this new-found prosperity lay **Falun**, Dalarna's administrative centre and the start of this itinerary.

Falun is known as the 'Copper Town'. According to one dubious story it effectively owes its existence to a white goat which is said to have been found by its Viking owners covered in a strange red dust. Curiosity was aroused and copper was discovered — the rest is history as they say. What is certain is that copper ore has been mined at Falun for over 1,000 years and that a documented thirteenth-century share purchase proves it to be the oldest mining enterprise in Sweden. A sizeable town, once the second largest in the land, grew alongside 'Copper Mountain' which had begun to resemble a Swiss cheese with its disorganised labyrinth of holes and tunnels. In 1687 the mine paid the price of over-eager exploitation and the whole unstable honeycomb collapsed creating a massive crater that can still be seen today. But the Falun miners had luck on their side — not only was no-one killed, but the 'disaster' opened up new ore seams which could be mined by open cast methods for the next 50 years. The huge hole also turned seventeenth-century Falun into a major tourist attraction.

Falu Gruva (Falun Coppermine) is worth a stop even today. Although ❈ commercial mining finally came to an end in 1992 regular tours take visitors 60m (197ft) down in a modern elevator and then along old drifts worked between the seventeenth and nineteenth centuries. A doleful bell rings continuously as a reminder of the days when its chimes signalled that the water pumps were operating. Silence would have meant imminent danger to the miners who worked by the light of flaming torches. Ore was extracted by lighting fires to crack the rock and Swedish botanist Carl von Linné who visited the mine in the eighteenth century commented that conditions down there were as dreadful 'as hell itself'. More recent VIP tourists such as Scandinavian crowned heads have had their signatures etched and gilded on a rough rock wall. Visitors to the mine are advised to wear warm clothes and sensible shoes — waterproof capes and hard hats are provided.

At its peak Falun copper mine produced two-thirds of the world's copper. But it did more than fill Sweden's coffers — it effectively changed the face of towns and villages throughout the country. The familiar red colour used to preserve and brighten the nation's timber houses is based on copper vitriol, a bi-product of the mine. Recent reports that the production of 'Falu Röd Färg' (Falu Red Colour) was to cease were met with dismay from traditionalists even though equally good products are now made elsewhere. Tour guides illustrate the amazing properties of Falun mine's copper vitriol with the story of a young miner who disappeared in 1670 and whose perfectly preserved body was found some 50 years later. It was put in a glass coffin as a local curiosity but remained unidentified until his former fiancé, by now an old lady, recognised the body as that of her betrothed.

The mine tour lasts about 40 minutes and afterwards it is worth having a look in the Mining Museum opposite the entrance with its collection of mining memorabilia including a thirteenth-century 'share certificate' or deed of exchange relating to one eighth of 'Copper Mountain'. There is a small shop which sells the famous red paint and a cafeteria. Near the mine lies Trädstaden (the Wooden Town), an old miners' quarter and now popular among local artists and craftsmen.

The mine and its associated industries are operated by a large conglomerate called Stora Kopparberg's Bergslags AB whose shortened form 'STORA' meaning simply 'Big' can be seen everywhere. Stora

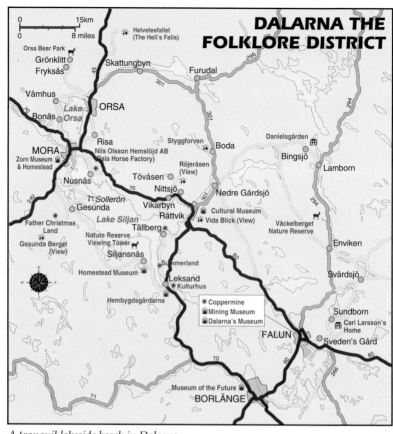

DALARNA THE FOLKLORE DISTRICT

0 — 15km
0 — 8 miles

Helvetesfallet (The Hell's Falls)

Orsa Bear Park
Grönklitt
Fryksås

Skattungbyn

Furudal

296

301

Våmhus
Bonäs

Lake Orsa

ORSA

301

294

Risa
Nils Olsson Hemslöjd AB (Pala Horse Factory)

Styggforven

Boda

Danielsgården

MORA
Zorn Museum & Homestead

Nusnäs

242

Sollerön
Gesunda

Father Christmas Land

Gesunda Berget (View)

Lake Siljan

Tövåsen

Röjeråsen (View)

Nittsjö

Vikarbyn
Rättvik

Tällberg

Nature Reserve
Viewing Tower

Siljansnäs

Homestead Museum

70

Nedre Gärdsjö

Cultural Museum
Vida Blick (View)

301

Bingsjö

Lamborn

Våckelberget
Nature Reserve

294

Enviken

Svärdsjö

Summerland

Leksand
Kulturhus

Hembygdsgårdarna

80

* Coppermine
▲ Mining Museum
🏛 Dalarna's Museum

Sundborn
Carl Larsson's Home

FALUN
Sveden's Gård

70

80

296

Museum of the Future
BORLÄNGE

71

A tranquil lakeside beach in Dalarna

Summer in Dalarna is a time of festivities and nostalgic folk dancing

One of the festivities celebrated in Dalarna is the 'Church Boat Race' on Lake Siljan

Kopparberg is also the name of Falun's oldest church, parts of which date back to the 1300s. In the past the fortunes of the town were directly linked to those of Copper Mountain and the elegant gently sloping square, town hall and the Kristine church date from the prosperous 1600s. Modern paper, chemical and graphics industries have taken over the vacuum left by mining and the busy pedestrian shopping streets still have an air of well-being. Large sums of money were also invested in turning Falun, already a frequent host to major Nordic ski competitions, into a centre for sports. The Lugnet recreation area is crowned by a 90m (295ft) and a 70m (230ft) ski jump and if you ever wondered how it feels to stand at the top of such an edifice in the secure knowledge that you do not have to whizz down it this is your chance. Visitors can take the lift up the 90m (295ft) jump in summer and the view from the top is spectacular. You could even be lucky enough to see the Swedish ski jump team getting some out of season practice — not on snow but on something akin to astro-turf.

As the main administrative centre for Dalarna, Falun also houses the splendid little Dalarna's Museum with a rich and varied collection of Dalecarlian folk paintings, costumes and domestic interiors. A smashed up Stradivarius on one wall demonstrates how religious piety of the nineteenth century clashed with popular fiddle music and dancing. Local *spelmen* (literally music-men) sometimes had their instruments destroyed by God fearing citizens who considered such frivolity to be sinful. Fortunately those days are gone and a room devoted to famous Dalecarlian musicians includes a selection of cassette recordings for visitors to play. Far removed from the unsophisticated folk culture is the elegantly reconstructed writing room that once belonged to Sweden's Nobel Prize winning author Selma Lagerlöf who spent some of her most productive years in Falun at the beginning of the twentieth century.

Leave Falun on route 80 in the direction of Gävle but turn almost immediately left following the signposts for Sundborn. **Svedens Gård** signposted on the right is known as the place where Linné the botanist celebrated his wedding to a local girl. But the main attraction in this area lies about 8km (5 miles) further on at the village of **Sundborn**, home of popular Swedish artist Carl Larsson whose idealised turn-of-the-century domestic scenes now grace postcards, plates and writing paper. Some 70,000 visitors descend on the odd but picturesque Carl Larsson Gård every year and on holiday weekends waiting times for guided tours can run to 3 hours — a testimony to his popularity. Carl Larsson was a gifted artist who spent his early years in Paris. But it was his talent for depicting scenes of domestic bliss in gentle watercolour and finally the publication of his illustrations in a book called *Ett Hem* (A Home) that endeared him to the public. Anyone familiar with his work should in fact feel quite at home in the house which is kept as it was in Larsson's day by members of the 200-strong family association. But if the cluttered interiors look familiar they are also a good deal more cramped than the artist would have us believe in his works. Enthusiastic guides, dressed to look the part in ankle length pinafore dresses point out Larsson's penchant for painting family portraits on interior doors and decorating just about anything else that stood still long enough. Meaningful texts are scattered around the house and a welcoming rhyme greets visitors above the front door. The coloured interiors must have been distinctly avant garde in their day, and one cannot help but wonder what the down to earth villagers of Sundborn made of this strange artist family when it first moved in. As Carl Larsson's finances improved he was able to add no less than seven extensions to his home, including a large, light studio and a guest room where occupants names were inscribed for posterity. It was a perfect picture of domestic bliss, but the reality according to some sceptics was rather different. Larsson, the devoted family man, is also said to have been a chauvinist who ruled supreme over his Sundborn nest.

More Carl Larsson portraits can be seen at the nearby Sundborn Community House (Församlingshem) and there are also works by him in Sundborn's church. From Sundborn follow the signs for Svärdsjö through undulating countryside dotted with lakes and red-painted farm houses. Parts of Svärdsjö church date from the fourteenth century and the font is from the 1200s. Follow the lakeside to Enviken. The area offers plenty of outdoor recreation possibilities including swimming, fishing, canoeing and walking. From Enviken turn north along route 294 in the direction of Edsbyn. The road follows the lake but the fields and farms are replaced by forest and the countryside takes on an altogether wilder look. **Våckelberget**, about 10km (6 miles) north of Enviken is a nature reserve.

Turn left off the 294 at Lamborn towards **Bingsjö**, a village that features on the calendar of every self-respecting Dalecarlian fiddle player. Most of the year Bingsjö looks like any other peaceful collection of red-painted timber houses but on the first Wednesday of every July it plays host to anything up to 30,000 people for the annual Bingsjö music festival. It is worth calling in at the Danielsgården homestead to see the work of one of the greatest Dalecarlian folk painters, Winter Carl Hansson who died in 1805 aged just 28. He was invited by the affluent farmer to paint the interior of his summerhouse and it took the young artist almost 3 years to complete his task. Among the best known images are *The Ages Of Man* in the kitchen. The characteristic flower which recurs in all Dalecarlian painting is a *kurbits*, based on the biblical tree provided by God to shade Jonah from the sun outside the city of Ninevah.

After Bingsjö the road sweeps off through a large area of undisturbed forest before joining the main 301 at Nedre Gårdsjö some 10km (6 miles) north-east of Rättvik. An increased volume of traffic is likely to be the first indication that you are nearing Lake Siljan, the heart of Dalarana and a perennially popular holiday destination. But if time allows make a short detour along the 301 towards **Boda** where 1km (½ mile) south-west of the church signs direct visitors to a 36m (118ft) high waterfall called Styggforsen. You can drive almost right up to the fall which features not only in countless troll legends but also in an Ingmar Bergman movie.

The Swedish ski-jumping team practice on 'astro turf' in summer at Lugnet ski jump, Falun

Swedish artist Carl Larsson's old home at Sundborn is now a major tourist attraction

Huts surrounding the church at Rättvik were used by churchgoers to stable their horses

The long pier at Rättvik is such a national landmark that people from all over Sweden paid to have their names carved on it

Return to Nedre Gårdsjö and continue into **Rättvik**, a modern looking town on the banks of Lake Siljan which is better known for its Dalecarlian heritage than for its architecture. Standing in the uninspiring central square you could be forgiven for thinking there can be little to see and do in this backwater. But the large and efficient tourist office has other ideas. Rättvik is one of the biggest tourist centres around Siljan with two camp sites, beaches, boat hire, fishing, golf and a range of other activities. It also has what is billed as Sweden's longest wooden pier stretching an impressive 628m (2,060ft) out into the lake. First built in the late 1800s, it was renovated in 1992 with the help of an imaginative fund-raising scheme in which sponsors could buy a plank and have their names engraved on it for 500kr. Such was the demand for immortality that the organisers ran out of pier before they did sponsors. They managed to fit a total of 3,000 named planks before the pier was finished.

The pier is a focal point for local festivals although it was originally built so that the Siljan steamers could berth in the shallow water. One of them, *M/S Gustav Wasa* still calls in regularly during lake excursions. The placid bay at Rättvik has sandy beaches for swimming and sunbathing and there are lovely views across the surrounding area from Vidablick on the 345m (1,131ft) high Lerdalshöjden just to the south. **Tolvåstugan** nearby has slalom runs in winter and a 750m (2,460ft) long rodel-slide in summer.

Overlooking the lake on the other side of the community is Rättvik church from the fourteenth century. The clusters of lopsided wooden cabins nearby could effectively be described as sixteenth and seventeenth-century 'garages' because this is where churchgoers used to stable their horses — or ponies judging by the size of some doorways. A small jetty is still used by traditional church boats when the weather allows.

The men of Dalarna played a crucial role in helping one of Sweden's most important historical figures, Gustav Vasa to free the country of Danish rule. A monument near the church commemorates the fugitive nobleman's call on dubious Dalecarlians to take up arms against King Christian of Denmark. About 2km (1 mile) from the town centre is Rättvik's open-air museum (Gammelgård) with Dalecarlian paintings, costumes and furniture. The Culture Centre (Kulturhuset) by Enån river also contains folk-art alongside an exhibition of local geology which helps to explain the devastating effects of the giant meteorite that once struck the area. A more manageable phenomenon in this very tourist oriented community is the natural fountain (Springkälla) some 7km (4 miles) from the centre of Rättvik (head for the race course and then follow the signs down a dirt road). The water spurts 3 to 4m (10 to 13ft) out of the ground in a picturesque forest clearing near the Draggå river and is especially spectacular in winter when it turns into a column of ice. It has been gushing continually since local oil prospectors struck it by accident in the nineteenth century.

In many ways the charm of the Siljan area lies not in its towns but in the villages and farms around the lake shore. The increase in tourism means that traditional crafts otherwise destined to die out have been kept alive.

Route 70 from Rättvik to Mora passes Nittsjö where ceramics are made and then the village of Vikarbyn with *tunnbröd* bakeries (*tunnbröd* is white unleavened bread which is rolled like a pancake around meat or cheese) and a weaving house in which visitors can make themselves a souvenir of the area. A small road to the right leads to Karl Tövåsen's hill farm, a group of traditional wooden buildings known as *fäbodar* in Swedish and a living reminder of the days when animals and people moved en masse to hillside pastureland in summer. It is one of three such farms still in use around Rättvik and in peak season is open for the sale of cheese and butter to visitors.

Back on route 70 the road passes red painted villages with glimpses of the lake and patches of forest before reaching a left turn signposted **Nusnäs**. A visit to the traditional home of the Dalecarlian horse is one of those obligatory stops on every Dalecarlian tourist map and the result is a steady stream of cars and coaches. The two main manufacturers virtually face each other on opposite sides of the road and advertise under the confusingly similar names of Nils Olsson Hemslöjd AB and Grannas A Olsson Hemslöjd AB. It is a relatively friendly rivalry because the local Dala horse moguls are in fact cousins. Visitors are welcome to watch the horses being carved, dipped in basic colour and painted in their traditional stylised patterns. The artists work at astonishing speed apparently oblivious to the jostling tour groups that lean over them with cameras poised. You can even buy a piece of wood which has been cut into the basic shape and make your own. There is a cafeteria at Nils Olsson and inevitable souvenir shops offering anything from a metre high beast to miniscule horse earrings.

Dalecarlian horses were originally carved by local farmers and woodsmen during the long dark evenings spent in isolated cabins. They chose the horse as a model because of its importance in day-to-day life and would take their handywork home for their children. As years passed the carved Dala horses were handed on to travelling peddlers who took them as part of their stock and used them to pay for food and board.

The thriving tourist centre of **Mora** lies 10km (6 miles) north of Nusnäs; to get there continue through the village and rejoin the main road.

Mention Mora to Swedes and they will automatically think of Dalecarlian horses, curvacious Mora clocks and above all Vasaloppet, the world's biggest ski race. Every March some 12,000 skiers, most of them amateurs, stagger past the finishing post in Mora at the end of a gruelling 90km (56 miles) run from Sälen sustained by, of all things, hot billberry soup! The first 'runner' was none other than King Gustav Vasa who, as plain Gustav Eriksson Vasa, had been trying to inspire the fierce Dalecarlians into revolt against Danish rule (King Christian had not exactly endeared himself by executing eighty Swedish noblemen in the so-called Stockholm bloodbath). At first Vasa got little support and, facing life as a fugitive, made a dash on skis for the Norwegian border. But the men of Mora had a change of heart — messengers were sent in hot pursuit and finally caught up with him at Sälen. He returned to Mora and raised

The thriving tourist centre of Mora

Dalarna horses, the most familiar international symbol of Sweden

his army. This changed the course of Sweden's history and Gustav Vasa went on to become one of its greatest monarchs. The modern Vasalopp has been run annually since 1922 and the finishing post is a permanent fixture spanning the road near the church with statistics and information about the race in the adjacent building.

Mora also owes much to its most famous citizen, the illegitimate son of a local farm girl turned internationally-renowned artist, Anders Zorn. 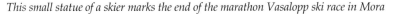 Zornmuseet (the Zorn Museum) and Zorngården (the Zorn Homestead) are among the area's most popular tourist attractions even though many of Zorn's greatest works now hang in major galleries around the world. The museum, a severe looking red brick building, has several of the great man's etchings and paintings including a graceful portrait of his wife Emma in a red dress and a self-portrait where the size of his girth shows that he enjoyed his success to the full. Zorn became one of Sweden's wealthiest men before his death in 1920. He made much of his money painting portraits of rich and influential sitters such as the then USA president Taft, but in his native Sweden he is most famous for his nudes. Money enabled Zorn to return to Mora and extend his grandparents cottage into what must by the rural standards of the day have been an exotic mansion. The result was Zorngården, a rambling and elegant home with an eccentric Viking Room that resembles a scaled-down baronial hall. Another part of the house has panelling made from seventeenth-century church pews.

This small statue of a skier marks the end of the marathon Vasalopp ski race in Mora

The artist was feted by royalty and other eminent figures who came to stay. He was treated as a local 'king' and his home telephone number was '4' at a time when the only other three phones in town belonged to the police, the fire brigade and the vicar. Zorngården which lies only a few metres from the museum was left to the state when Emma Zorn died in 1942 and is open for guided tours. But do not expect to see many Zorn paintings. The artist did not approve of having his own art on the walls preferring to hang work by friends such as Prince Eugen and Carl Larsson. Emma's room was an exception.

Just along the road is Mora church, the subject of at least one well-known Zorn painting. The oldest parts of it date from the thirteenth century although a spire was added 400 years later and the separate seventeenth-century bell tower is a well-known Mora landmark. Other local landmarks predictably include statues of both Zorn, opposite the church and Gustav Vasa, overlooking the main road into Mora. Zorn had something of a missionary zeal when it came to local culture and helped start up an open-air museum on the outskirts of town. The Zorn Gammelgård is next to the high school and has about forty old houses.

Mora itelf is a thriving modern community with a large batch of hotels and restaurants, two campsites and plenty of recreation facilities such as swimming, boat hire, fishing and a golf course. Although it has a population of just 10,000 its administrative area covers several smaller communities and the busy pedestrian shopping street has a good selection of boutiques and chainstores. There is a local airport and a railway station.

The itinerary will unavoidably pass through Mora once more as it weaves a figure of eight around the adjacent lakes Siljan and Orsa. But for the moment continue along route 70 in the direction of Älvdalen and turn right after a few kilometres onto a smaller road towards Bonäs and Våmhus. Villages rub shoulders with each other in this busy farming area which was also famous for its basket weaving and for handicrafts made from women's hair. Many Våmhus 'hair girls' as they were known took their skills abroad during the 1800s and are said to have made sizeable sums producing wigs, watch chains and brooches for fashion conscious city-dwellers. The skills have been passed down through the generations and are still demonstrated during summer at the Hembygdsgård (Våmhus Homestead Museum) at Sivarsbacken.

Follow the signs for Orsa, a small community and tourist resort at the northern end of the lake and effectively the last centre of any size before a large tract of wilderness. The neighbouring forests and marshes are the natural environment of Sweden's largest predator, the elusive brown bear. The local authorities have understandably taken advantage of the fact that few if any visitors are ever likely to see a bear in the wild and have established a large Björnpark (Bear Park) at **Grönklitt** some 13km (8 miles) north of Orsa. It is well signposted from the main road. There are between twenty and twenty-five bears in the park which stretches across 80,000sq m (861,000sq ft) of sloping forest dotted with small ponds and patches of open ground. Visitors who enter the park through a cafeteria perched at its highest point can look down on the area from large viewing ramps and walkways. Binoculars are useful, but even without them you will generally see some of the lumbering and genuinely cuddly looking inmates playing among the trees or dunking each other in the water. The bears appear to thrive and in spring there are usually several cubs.

Grönklitt is a popular recreation area both in summer and winter with a batch of holiday cottages for rent, an exceptionally comfortable youth hostel and a hotel. There are marked walking routes which double up as ski trails and eleven downhill runs. Crafty bear park wardens have installed video cameras in the bears' lair so that winter visitors can watch them in hibernation. The pictures are transmitted to the hotel and holiday cottages on a special 24-hour TV channel. There are some 600 wild bears in Sweden but apart from occasional sightings the creatures are shy and elusive. Grönklitt, billed as Europe's biggest bear park, offers the best chance of seeing one in a near natural environment and is well worth a detour. As the road descends gently through forest to the shores of Lake Orsa it passes signs for Fryksås, a large collection of old hill farm buildings with a hotel, holiday cottages and extensive views.

There is little to see in the centre of **Orsa**, a small modern community with a smattering of shops and restaurants and the improbably named Buffalo Bill Pub opposite a local cultural centre. There is a good handicraft shop and a memorial to a certain Corporal Gifting of the Orsa Regiment whose comment 'Orsa Company promises nothing definite' when instructed not to sample the wares of a local tavern is now a popular Swedish saying. The town lies at the point where the Orsa river meets the lake and was once renowned for making whet-stones from local sandstone. The church, parts of which date from the thirteenth century, has a floor of Orsa sandstone with the signatures of craftsmen visible on some of the stones.

Orsa may not be much to see in itself but it is a good centre from which to explore the wilderness to the north and the cosy villages and lakeside meadows to the south. It also has one of the best sandy beaches in the area and a large well organised camping and recreation area with holiday cottages, swimming pools, a water slide; fishing, boat and canoe hire. Possible excursions include a visit to the so-called Hell's Falls (Helvetesfallet) some 25km (15½ miles) north of Orsa where a hanging bridge crosses the Emå river as it cascades down a 25m (82ft) deep gorge, or a similar fall further south called Storstupet which is spanned by a railway bridge. To the north lies a wild rugged area named Orsa Finnmark because of the many Finnish settlers who made their homes there in the 1600s. The vast forests and marshlands dissected by fast flowing rivers were a nostalgic reminder of Finland and local placenames still look more Finnish than Swedish. Route number 45 from Orsa passes through the area and anyone prepared for a lengthy but undemanding 300km (186 mile) plus drive can follow it north via Sveg to link with the itinerary in

Chapter 6. Skattugnbyn to the east has widespread views over the wilderness from the church.

The main route 45 heads south to Mora on the eastern side of Lake Orsa, but if time allows try the more picturesque 'Tourist Way' further inland. It passes old timbered villages and good views of the lake. Continue through Mora on route 45 to the western lake shore, then turn left following the signs for **Sollerön**. A short bridge crosses to this lush green island said to have the most fertile soil and the mildest climate in the Siljan area. The fruit trees, flower-filled meadows and pristine gardens are evidence enough that nature has been kind and the island's prime location attracts a sizeable sprinkling of summer visitors. There is a chalet village and an 18 and 9 hole golfcourse on the south-west side. Before the bridge was built the islanders used boats to get to the mainland or, most importantly, to Mora church on Sundays. Apparently there was little love lost between the two communities and after being fined one Sunday for not turning up (in those days people really did have to pay for their sins) the islanders petitioned the king for money to build their own church. The cash duly arrived and the result, a church big enough to hold the entire community, can still be seen today. The grateful islanders called it Sofia Magdalena in honour of the queen. Sollerön was inhabited even in Viking times and a large Viking burial field was discovered when the first bridge was constructed at the turn of the century. There are more than 100 graves, most of them on windswept meadows at **Bengtsarvet** near the local Heritage Museum in the northern part of the island. It is not surprising that with its Viking past and later dependence on church boats the Sollerön islanders have an old boat building tradition.

Fortunately there is no need to take to the water to reach **Gesunda**. A couple of bridges whisk motorists across the lake and road signs point them up a long incline to Gesunda Mountain ski centre and its neighbour Tomteland (Father Christmas Land). Father Christmas's timber gatehouse with decorative pained shutters lies temptingly along the road. Once inside children can play in his forest theme park, watch his helpers busy themselves with next season's toys, meet his animals and eat a bowl of porridge (as favoured by Swedish Santas) in his cafeteria. Just a few hundred yards further up Gesundaberget is a ski centre and hotel with wonderful views across Lake Siljan. There are five ski lifts and seven downhill runs, the longest of which is about 2km (1 mile).

Head south along the main road — a gnarled old water mill hidden from view in a wooded clearing is signposted to the left — and on to **Siljansnäs**. Here Björkberget, a forested knoll jutting out into the lake, has been turned into a nature reserve complete with short trails and other more demanding walks. The modern Naturum (Nature Centre) has exhibitions and information about local flora, fauna, wildlife and geology and there is a tall viewing tower. Near its base is a pleasant restaurant and cafeteria with yet more panoramic views from the log terrace. Siljansnäs also has its obligatory heritage museum — a must in every self-respecting

Fiddle players in national dress, Tällberg

A profusion of dandelions in a field near Tällberg

community — and if you haven't had enough of them by now, this one is called Masolles Gammelgård and is situated down the slope at the edge of the village. The old farm buildings house a collection of costumes from the surrounding area.

The road now loops around the southern end of Siljan and reaches Leksand, the last of the sizeable communities around the lake and the one that most proudly preserves its Dalecarlian traditions today. Some 30,000 people gather here each Midsummer to see what is billed as 'Sweden's tallest maypole' and to take part in the music and dancing that goes on around it. Folk costumes are dragged out from the back of closets and violins are tuned for what is the undisputed highlight of the year. The festivities are focused on Sammilsdalen, an open area in the centre of town which is also used for the annual 'Himmlaspelet' outdoor play described at the beginning of this chapter. In fact so fond are the Dalecarlians of their maypoles that they tend to leave them standing all year round, taking them down only briefly just before Midsummer to dress them with new leaves and flowers. The onion domed church has room for 2,000 people but even that is insufficient on Midsummer's Day when services are relayed by loudspeaker to those who could not squeeze in. The outsize congregation is not due to any great awakening of religious fervour but to the traditional role played by the church at seasonal celebrations. In the nineteenth century flotillas of church boats, some carrying up to seventy men, women and children would be rowed to Leksand from villages all around for the Midsummer service. Most of today's congregation arrive by private car or tourist coach but if you happen to be there at Midsummer you should still see decorated churchboats reviving the old traditions. Swedish composer Hugo Alfven lies buried in the churchyard, his grave marked by a sculpture by Carl Milles.

Leksand's traditions may lie in the past but the town itself certainly does not and its characterless modern centre is something of a disappointment. For a bit more colour call in at the Kulturhus (Culture House) on the Kyrkallé where there are displays of local costume, Dalecarlian paintings and textiles and a film show with English commentary. There are no less than six heritage museums in Leksand's local administrative district and the oldest of them, 'Hembygdsgårdarna', is near the church. It includes several elderly farm and village buildings as well as a reconstructed painting studio that belonged to Dalecarlian artist Winter Carl Hansson.

With its emphasis on summer tourism, Leksand is not surprisingly awash with craft workshops and boutiques and its homecraft association is said to be the oldest in the country. The town is pleasantly situated at the point where the Österdalälv meets Siljan and is another starting point for waterborn tours of the lake onboard the *M/S Gustaf Wasa*. The main route 70 south follows the river to **Borlänge**, a major industrial and commercial centre and quite a contrast to the rural Siljan communities. If the steel and paper mills do not appeal you could try Borlänge's Framtidsmuseum (Museum of the Future) with a planetarium and exhibitions concentrating on technical and industrial developments with plenty of 'visitor participation'.

But to complete the tour of the lake head north on the road signposted Tällberg and past one of Leksand's rather more modern attractions, Sommarland. A tangle of waterslides, and stepped swimming pools occupy the sloping lakeshore 3km (2 miles) north of the town. This artificial tourist trap has suffered the wrath of Dalecarlian purists but its young visitors vote with their feet. A pleasant country road follows the lake to the final port of call on the circuit, the village of **Tällberg**, known to the locals as 'Hotellberg'. It does not take long to see why, with seven hotels the 900 inhabitants are outnumbered by almost 1,000 tourist beds. Fortunately Tällberg is not in danger of becoming the local 'Costa'. Dalecarlian sensitivities ensured that all buildings in the village are constructed of wood leaving an atmosphere that remains remarkably sedate despite the tourist coaches. It has attracted visitors since the turn of the century because of its attractive position on wooded slopes running down to the lake. Many city dwellers built their own summer houses there in old Dalecarlian style while the hotels also have something of the 'olde worlde' Dalecarlian character. One is housed in a seventeenth-century farm homestead. Local specialities such as fish from the lake are usually on the menu, but be prepared to do battle in peak season with coach parties who descend on the most popular restaurants like a hoard of hungry locusts ready to gobble everything down to the last pickled herring.

Luckily most of them are too busy enjoying their afternoon coffee to invade Tällberg's secluded beach. It is sheltered by small offshore islands and there is a pleasant campsite for those not tempted by one of the hotels. At the top of the village is the inevitable local museum, a collection of timber buildings called Holen which house local folk art, tools and farming equipment. Those who have not seen enough of Siljan can enjoy still more views over the lake from here and if exercise is in order, the village has four marked summer walking trails ranging from 1½km (1 mile) to 12km (7 miles). All that now remains is to continue either the gently meandering coast road or to join the main route 70 and head for Rättvik. Turn right just before the centre onto road number 80 to return to Falun, the starting point of this tour.

Additional Information

Places to Visit

Bingsjö
Danielsgården
☎ 0246 40018
Open: 1 June to 15 August 11am-5pm (Monday, Tuesday closed). Collect the key from Pekkosgården.

Borlänge
Framtidsmuseum (Museum of the Future)
Jussi Björlings väg
☎ 0243 81085
Open: all year, Monday to Friday 10am-5pm, Saturday and Sunday 12noon-5pm.

Falun
Falu Gruva (Coppermine)
☎ 023 15825/11475
Open: daily for guided tours 1 May to 31
August 10am-4.30pm. Weekends only in
autumn. Closed December to March.

Stora Museet (Mining Museum)
Opposite mine entrance
☎ 023 11475
Open: daily 1 May to 31 August 10am-
4.30pm. 1 September to 30 April 12.30-
4.30pm.

Dalarna's Museum
Stigaregatan 2-4
☎ 023 18160
Open: Monday to Thursday 10am-6pm,
Friday to Sunday 12noon-5pm. Winter
10am-5pm.

Gesunda
Tomteland (Father Christmas Land)
17km (10 miles) south of Mora
☎ 0250 29000
Open: peak summer and winter season.

Grönklitt
Björnpark (Orsa Bearpark)
15km (9 miles) north of Orsa
☎ 0250 46200
Open: daily 30 April to 27 September 10am-
3pm (13 June to 9 August 10am-5pm).

Leksand
Kulturhus (Cultural Centre and Museum)
☎ 0247 80245
Open: all year 11am-4pm, summer 11am-
5pm. Closed Monday except 15 June to 15
August. Limited hours at weekends.

Mora
Zornmuseet (Zorn Museum)
☎ 0250 16560
Vasagatan 36
Open: all year, summer 9am-5pm, winter
10am-5pm, limited hours on Sundays.

Zorngården (Zorn Homestead)
Next to the museum
☎ 0250 10004
Open: all year. Summer 10am-5pm, winter 12.30-5pm, limited hours on Sundays.

Nusnäs (Dala Horse Manufacture)
Nils Olsson Hemslöjd AB
About 10km (6 miles) south of Mora
☎ 0250 37200

Open: summer (shop) 8am-6pm,
(workshop) 8am-4pm. Limited hours
weekends. Winter 8am-5pm (workshop) 8am-3pm weekdays only.

Rättvik
Gammelgård (Open-Air Museum)
2km (1 mile) from centre near church
☎ 0248 11445
Open: June to August 11am-6pm
weekdays, 12.30-6pm Sundays.

Culture Centre (Kulturhuset)
By the Enå bridge
☎ 0248 70195
Open: Monday to Thursday 11am-7pm,
limited hours at weekends.

Siljansnäs
Nature Centre and Viewing Tower
Björkberget
☎ 0247 22105
Open: daily 17 May to 30 August 11am-
4pm.

Mas Olles Gammelgård (Homestead Museum)
13km (8 miles) from Leksand
☎ 0247 22784
Open: 29 June to 2 August 12noon-5pm.

Sommarland (Summerland)
North of Leksand on the Tällberg Road
☎ 0247 13939
Open: daily 23 May to 16 August 10am-
5pm. Extended to 6pm and 7pm June
and July.

Sundborn
Carl Larsson's Home
☎ 023 60053
15km (9 miles) north-east of Falun
Open: 1 May to 30 September Monday
to Saturday 10am-5pm. Sunday 1-5pm.

Tourist Information Centres

Falun
Stora Torget ☎ 023 83637

Leksand
Norsgatan ☎ 0247 80300

Mora
Ångbåtskajen ☎ 0250 26550

Rättvik
Torget ☎ 0248 10910

6

THE MOUNTAINS OF CENTRAL SWEDEN

The city of Östersund lies almost 1,000km (620 miles) from Malmö in the south and 775km (480 miles) from the west coast port of Göteborg, yet it is little more than half-way to Sweden's most northerly point. That can be a sobering thought for anyone with limited time and an ambition to see the Arctic. Fortunately much of what the far north has to offer can also be found in the highlands west of Östersund as they rise gradually towards the Norwegian border and then drop into Trondheim Fjord beyond. They have the same remote beauty, clear air, mirror calm lakes and turbulent rapids and they take considerably less time to get to than their more distant neighbours. But do not expect to find rugged Alpine peaks. The Swedes call these highlands *fjäll* or fells. Although some reach 1,700m (5,571ft) the Ice Age has given them gentle rounded contours which can easily be conquered by walkers and skiers alike. For hints and advice see the feature box, Walking Tours In The Swedish Mountains.

Östersund is by far the largest community — in fact it is really the only sizeable town in an area covering the provinces of Jämtland and Härjedalen. Swedish winter sports enthusiasts have been coming here for years. The nation's biggest downhill resort, Åre lies less than 2 hours away and further west is Storlien, a major ski touring centre and a popular walking region. Summer visitors share the trails with herds of reindeer, moved by their Lapp owners to higher pasture as the snows melt. In fact do not be surprised to find the ungainly creatures wandering like a herd of cows down the road, stubbornly refusing to get out of the way of the traffic. Until recently tourism in this part of the country centred on winter sports. But local entrepreneurs based around the ski resorts now tempt summer tourists with canoeing, white water rafting, trekking on Icelandic horses, fishing and even the odd bear safari. Fortunately accommodation prices which can be horrendous during the peak ski season plummet for the rest of the year as hotels vie with each other for business. There is no doubt that a keen interest in the great outdoors will help visitors to make the most of the area, and indeed northern Sweden in general. No-one travels all the way to Jämtland and Härjedalen for glitzy nightclubs, top restaurants or smart shopping. But it would be wrong to leave the impression that there is nothing more to the area than a few forests and fells. The natural starting point for this itinerary is therefore **Östersund**, a town of some 40,000 people situated on the shores of Sweden's fifth largest lake.

Storsjön or the Big Lake as it is called is not just any old Swedish lake. Beneath its sometimes choppy water is said to lurk a monster. Numerous 'sightings' of the Storsjö Odjur (Big Lake Monster) have been recorded over the centuries. It was once even accused of polishing off an entire potato crop on the lake shore, but funnily enough none of these incidents have ever been substantiated. All attempts to catch it failed and in 1986 the local council took a tongue-in-cheek decision to officially declare the local celebrity a 'protected species'. It has been adopted as Östersund's symbol and the tourist office not surprisingly does a healthy trade in monster souvenirs.

Would-be monster catchers may have had to hang up their gear but you can still see some of the strange devices they planned to use at the Jämtland Läns Museum (County Museum) about 10 minutes walk or a short bus ride from the town centre. Near the museum is one of Östersund's most popular attractions, the Jämtli Open-Air historical park. This is no ordinary 'theme park' but a well orchestrated reconstruction of local life as it was in the nineteenth century. In summer volunteer 'actors' of all ages live and work in painstakingly re-assembled buildings; baking, harvesting, tending farm animals and going about life as they would have done last century. Visitors are encouraged to enter the houses and to join in the activities.

Back in the centre of town the streets slope in a grid pattern to the lake shore with views across to its suburbs on the island of Frösön. Busy pedestrian shopping streets converge on Stortorget, the main square while Östersund's large and efficient tourist bureau lies a few minutes walk away on Krykgatan. Östersund is the undisputed regional centre with a good selection of shops and a liberal smattering of restaurants. But although it has a pleasant, relaxed atmosphere there is not much else in the way of sights. Keen museum fans may want to call in at the small Stadsmuseet (Town Museum) between the tourist office and Gamla Krykan (the Old Church). Down by the lake the Badhuspark has a mini golf course and outdoor entertainment in summer and just along the waterfront is the *SS Thomee*, Sweden's oldest working steamship which makes regular lake excursions in summer. A road bridge and separate pedestrian walkway links **Frösön** with the mainland. Although effectively a suburb of Östersund these days, the island was an important centre long before the town was even thought of. Its name comes from the pagan fertility god Frö and it was once a focal point for pre-Christian rites and rituals. Frösön also boasts Sweden's most northerly rune stone, dating from AD1000 with the inscription; Östman, son of Gudfast had this stone raised and this bridge made and brought Christianity to Jämtland. Asbjörn made the bridge, Tryn and Sten wrote these runes'. The stone has been moved from its original spot and unfortunately the only 'bridge' within reach nowadays is the modern highway onto the island. To get there follow the signs from the main road through a residential area and finally via a walkway to its somewhat obscure location outside a modern municipal office block. The main road heads on to Frösö Djurpark (Zoo) 3km (2 miles) away where a small amusement park in the grounds helps attract the crowds. You can get there by bus from the centre. Past the zoo and off to the left is an unassuming viewing tower with a cafeteria called Frösötornet. It is not terribly high, but it does help put the island in its context as just one of many lush green stepping stones dotted around Lake Storsjön.

In the southern part of Frösön (turn right after the tower and then bear left — it is reasonably well signposted) is Frösö's attractive old church. It dates from the twelfth century and has a separate wooden bell tower, a later addition which is characteristic of many churches in northern Sweden. There are lovely views out over the lake to the highlands beyond. Every year during the first or second week of July a well-known Viking drama called *Arnljot* is acted out near the church. Its creator, composer and music critic Wilhelm Peterson-Berger lived just a short distance away at Sommarhagen. His former home is now a museum. The group of old wooden buildings west of the church are also open to the public as a local history centre. On the other side of the road is an 18 hole golf course and driving range with superlative views across the lake although your swing may suffer from the occasional roar of military and civilian flights at the nearby airfield.

Anyone planning to spend time in the Östersund area during summer would do well to invest in the so-called Storsjökortet or Big Lake Card. It is valid for 9 days and gives holders free or half-price access to most of the attractions including local sporting events and cut-price excursions on the *SS Thomee*. It also allows holders to park free in the city's covered car park. The card is available from the tourist office.

Continue the itinerary from Frösön using one of the 'commuter' ferries that run every 30 minutes between the island and Rödön to the north (follow the signs past the airfield). The squat, ugly vessels may not look much, but they can load cars in seconds so there should not be a long wait. Once across the narrow straight head for **Ytterån**, skirting the lakeside past fertile agricultural land with prosperous looking farms. Two earlier cultures have left their mark here with a couple of prehistoric burial fields close to where the ferry berths and a ruined fortress from medieval times. An eccentric known by the evocative name of Mus Olle (Olle the Mouse) left a different sort of legacy at the small community of Ytterån—a bizzare museum containing the fruits of his unparalleled collectors mania. Mus Olle is said to have peddled around the local area on an old bicycle at the turn of the nineteenth century collecting any packaged item of household goods he could lay his hands on. He then turned to coins, photographs, stamps, ceramics and just about anything else that he could cram into his

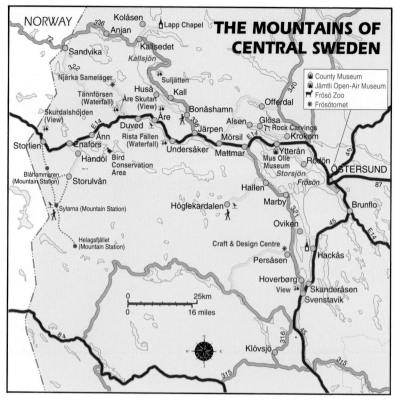

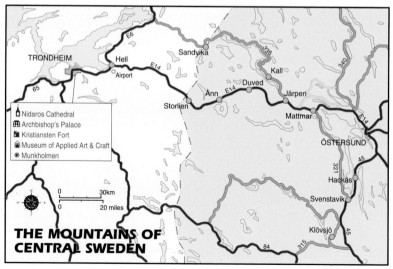

Many churches in northern Sweden have separate wooden bell towers

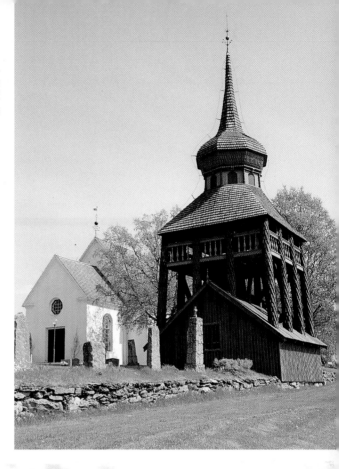

Driving range at Frösön golf course with views across Storsjön

tiny timber house. By the time he died in 1955 it contained some 150,000 exhibits most of which can still be seen at the Mus Olle Museum. Turn right along the busy E14 and then immediately left to Nälden followed by another left turn toward **Glösa** about 15km (9 miles) away. This part of Jämtland has been inhabited for thousands of years and the best evidence can be seen not far from the parking area at Glösabackens Hällristningar (Rock Carvings). The naive but appealing pictures of reindeer, elk and other symbols were etched into the rock between 4,000 and 5,000 years ago, their outlines now highlighted in red paint to make them easier to see. Nearby is a series of ancient elk traps or ditches used by hunters centuries ago. It was probably a marginally safer method than today's elk shoots which have been known to result in the accidental 'bagging' of the odd homo sapien huntsman or berry picker whose rustling steps were mistaken for those of an elk. There are some 60 ditches stretching 3km (2 miles) into the forest. The area around Offerdal, further to the north, is also famous for its cultural history and there are three lifesize rock carvings of elks at Gärde. Should you venture to **Offerdal** church spare a thought for the local farmers who once had to give a tenth of their crops to the local vicar. He gave them a beer in return, which he scooped from the red seventeenth-century wooden bowl still on display in the church.

Continue to the end of Alsensjön (Lake Alsen) and then cut across the low fells to **Mörsil**, once the most important tourist centre in Jämtland but left somewhat stranded as holidaymakers headed further west. The reason for this becomes obvious as you look across the open countryside towards one of Sweden's best loved and most popular 'holiday mountains', **Åre Skutan**. At 1,420m (4,658ft) it is not particularly high, but its solitary position between the valley of the powerful Indalsälv and Lake Kall on the other side makes 'Skutan' appear more majestic than it perhaps deserves. Follow the main E14 in the direction of Järpen. Restaurants and filling stations can now be found at regular intervals as the tourist pace quickens. But the problem with any itinerary in this sparsely populated part of Sweden is that the choice of roads becomes increasingly limited and their quality may not quite be up to international highway standards. With that in mind, turn off to the right along route 336 bound for the village of Kall. Some of the more remote sections of this road has a gravel rather than tarmac surface although the entire stretch to the Norwegian border is wide enough for caravans and larger vehicles. There were signs however that improvements are planned.

The road follows the shore of Lake Kall as the valley opens out to reveal the Åre mountain rising up to the left, streaked with snow late into spring and early summer. The 336 first passes **Bonäshamn** with a major freshwater fish farm which is often open to visitors. At Kall the white nineteenth-century village church is dwarfed against its mountain backdrop. Its most important artefact is the so called Kall Madonna from the twelfth century. There is a combined hotel and youth hostel and anyone who feels like

donning their walking boots can head up to the right from the village to
an area of marked trails 6km (4 miles) away. The shortest is just 1½km (1
mile) and the longest 20km (12 miles), heading through peaceful birch and
pine woods and past isolated lakes and streams. Before setting out check
that the route you choose will take you in a loop back to the starting point.
After Kall the road deteriorates in quality but remains plenty wide
enough for two vehicles to pass comfortably. It follows the lake, swinging
to the right at Konäs from where there are marvellous views towards
higher fells, their reflections mirrored in the water on calm days. The
oddly shaped rocky protuberance to the right is known as Suljätten (the
Sul Giant) and legend has it that he is crying down with his nose in the air
because he lost a fight with his neighbour, Åre Skutan. There are a number
of marked walks from Konäs and, as elsewhere, plenty of chances to buy
a fishing licence and catch supper in the lake. The road winds on along
Kallsjön, passing small farms, and areas of forest to the community of
Kallsedet at the point where the Kall rapids meet the lake. For some reason
the road improves just here, a welcome relief after some 40km (25 miles)
of gravel surface. The village boasts the remains of a seventeenth-century
fortress although it is not much to see. More importantly there is a shop
and a camping site. Stay on the 336, which unfortunately soon degener-
ates back into gravel and after 20km (12 miles) you will reach **Anjan**, a
rambling and fishing centre and highland hotel with a batch of picturesque grass-roofed wooden houses. The walking trails here are generally
longer and rather more gruelling than those in the gentle fells further east,
heading off to evocative sounding places like the Great Reindeer Lake.

It is now less than 20km (12 miles) to Norway and the countryside is
rougher, more desolate and remote. The border post tends to be pretty
devoid of human activity too as Norwegian customs lurk several kilometres down the road at Ådalsvollen. You are unlikely to encounter an
official at either. Once across the border the road surface improves but
ironically the general speed limit goes down to 80kph (50mph) — and
beware, it is strictly enforced. There is a hotel at the border community of
Sandvika before the long winding descent to Trondheim Fjord. The steep
sided valleys offer a different type of scenery compared with the rolling
fells and open views on the Swedish side. There are a couple of impressive
waterfalls just the other side of the border and plenty of idyllic picnic spots
along the Inna river on the way down. The valley opens out into farmland
at Steine and goes on to meet the main E6 which runs a tortuous route
along the frayed length of Norway. Turn left for the 89km (55 mile) drive
south to Trondheim with the broad Trondheim Fjord on the right and a
narrow band of farmland backed up against craggy wooded hills to the
left. The road climbs over a couple of rocky knolls before dropping down
to the coast again near the unfortunately named town of Hell (by way of
contrast you may have noticed the village of 'Hello' further north). A
number of large industrial plants for timber and fish canning dot the
coastline along this part of the E6 as it edges round the bay and turns into

Walking Tours In The Swedish Mountains

The Swedish mountains stretch 1,000 kilometres from far above the Arctic Circle to the central province of Dalarna. They are not very high (Kebnekaise, the tallest peak, is only 2,117m/6,944ft) so serious climbers tend to look elsewhere. But their rugged remoteness and unspoilt beauty have turned them into a mecca for hikers in summer and ski tourists in spring. As there are comparatively few difficult ascents and descents and well marked trails you do not have to be super-fit or an outward bound expert to go there.

Recognising this, the Swedish Touring Association (STF) has some fifty huts dotted along the mountain tracks, usually spaced a day's walk from each other. You cannot book in advance, but if the hut is open you will never be turned away. They are often basic with no electricity and it is up to visitors to fetch water, chop firewood and so on. There are beds, blankets, cooking facilities and sometimes provisions for sale.

The most popular areas, and therefore those with the most huts, are the Jämtland mountains (Central Sweden) and western Lappland. The huts are generally open from early March until May for ski touring and from the end of June to September for the walking season. The busiest time is from mid-July to mid-August.

The summer trails are marked by cairns, painted posts or trees while winter trails for skiers have posts with a red cross. Where a track crosses a stream there may be a bridge or a rowing boat, if not you have to ford it. Do not try taking a ski trail in summer, you could end up in the middle of a lake or bog! The STF also has eight so-called Fjällstationer or mountain 'stations' which act as points of departure or rendezvous places in

Unspoilt fells and mirror-calm lakes — it is easy to see why Jämtland is popular with walkers

popular walking regions. These have full hotel facilities and restaurants and offer a range of local activities.

For a hiking trip with overnight stops you will need strong windproof clothing even in summer because this far north an altitude of 1,000m (3,280ft) is equivalent to 2,500m (8,200ft) in the Alps. Pack gloves, a hat, and a waterproof jacket and trousers. Wellingtons are the best footwear because the ground can be wet, especially early in early season, and there are streams to ford. But do not forget the shorts and tee-shirts too as it can be very warm. You are always advised to tell staff at your last port of call where you are going and how long you expect to take.

The most famous and well-beaten trail in Sweden is Kungsleden, the 'King's Route' which stretches 500km (310 miles) from Abisko in the north to Hemavan. The northern and southern parts of the track have huts every 15 to 20km (9 to 12 miles) although there is a gap in the middle. The most popular section is the 86km (53 miles) stretch from Abisko to Kebnekaise, scathingly described as 'the E4' by more solitary types. The route passes river valleys, moorland, forest and Sweden's highest mountain massif. There are five overnight huts on the way as well as the Kebnekaise mountain hotel from where it is a further 19km (12 miles) to the Lapp village of Nikkaluokta. Part of the final stretch is covered by boat and once at Nikkaluokta there are regular buses to Kiruna. This section of Kungsleden takes about a week to walk. The trail is not particularly difficult and the availablility of overnight accommodation helps keep the size of the backpack down. For more information on walking in Jämtland see the main text of Chapter 6. The Additional Information section at the end of this chapter lists addresses of mountain stations.

The church at Kall is dwarfed by Åre Skutan, its northern slopes streaked with snow until early summer

a toll road for the last 25km (15½ miles) to Trondheim (Swedish money is accepted).

✳ **Trondheim** has been welcoming a steady trail of visitors since the eleventh century when King Olav Haraldsson who brought Christianity to Norway was declared a saint. The king apparently converted from paganism during a Viking visit to England. He went on to spread the word at home before he was killed in a battle north of Trondheim in 1030. A stone church and later a mighty cathedral were built over his original grave although by then his bones had been exhumed and put in a shrine. ♦ The cathedral, parts of which date from the twelfth century, became the focus for pilgrims from all over Scandinavia and northern Europe who in turn left an idelible mark on the old pilgrim routes. Trondheim, Norway's oldest city was called Nidaros until the 1400s and the huge grey stone church is still referred to as Nidaros Cathedral.

It is an impressive structure, one of the largest medieval buildings in Scandinavia and adorned with countless stone gargoyles and statues. It is difficult not to marvel that a church of these Notre Dame proportions should be built in such a far corner of northern Europe. The interior is dark, relatively uncluttered and cavernous with what little natural light there is penetrating through intricate stained glass windows. The cathedral is now both Trondheim's parish church and Norway's national sanctuary. Royal Coronations take place here and since 1988 the crown jewels have been kept in one of the cathedral chapels. They were most recently used in 1991 for the Coronation of King Harald V of Norway.

⊞ Next to the cathedral lies the former Archbishop's Palace dating from the twelfth century. It has had a variety of uses since the Archbishop was turned out during the Reformation and parts of it today host official functions. Beyond, an open grassy area slopes down to the Nidelva river with views of prosperous suburbs sprawling over the hills beyond. They � in turn stretch up to the seventeenth-century Kristiansten Festning (Fort) with its commanding views over Trondheim Fjord. The grassed area itself is a popular spot for weekend sun-worshipping, frisbee throwing and summer picnics.

⬛ Just along the road from the cathedral lies Trondheim's Nordenfjeldske Kustindustrimuseum (Museum of Applied Art and Crafts) with a good collection of Norwegian paintings from the 1800s onwards. The heart of the city and the tourist office are a few minutes walk away at Trondheim Torg and beyond is Trondheim's commercial and shopping centre. Unfortunately prices in general are as high, if not higher than those in Sweden. The old part of the city lies on the other side of the river at Bakklandet where the narrow Bybrua (Town Bridge) crosses to a district of winding cobbled streets and rambling wooden houses. Along the river ⊞ is a much photographed row of colourful waterside warehouses many of which date from the 1700s. Trondheim once had two fortresses, Kristiansten on the mainland and Munkholmen an island fortification just beyond the harbour. The latter was originally an eleventh-century Benedictine monastery and later became a sort of Norwegian 'Alcatraz', then a customs post. It is a rather more relaxed place these days with a restaurant, swimming and recreation area. Regular boat excursions leave in summer from Ravnkloa near the city fish hall.

This has been only the briefest of guides to Trondheim. Anyone wishing to explore the area in more detail or planning a longer stay on the Norwegian side of the border should invest in the *Visitor's Guide to Norway* published by Moorland Publishing. But for the purposes of the current itinerary it is time to pay for the toll road and return quite literally to 'Hell'. Turn right onto the E14 a few kilometres further on at Stjördalshalsen and follow the road as it starts to climb back towards the Swedish border. The fortress at Hegra played an important role in the days when the Swedes and Norwegians were not the best of neighbours and there are some rock carvings to the left a few kilometres further east. The valley closes in as the road follows the river upstream. This is a much busier tourist route than the one to the north with camp sites at Sona and at Meråker and a number of hotels along the way. The main road climbs steeply near the border and joins the railway line as it heads over a treeless pass with lovely views back across the valley. Once in Sweden it is only a couple of kilometres to the large skiing and outdoor recreation centre of **Storlien**.

The area has been the country's premier Nordic skiing destination for generations with activities centred on a large 500 bed hotel and more than 30 self-catering holiday cottages. The fells may look a bit bleak off season, but in early spring they are criss-crossed with ski trails connecting far flung mountain cabins and remote fell hotels accessible only on skis or by snow scooter. In summer, after the snows have melted and the ground has dried the trails are adapted for walkers and ramblers. Storlien's venerable old Högfjällshotel lies at some 600m (1,968ft) above sea level and has just about every facility you would expect in an establishment that size; restaurants, a 'pub', swimming pool, sauna, conference rooms, a tennis court and a sports centre from which you can hire equipment. As such it is a good, if not exactly bargain, place from which to sample some of the surrounding countryside. There are good views from the 840m (2,755ft) high Skurudalsheight which involves a relatively undemanding walk of about 2km (1 mile). Four kilometres (2 miles) away to the west is Brudslöjan or the Bride's Veil waterfall, which drops 24m (79ft) into an isolated river canyon. The hotel also advertises guided rambles and, for those who do not mind paying the extra, fishing tours and fly fishing to what it bills as secret waters. The hotel can arrange just about any other outdoor activity that takes your fancy such as riding, canoeing, white water rafting, hunting (including a special week's course for women!) mushrooming, painting, mountain cookery and so on.

Storlien lies at the edge of a highland area where conveniently spaced mountain huts provide ramblers and skiers with a guaranteed roof over their heads at night. Each hut is effectivley run as a mini youth hostel with self catering facilities. You cannot book ahead but no-one is ever turned

Trondheim Cathedral, one of the largest Gothic buildings in Scandinavia

A row of colourful warehouses many dating from the 1700s, Trondheim

Tännförsen is one of Sweden's most spectacular waterfalls

Reindeer still provide a vital source of income for many Sami

away. This can predictably cause a bit of a squeeze at peak holiday times, but with so much space and rugged wilderness outside the door, no-one seems to mind a little overcrowding inside.

One of the best places to start a walking holiday in the Jämtland fells is at **Storulvån**, an hotel with restaurant and self catering facilities proudly described as the 'front door' to the mountains. To get there from Storlien continue down the main E14 (there is a youth hostel and another fell centre at Storvallen, 2km/1 mile further on) and turn right at Enafors. The main road in this remote part of the highlands is called Karolinerleden (Carolean Route) in honour of 4,000 soldiers who froze to death in the mountains in 1719. They were hit by a winter storm as they tried to return to base after a campaign in Norway and their bodies were found huddled together, some even frozen solid as they stood. Relics such as uniform buttons and buckles are sometimes still found in isolated spots. The soldiers were called Karoliner because they served King Karl XII and various monuments have been raised to their memory.

The route from Enafors passes over moors and through the village of **Handöl** with its small Lapp chapel. The Handöl river drops more than 100m (328ft) in this area in a series of falls and rapids. The hotel, or more properly 'fell station' at Storulvån lies surrounded by birch trees at a height of 700m (2,296ft). Do not let the 12m (39ft) tall indoor climbing wall put you off, rambling in the Jämtland fells does not generally require rock-climbing skills although the indoor 'face' is a popular attraction. The centre is literally at the end of the road, beyond it the fells are left to the reindeer, wildlife and walkers. More than 300km (186 miles) of trails link a network of eight mountain cabins and two other comfortable fell hotels. Each is within a relatively comfortable 15 to 20km (9 to 12 mile) distance of the next and all are operated by the highly efficient Swedish Touring Association (STF) — details in Fact File at the back of this guidebook. The fell hotel at **Sylarna** for example is a 16km (10 mile) walk from Storulvån and a good spot from which to explore the 1,762m (5,799ft) high Storsylen. **Blåhammaren**, 19km (12 miles) from Sylarna and 12km (7 miles) from Storulvån lies at 1,000m (3,280ft). It is the smallest of the three 'fell stations' and can only be reached on foot or skis, but nevertheless boasts a licensed restaurant. Just above the Helags hostel, a 19km (12 mile) walk from Sylarna and 12km (7 miles) from the nearest road is Sweden's most southerly glacier. The Helag hostel is one of the largest shelters and has a shop and refreshments such as light snacks, soup or sandwiches. All hotels and hostels have self catering facilities and about half of them have food for sale enabling walkers to travel light.

As many highland hotels and hostels close out of season it is always worth checking with the STF on current opening times. The tourist season generally runs from February until the beginning of May for skiing and June until September for summer visitors. While hostels are not bookable, rooms in the Fjällstationer (Fell Hotels) can be reserved in advance.

Return to the main E14 from Storulvån and turn right passing Ånn

Lake, a local bird watching centre with a number of marked trails and hides. A large information board by the lake lists the likely feathered visitors and where to see them. They include Arctic Terns, Pintails, Rough Legged Buzzards and Hawk Owls. There is also a local canoe hire centre. The next stop is **Duved**, a well-known tourist resort in its own right but somewhat overshadowed by its trendier neighbour Åre. The predominance of Nordic skiing in the highlands near the border gives way to an emphasis on the racier downhill variety in this part of the Indalsälv valley. Duved lies at the edge of an area where popular skiing culture has reached near Alpine proportions. There are nine ski lifts near the village and double that number of hotels and holiday villages. Standards are generally high but if you want a taste of regional cooking one hotel does warrant a special mention. Millesgården which translated means the Middle Farm is renowned locally for its Jämtland specialities with a menu that includes fillet of bear (exclusive even in Sweden and therefore the most expensive item), reindeer with morrels or chantarelles, roast elk, hare, ptarmigen and other game birds or fresh fish from a local lake. Sometimes there is a game or 'Jämtland's' buffet.

Millesgården lies on the edge of Duved next to one of the monuments commemorating the Karoliners 'death march'. The village has two small supermarkets, several banks, sports equipment hire, a station and a post office. There are marked ski tracks and walking trails around Mulfjället mountain, a junior partner of the mightier Åre Skutan to the east.

A couple of kilometres to the west, near where the E14 crosses the Indalsälv river is a minor road signposted to one of Sweden's most spectacular waterfalls, **Tännförsen**. It can be a bone shaking few kilometres but the 37m (121ft) fall at the end of it is worth the effort. To describe Tännförsen as a 'Nordic Niagara' may be a little exaggerated, but it is one of the country's largest falls and the sheer force of the water during the late spring flood is impressive. For the best effect walk onto the rocky platform jutting into the middle of the fall — you will probably be glad of the surrounding railings. Tännförsen is easy to reach from the road — the deafening roar can be heard as you head down the short path from the carpark. There is a pleasant little cafeteria and, close to where the minor road joins the E14, an 18 hole golf course open for a short season from 15 June to 15 October.

The provinces of Jämtland and Härjedalen are home to a fair number of local Sami although visitors could be forgiven for not realising that. Forget the picture postcard image of leathery, weatherbeaten figures in colourful woollen tunics and pom-pom hats living in Nordic style tee-pees. Most Sami these days are indistinguishable from other Swedes favouring jeans, Volvo estates and comfortable centrally heated homes. But reindeer herds still provide a vital source of income for many. Visitors can learn something of the Samen way of life at **Njärka Sameläger** (Sami Camp) signposted 20km (12 miles) from the E14 at Duved. The long, bumpy drive — you can just make out Tännförsen waterfall on the left — comes to an abrupt end at an isolated holiday village on the banks of Häggsjön. The Sami camp at the far end of the village consists of a number of 'Kåtor' (pronounced Kawtor), traditional triangular shaped dwellings which can be made of wood, stretched skins or even turf and a few token reindeer from a 2,000 strong herd. Paying guests are offered coffee served with salt in the traditional Samen way, cake and perhaps some smoked reindeer meat or fish. Canoes are available and visitors are permitted to fish in the lake. The camp's owners also have a small collection of Lapp artefacts stored in a mini museum including a decorated drum used to call up the spirits, Samen knives, tools and photographs.

Once back on the E14 continue through Duved to Åre. The valley opens up as the Indalsälv river and runs into a long thin lake flanked on the left by Åre Skutan and the village of **Åre** at its base. This is Sweden's closest approximation to an Alpine ski resort with modern hotels, holiday chalets, high rise apartments and twenty-four restaurants — quite an achievement in this part of the world! Planners apparently set out to recreate the character of a continental ski resort but inevitably achieved their aims at the expense of the traditional village atmosphere. Fortunately Åre is still relatively restrained when compared with the excesses of purpose built resorts elsewhere in Europe. Its hotels are listed on information boards along the main road and an efficient little tourist office in the central square can help with accommodation enquiries and local activities. Hotel and chalet prices tend to be astronomic during the ski season and a real bargain at other times of the year as owners try to boost occupancy rates. Many close between the winter season which runs through to the end of April and the summer season which begins in mid-June. The same applies in autumn, so it is worth checking on current opening times. The village also has a camp site and a youth hostel.

The combined resorts of Duved, Åre and the smaller Tegefjäll in between have a total of forty-two ski lifts. These include a 3km (2 mile) long cable car (Kabinbanan) which offers wonderful views as it rises from Åre to a mountain restaurant 1,274m (4,179ft) above sea level. A World Cup downhill ski run starts from nearby and from the top station it is only a 700m (2,296ft) scramble to the summit. The cable car is open in summer and winter but may be closed for servicing between seasons. There is also a funicular railway which runs to Hotell Fjällgården and a parking area from where marked walking trails criss-cross the mountain. Åre is best known as a winter sports resort, but after the skiers have left it is the turn of ramblers and out-door enthusiasts who take advantage of the lower summer prices and empty hotel rooms. The tourist office has information about local activities such as white water rafting, canoeing, fishing, rambling or horse riding tours. Homegrown summer entertainment is provided by the village of Huså on the other side of the mountain which stages traditional outdoor plays — unfortunately you need a knowledge of Swedish to understand the finer nuances of dramatised nineteenth-century village life.

Continue on the E14 as it heads east towards Järpen. There are several small communities along the valley with narrow roads leading up across the highlands, including one to Huså. Near Undersåker a signpost indicates a right turn to Ristafallen, another impressive waterfall in which the Indalsälv river thunders over two drops totalling 14m (46ft). The fall is less than 1km ($^1/_2$ mile) from the main road and you can hear the roar above the sound of the traffic. Neighbouring Hålland has a school and an old people's home especially for the Samen. **Järpen**, the largest centre in Åre's administrative district lies at the confluence of the Indalsälv river and Järpenströmmen but little remains of its strategic seventeenth-century fortifications. Stockholmers however have reason to be grateful to this unassuming little community as it provides much of the capital's hydroelectric power. At Järpen the itinerary doubles back on itself following the main the E14 eastward to Mörsil. Continue on to **Mattmar** where a picturesque church with typical Jämtland-style bell tower looks out over the broad valley.

Shortly after Mattmar turn right along the 321 crossing a small inlet onto the western shore of Storsjön. The highlands are never far away. Oviksfjällen to the right rise to well over 1,000m (3,220ft) while in contrast the lake shore is dotted with small agricultural villages. One of them, Hallen is a good base from which to explore Drommen, Västfjället and

The impressive waterfall at Ristafallen

Jämtland's second biggest ski area at the linked centres of Höglekardalen and Bydalen some 20km (12 miles) away. The Dammån river shares its valley with the road as it cuts through the highlands to one of the province's oldest tourist areas. Apparently it was the British who first discovered its possibilities, already building cottages and buying up local fishing rights at the end of the nineteenth century. **Dammån** is still popular with fly fishermen and anglers while the highland lakes on Västfjället are rich in trout and arctic char. Fishing tours are run by local guides and there are plenty of rambling trails once the snow has melted. The area trades on its low-key 'away from it all' image so do not expect a large range of hotels although there are a number of holiday villages and tourist centres with self catering facilities whose staff can give advice on local activities.

Back at Hallen the main road follows the lakeside to Marby from where it is possible to 'island hop' by ferry back across Storsjön to Östersund. The first leg goes to the island of Norderö, the second to Sunne on a peninsula which nudges out into the lake and the third, onto Frösön. Timetables vary but ferries generally run at 30-minute intervals during the day. In winter it is often possible to get across the lake under your own steam, using one of the 'ice roads' marked out by the local authority. These routes are carefully monitored and signposted and may be open from January until April depending on the temperature. There is a popular nature reserve on Andersön island just north of Sunne and the ruins of a medieval church with a foritified tower in the village itself.

Continuing along the west side of the lake the road edges away from the water for a while passing farming villages and woodland. On the left is the Oviken peninsula, a fertile agricultural area linked to the eastern lakeshore by the 1,300m (4,264ft) long Sannsundsbron, Sweden's third longest bridge. The 'Big Lake' is reduced to a long, narrow finger of water at this point and the decision to span it saved time-consuming detours around its southern tip. Oviken's little stone church was consecrated in some style in 1503 by the then archbishop and its wall contains a number of compartments built for the slightly macabre but highly practical purpose of storing bodies when the ground was too frozen for proper burial. Many churches in northern Sweden were built with these makeshift morgues so that with constant winter temperatures below zero the dead could effectively lie on consecrated ground for weeks or even months until it thawed sufficiently for a grave to be dug.

Back on the western lakeshore route 321 arrives at **Persåsen**, an insignificant looking place until you venture inside the cavernous showrooms belonging to local craftsman Leif Wikner. It does not take long to see where his talent lies. Most of the chunky Scandinavian looking ornaments, tables, chairs, lamps and conical cockerils are made out of pine culled from the surrounding forests. Blue pine is Mr Wikner's favourite although there are also works in ceramic, metal and textiles by other artists. Many are exhibited in modernistic subterranean rooms beneath Persåsen's hotel and a restaurant called the Blue Lamp. The complex also has an exceptionally comfortable youth hostel, holiday cottages and a couple of small ski runs and trails nearby. Just past Persåsen is a long winding dirt road called 'Fäbodvägen' (Hillfarm road), because of the ❈ thirty small farms known as *fäbodar* along the way. For Swedes it is a piece of unashamed nostalgia reminding them of the days when cattle, sheep and goats would be herded up to these highland pastures in summer staying there with their owners until the first snows came. The characteristic timber-built hill farms still lie in tranquil forest clearings although living in them is rather less idyllic as most have no modern services. A few hardy farm families nevertheless venture up there still and may well agree to sell homemade cheese and butter to passing travellers. Each *fäbod* is signposted with its name followed by the word *bua*, local dialect for *fäbod*. Look out for herds of reindeer up here too, you are more than likely to come across small groups grazing along the road.

Fäbodvägen continues on to the ski resort of Ljungdalen near the Norwegian border, but to complete this itinerary head back to the 321 and turn south to **Hoverberg**, a bun-shaped outcrop of rock at the southern tip 🦌 of Storsjön. Hoverberg's main claim to fame is its grotto or cave which according to legend once housed an ill-humoured giant who liked to throw rocks at a neighbouring village in an effort to frighten people away. He did not succeed and eventually moved in disgust to the province of Hälsingland coining a common Swedish utterance 'go to Hälsingland' — a sentiment that is undoubtedly preferable to the more obvious alternative! The grotto is signposted from the 321 and there is a small pay kiosk nearby. It lies at the base of the rock and measures some 187m (613ft) although that includes an inner chamber which is difficult to reach. Continue along the minor road that passes the cave and you reach a steep incline leading up to Hoverberg's Top Stuga where a viewing tower offers a superb panorama across the southern end of Storsjön — and a birds eye 🦌 view should the 'monster' put in an appearance. The *stuga* itself serves coffees and snacks in summer and there are a number of pleasant walking trails.

From Hoverberg it is less than 10km (6 miles) to Svenstavik, the largest community in the area but with little to merit a stop. Just the other side of the village is the busy trunk road number 45. To complete the circuit turn left, heading north along the Storsjö shore. **Skanderåsen**, the village that according to legend suffered the Hoverberg giant's wrath is thankfully still there! Take time 15km (9 miles) further on to pause at the lovely little church at **Hackås**, one of the oldest in northern Sweden and worth a visit ⛪ for its picture postcard setting alone. It dates from the twelfth century and its interior decoration and altar are highly prized. Hoflinsgården next door is described as Sweden's oldest family homestead having been passed on from father to son for 600 years. A couple of marked trails nearby trace the local history which includes a scattering of some seventy 𝝥 burial mounds from AD400.

Continue past Hackås and across an agricultural peninsula joining the main E14 at Brunflo for the homestretch back to Östersund. It is worth mentioning that some 200km (124 miles) to the east along the main road is a popular stretch of coastline known as 'The High Coast' or Höga Kusten in Swedish. Here steep sided forested hills rise 200m to 300m (656ft to 984ft) straight out of the water forming a picturesque series of bays, islands, inlets and some fifty small lakes. The frayed coastline is broken by two large rivers, the now familiar Indalsälv and further north the Ångermanälv while tucked in between the folds of the coastal hills are small farming and fishing communities. The 'High Coast' effectively stretches from the town of Sundsvall in the south to Örnsköldsvik in the north.

This itinerary has by necessity been little more than a taster when it comes to Sweden's wilder regions. Outdoor enthusiasts who return year after year all have their own favourite fell, their preferred fishing spot and probably a 'secret' cloudberry marsh the location of which they keep to themselves. There really are endless possibilities and visitors can decide for themselves just how far they want to go to 'get away from it all'. The best advice is to consult the tourist office where staff are generally happy to make holiday suggestions based on individual preferences for walking, fishing, sports or relaxation.

But before concluding this chapter it would be a shame not to mention the area around Vemdalen, some 120km (74 miles) south-east of Östersund. It is best known as a winter sports and ski centre with more than fifty downhill slopes but also boasts the picturesque village of **Klövsjö**, hailed as the prettiest in Sweden by local tourist brochures. Klövsjö's timber houses date from the 1500s and 1600s and the village enjoys an enviable position on the sloping shore of its very own lake. Its long agricultural traditions are kept alive in a number of working hillfarms.

Klövsjön lies on road 316 which turns into the 315 as it climbs over the fells at Vemdalen itself. Further west is Sånfjället, a small National Park which attracts hundreds of visitors all hoping for a glimpse of its most famous resident, the brown bear. There are known to be several in the area and special 'bear safaris' are run to Sånfjället to look for them. Contact the tourist office at Östersund for more information although even the staff there will admit that you need both patience and luck to spot one.

Additional Information

Places to Visit

Frösön
Frösö Djurpark (Zoo)
☎ 063 114743
Open: daily May to August.

Frösötornet (Frösö Viewing Tower)
Open: daily mid-May to mid-September.

Hoverberg
Hoverbergsgrottan (The Hoverberg Grotto)
☎ 0687 12097
Open: 8am-8pm in summer.

Mountain Stations
Storulvån Fjällstation (STF mountain centre)
Duved
☎ 0647 72007
For more information about mountain stations contact STF (The Swedish Touring Association)
Drottninggatan 33
Box 25, 10120 Stockholm
☎ 08 7903100

Njärka Sameläger (Sami Camp)
Häggsjönäs
Duved
☎ 0647 25042
Open: daily June to August.

Persåsen
Craft centre with hotel, youth hostel and chalets
Oviken
☎ 0643 40141
Open: all year.

Trondheim
Trondheim Kunstgalleri
Bispegt. 7B
☎ 07 526671
Open: daily June to August 11am-4pm, Tuesday to Sunday 12noon-4pm rest of the year.

Kristiansten Festning (Fort)
☎ 07 995997
Open: June, July, August Monday to Friday 10am-3pm, weekends 11am-3pm.

Nordenfjeldske Kunstindustrimuseum (Museum of Applied Art and Craft)
Munkegt 5
☎ 07 521311
Open: weekdays 9am-3pm (Sunday 12noon-4pm), 20 June to 20 August 9am-5pm (Sunday 12noon-5pm).

Ytterån
Mus Olle Museum
Open: daily 29 June to 16 August.

Östersund
Jämtli Open-Air Museum
North of the centre off Rådhusgatan
Open: daily June to August 11am-5pm.

Läns Museum (Jämtlands County Museum)
Next to Jämtli
☎ 063 127125
Open: all year, weekdays 9am-4pm (Tuesday to 9pm), weekends 12noon-4pm.

Stadmuseet (Östersund Town Museum)
Biblioteksgatan
Open: 22 June to 9 August, afternoons only.

Tourist Information Centres

Storlienfjällens
Storlien
☎ 0647 70570

Storlien Högfjällshotell (mountain hotel) and Chalet Village
Storlien
☎ 0647 70170

Trondheim
Trondheim Torg
☎ 07 527201

Åre
Torget
☎ 0647 51220

Östersund
Rådhusgatan 44
☎ 063 144001

7

LAPPLAND

Call it the land of the Midnight Sun, the top of Europe or the continent's last wilderness — there is something rather exotic about Lappland. It is, after all, full of un-Swedish sounding places like Karesuando, Jokkmokk and Svappavaara. Its original inhabitants were not blond Swedes but the culturally distinct Lapps or Sami whose reindeer roam the fells like herds of sheep. It is a land of forests, mountains and fast flowing rivers where a miniscule population of under 300,000 is spread across an area equal to that of Belgium, Holland and Switzerland combined. Lappland is also remote. About half of it lies north of the Arctic Circle and getting to say, Kiruna involves a 1,900km (1,178 mile) haul from Malmö in the south and 1,700km (1,054 miles) from the west coast port of Göteborg. Visitors who make the journey in June and July are rewarded with 24 hours of daylight while in the depth of winter the sun does not rise at all and the brightest spectacle in the night sky are the Northern Lights.

It is the very remoteness of Lappland that makes it appealing to tourists. Every summer the main inland route number 45 and the busier E4 along the coast are sprinkled with campervans, caravans, hitchhikers and cyclists keen to escape their own cramped parts of Europe. This is the great Swedish outdoors at its most majestic. To get the best out of it pack a pair of walking shoes or wellington boots, a fishing rod if you are a keen angler, and a good insect repellent. Mosquitos can be a real nuisance once the snows have melted and ammunition is essential if you do not want to become a mobile buffet! Fortunately the mosquitos disappear as suddenly as they came with the first frost of autumn.

Visitors are also governed by the climate which is at its most agreeable between June and September. If you go in May or June you should be one step ahead of the mosquitos but may find the going underfoot a little wet as the ground recovers from the winter. This is more than made up for by the riot of spring flowers. In July and August the trails are dry, the days are long but the mosquitos are at their most active. September is one of the most popular months because of the glorious autumn colours.

The decision whether to travel the inland or coastal route to Lappland will probably depend on where your journey starts. Both involve long sections of fairly tedious countryside by the end of which you could be forgiven for never wanting to see another fir tree. But the roads are good and the low traffic density means that progress is often faster than expected. There are plenty of small communities and fuel stations along both routes.

With that in mind, this itinerary takes as its starting point the 'crossroads' community of **Arvidsjaur** on the inland route 45; close to where it meets the 95 from the Bothnian coast to the Norwegian border. The word *jaur* means lake in Sami which is not surprising as there are 4,000 in the area — the tourist office by the central square can arrange canoe or boat hire and fishing licences. Once at Arvidsjaur you are already well inside the borders of Lappland. The uninspiring shops and offices strung along the main street form an administrative centre for a community spread across an area the size of Skåne. At first glance it would hardly seem worth a stop. But Arvidsjaur has for hundreds of years been the meeting place of 'forest sami'. It was effectively superimposed on traditional Lapp territories or 'villages' whose boundaries are defined by the grazing limits of their reindeer herds. A 'Lapp Town' therefore developed near Arvidsjaur church so that Samen families from a wide area would have somewhere to stay when they attended Sunday service. Today **Lappstaden**, 'the Lapp Town' has some eighty squat-looking wooden Lapp dwellings (known as *kåtor*) and store houses. It can be found set back from the main road a few minutes walk from the centre. Many of the dwellings date from the 1700s and are still used by their owners. The best time to visit the town is during the last weekend in August when the local Sami hold a huge get-together with competitions auctions and handicraft displays. Church services are held there on Sundays in July and there are regular guided tours.

Today's well-educated and sophisticated Sami are acutely aware of the tourist potential arising out of their traditions and customs. Next door to Lappstaden is Samegården Arvas where you can buy handicrafts and taste local sami specialities. During the three weeks after Midsummer the centre also arranges for visitors to go with Sami herdsmen to watch them catch and mark the season's young reindeer. Hapless city dwellers are occasionally handed a lasso and told to get a reindeer themselves.

There is not really a great deal more to see in Arvidsjaur. Gamla Prästgården (the Old Vicarage) on the outskirts of the community houses a small local museum with mementos of indigenous Lapp culture and of the settlers from the south. For some strange reason it contains an ancient replica of the world's first lock — the original is apparently to be found in Afghanistan! Near the museum is a small ski slope and for a different kind of exercise, the tourist office can organise outings on railway inspection trolleys along a disused branchline from Arvidsjaur to Jörn. The centre has a fair number of shops including one on the main road which sells local handicrafts, a good campsite and a smattering of restaurants and hotels.

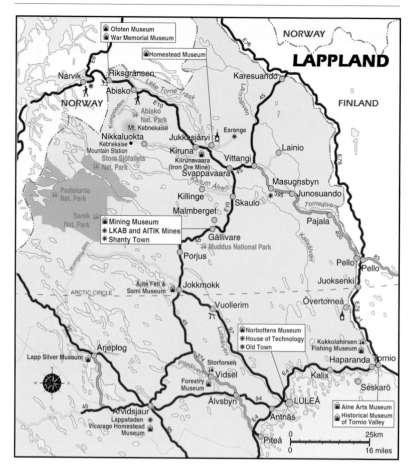

Continue north along route 45 past great tracts of forest and scrubland broken only by the odd lake or village. There is a campsite at Moskosel with holiday cottages and boat hire and a wilderness recreation area with hunting and fishing further on at Kåbdalis. Do not forget to look out for stray reindeer wandering along the verges. Like elk they can be a real traffic hazard up here although they generally cause fewer accidents because they tend to run alongside the road while elk barge straight across it. Even bears have been spotted from time to time but their appearance is such a rarity that when three were seen crossing the main road near Arvidsjaur they made the national news.

You know you are getting near **Polcirkeln** (the Arctic Circle) when you see the first 'certificates' for sale — usually alongside offers of smoked fish and Lapp souvenirs. The Arctic Circle itself, about 8km (5 miles) south of Jokkmokk, is a bit of a let down. A large blue roadsign in several languages marks the spot and there is a tiny picnic area across the road. The fact that there is nothing much to see does not deter travellers from proudly photographing each other under the landmark. In reality a bit of 'licence'

Young Lapp boy at Arvidsjaur

Backpackers at Jokkmokk railway station

was used when erecting the sign because the Arctic Circle does not remain absolutely still but moves slightly each year. Geographically it lies at 66 degrees and 33 minutes north, 3,330km (2,065 miles) from the North Pole and 6,660km (4,129 miles) from the Equator. It is also the generally recognised boundary of the Midnight Sun, long daylight hours further south are due largely to reflected light. The further north you travel, the longer the Midnight Sun is visible. So at Jokkmokk, for example it can be seen from around the 8 June to the 3 July while in Kiruna the period extends from the end of May through to mid-July. At the extreme northern tip of Scandinavia the sun is on show for 24 hours from the second week in May to the beginning of August — all depending on the weather of course.

Jokkmokk, a sprawling community of 7,000 and the centre for a huge area of sparsely populated marshland and forest means 'Bend in the Stream' in Sami. Some 10 per cent of its population are Sami and it is the only parish in Sweden that insists on its local vicar speaking Sami as well as Swedish. The community is most famous for its huge lively winter market held across the first Thursday, Friday and Saturday of February and therefore a pretty dark, chilly affair. The Lapp market is an annual tradition that goes back almost 400 years and is well worth a visit for anyone who happens to be in Lappland in the depth of winter. Quite a lot of people evidently are — the Danes apparently come on organised tours and hotels have to be booked months in advance. A more low-key market is held at the end of August.

The history of the Sami and of the settlers who were encouraged to move north in the 1600s and 1700s is eloquently told in the splendid Ájtte Swedish Fell and Sami Museum a few minutes walk from the tourist information office. Ájtte means storehouse and the museum uses slides and high tech to tell its story. Also near the tourist office is Jokkmokk's old church, a pretty red-painted timber building surrounded by a thick boundary wall which contains hidden compartments formerly used to store bodies while the ground was too frozen for a grave to be dug. It effectively meant that the dead could rest on consecrated ground awaiting a proper burial. The tourist office in the centre of the community just off Storgatan is the place to go if you really must have a certificate for crossing the Arctic Circle. It is also a useful first port of call for anyone interested in exploring the rugged National Parks that lie on Jokkmokk's doorstep: Muddus, Stora Sjöfallet, Padjelanta and Sarek. Staff will give advice on local fishing, small game hunting, and help book white water rafting on nearby Piteå.

Just over 40km (25 miles) south-east of Jokkmokk at **Vuollerim** archaeologists excavated the remains of a Stone Age village which was first discovered by chance in 1983. Parts have now been reconstructed nearby for visitors to see and there is a new information centre with a cafeteria which organises guided tours of the dig. To get there take route number 97.

Vuollerim, which also has a couple of good campsites lies at the confluence of two branches of the Luleälven (River Lule) in an area dominated
by huge hydroelectric power plants. The river's sixteen power stations
produce a quarter of Sweden's hydroelectric power. To continue north
return to Jokkmokk and follow route 45 past the largest of them,
Harsprånget and on to the oldest, **Porjus**. Porjus was originally built to
supply electricity for local ore trains and must have been quite an achievement when it was originally completed in 1914. Since then a new power
station has been constructed relegating the original building to a museum
and cafeteria.

From Porjus it is 50km (31 miles) to the great copper and iron ore mining
centre of Gällivare-Malmberget. A road to the left heads off towards the
Storasjöfallet National Park highlands while on the right is Muddus
National Park, a 500sq km (310sq mile) wilderness of dark forest and
inaccessible marshland inhabited by bear, lynx, elk and many rare species
of bird. There are a few trails and overnight huts within the area but it is
generally regarded as difficult terrain for unaccustomed ramblers.
Gällivare has its own nature reserve in the form of Dundret, an 800m
(2,624ft) high fell and popular recreation area just south of the community. A right turn from the trunk road leads to the top from where, weather
and time-of-year permitting you get a grandstand view of the Midnight
Sun. It appears at Gällivare from the beginning of June until 12 July and
Dundret is 'the' place to see it. The tourist office in the town centre runs
special Midnight Sun buses for visitors without their own transport.

Gällivare means 'Cracked Mountain' in Sami, a fitting name as the
community depends on iron and copper mining for its survival. It is
linked to its neighbour Malmberget (literally 'Ore Mountain') by a short
stretch of dual carriageway and the two are generally treated as a single
entity. No-one could describe the bleak looking sprawl of modern flats
and industry as beautiful. The local economy is dominated by two industrial giants; firstly AITIK, Europe's largest copper mine and Sweden's
most productive gold mine and secondly the huge LKAB iron ore mine.
Both run tours for visitors, bookable through the tourist office or at the
mine, which vividly demonstrate how machinery and high tech have
taken over from traditional methods. They usually include a stop at a
reconstructed 'shanty town' in Malmberget called Kåkstan, once dubbed
Lappland's Klondyke. The restored 'wild-west' lookalike with its 'Cafe
for the Sober' is a reminder of the influx of workers into the mining
community in the late 1800s. The local Mining Museum traces the development of the industry.

Gällivare is the older of the two neighbours although its dull looking
centre has little to show for it. But if you scratch the surface there are one
or two things worthy of mention. They include the eighteenth-century
'One Öre Church' known as the 'Old' or 'Lapp' Church. It got its name
because when the king decided to build this he demanded one *öre* per year
over 4 years from every family in Sweden to pay for it. A little further

The Midnight Sun, one of Sweden's most beautiful sights

Watch out for reindeer and elk wandering on the road sides in Lappland

along the riverbank on the edge of the town is a pleasant open-air museum (Hembygdsgård) with historic timber houses rescued from other parts of the community and a cafeteria overlooking the water. A 'Lapp Camp' next door has a collection of turf *kåtor* (dwellings) one of which boasts an incongruous front door that would look more at home on a suburban semi. The smaller wooden huts on tall poles are high rise larders which keep food out of reach of wild animals.

There are a number of open-air barbeque spots along the river bank and a good campsite while the other side has a 'children's wood' where youngsters learn about plants and trees from a fairytale character called 'Plupp' who dutifully appears out of his Lapp tent. Adults are not allowed because, says the literature, Plupp is afraid of them!

From Gällivare follow the signs for Kiruna, turning left onto route 45/E10 after about 10km (6 miles). The forest is sparse and patchy this far north with stunted, balding trees and surprisingly flat stony ground. A 1km (½ mile) track on the left leads to a gold panning camp where cluttered log cabins and a flagpole give it an authentic looking pioneer feel. Panning for gold is a popular holiday pastime up here and would-be prospectors often have to book well in advance.

Further north the main road passes some of Lappland's best fishing waters. Kaitumälven (the Kaitum River) which joins the Kalixälv (Kalix River) just upstream from the road bridge at Lappesuando is a popular destination for fishermen from all over the world. You have to be prepared to hike or pay for a helicopter flight to get to the remote fishing camp at Tjuonajokk in the upper reaches of the river, but a reasonable dirt road does lead from near Skaulo some 40km (25 miles) into the wilds. It skirts many fine fishing waters along the way and passes Killinge where non-fishermen can pan for gold or try their hand at white water rafting. There is a small tourist centre and an old Lapp school with residential school huts once used by the otherwise Nomadic Samen while they attended lessons. The road ends at **Kaitum** where a small chapel has been built to the memory of the late UN General Secretary Dag Hammarskjöld. A walking trail continues along the river for those who want to go further upstream. Fishermen can expect to catch trout, Arctic char, grayling and salmon. The tourist offices at Kiruna, Gällivare or the local information centre at Lappesuando can give additional advice and arrange fishing licences. Lappesuando is being developed into a roadside tourist centre and nowadays offers 'floating saunas' onboard a wooden river raft as one of its more off-beat attractions. There are holiday chalets, refreshments and, 5km (3 miles) further north at Piilijärvi a full-scale campsite.

Continue north staying on the E10 when it splits from the 45 just south of Svappavaara. You may not have realised it but you are already in **Kiruna**, Sweden's most northerly town and deceptively billed as 'the world's largest' because of its huge administrative area. It stretches over a thinly populated 19,447sq km (7,475sq miles) of lakes, wilderness, mountains and ore fields. Anyone approaching from the south will first see signs for the village of Jukkasjärvi on the banks of the Torne river. The name means 'Meeting Place' and it was once an important market where the local Sami traded with Swedish settlers. The sparse scatter of houses is centred around a well kept Homestead and Hembygdsgård (Lapp Museum) incorporating a first rate cafeteria in one of the old-style timber buildings. The home-baked waffles with whipped cream and cloudberry conserve can be thoroughly recommended. The village also has a well established *wärdshus* (inn) specialising in local dishes. At the far end of the main street is Lappland's oldest church with a spectacularly colourful altar triptych by the well-known twentieth-century Swedish artist Bror Hjorth. The naive raised images show preacher Lars Levi Laestadius, whose religious movement Laestadianism spread far beyond the borders of Lappland, preaching temperance to the Lapps.

The church also contains an odd little memorial to Lappland's first 'tourist', an intrepid frenchman called Jean-Francois Regnard de Corberon. In 1681 he and two friends thought they had come to 'the end of the world' and carved the following inscription now hanging in the entrance: 'We were born in Gaul. We have seen Africa and have drawn water from the River Ganges. We have observed Europe in its entirety, crossed over land and sea and by the vicissitudes of fortune, now finally we stand here at the end of the world.'

With such tourist appeal both past and present, **Jukkasjärvi** does a brisk business in adventure holidays, white water rafting, dog sledding, survival training and even Nordic saunas. Ask for more information at the homestead museum or at the holiday centre on the main road as you drive into the community. The latter has cottages for rent and whole flotilla of rubber rafts in which you can make 6-hour trips down the Torne river rapids with the odd stop for a camp fire lunch and hot coffee. Rafting is exciting but it does not come cheap. Remember also that river water in the Arctic is usually glacial and rarely reaches many degrees above zero, so it can be a chilly business even on the finest of summer days. Staff at the holiday centre should be able to give advice on other outdoor activities while the tourist office in Kiruna itself can offer several alternative, and possibly cheaper options.

A bumpy, unmade dirt road leads on from Jukkasjärvi to the isolated Esrange rocketbase and space research station some 20km (12 miles) away. The base is run by the European Space Agency and proudly proclaims to have been responsible for the launch of rockets 'as high as seven storey houses'. An international staff monitors many of the satellites that circle the earth and carries out vital research into the ozone layer. Guided tours are arranged by Kiruna tourist office in summertime.

Cross back over the Torne river to rejoin main E10. Anyone ready for an *al fresco* lunch could do worse than stop at the pleasant little picnic spot just before the bridge where ready-to-use camp fires complete with barbecue racks have been installed. Turn right on the main road for the 15km (9 miles) drive into Kiruna, the only major centre of population in this remote northern corner of Sweden. The town cannot be described as beautiful. The neat rows of suburban villas and flats are dominated by a brooding grey mountain of waste spewed up over the decades by Kiirunavaara, the world's largest underground mine. There is so much ✳ waste that locals calculate they have enough hardcore to construct a road from Lappland to Rome. The little that got used when the E10 was extended to Narvik some years ago barely scratched the surface; but high transport costs have put paid to all grandiose schemes and the pile just keeps growing.

There were only a couple of primitive turf *kåtor* inhabited by Sami here when a geologist called Hjalmar Lundbohm came to investigate local iron ore finds 100 years ago. He discovered the world's richest ore seam and even after a century of exploitation deposits are expected to last another couple of centuries. The mine has some 550km (341 miles) of underground 'roads' and looks like a huge landlocked ship at night when strings of lights define the old waste terraces. It is also Kiruna's number one tourist attraction. During the summer the tourist office runs several daily tours to a special 'visitors' section of the mine at 370m (1,214ft) depth. Participants (children have to be aged over 10) are given samples of ore pellets produced by the LKAB mining company and apparently make off with a total of 20 tons of these 'souvenirs' every year.

You get a good view of the mine, the town and the distant highlands from the top of Kiruna's local ski run at Loussavaara. From here you can see the endless ore trains crawling north-west towards the Norwegian border and the port of Narvik. Access to Lappland's iron ore was of immense importance during World War II and Narvik paid dearly for its strategic position at the end of the ore railway.

Kiruna's centre is a modern, draughty looking place with the usual array of shops, supermarkets and a couple of good but expensive handicraft boutiques selling samen souvenirs and other local artefacts. Land values were obviously not a problem when assembling this sparse jigsaw of apartments and office blocks. The town is proud of its Stadshus (Town Hall) easily identifiable by the tall clocktower and improbably described as 'Sweden's most beautiful official building' when first completed in 1964. The interior draws on the area's Samen culture and includes a local art collection. There are daily guided tours during the summer. Samegården (the Sami House) has a small museum about Sami culture and rents rooms to tourists. Kiruna's cavernous church is supposed to give the impression of a Sami Kåta inside and is remarkable for its lack of Christian symbolism. Hjalmar Lundbohm who funded it specifically wanted the building to be available to all religions although a subsequent bishop has since installed a small removable statue of Sami praying at a cross on the altar.

Downhill from the church is Hjalmar Lundbohm's home, Hjalmar ✳ Lundbohmsgården which is now a cultural centre full of memorabilia of the man credited with founding not only the ore mine but Kiruna itself.

Kiruna's tourist office lies just off the main thoroughfare named after Lundbohm and diagonally opposite the Town Hall. Staff there should be able to give information about wilderness tours, fishing, white water rafting and numerous other activities organised by enterprising 'outward bound' types in the area.

One popular excursion goes to the Sami village of **Nikkaluokta** 66km (41 miles) away in the shadow of **Kebnekaise**, Sweden's highest mountain massif. There are some twenty snow-capped peaks around the 2,000m (6,560ft) mark in this area. The highest, Kebnekaise's south peak, is 2,117m (6,944ft) but that has not prevented the Swedish Tourist Association from building a cabin up there. There is a good tarmac road all the way following a long finger of lake and passing one or two tiny settlements. Buses also run regularly from Kiruna. The road ends in a huge carpark at Nikkaluokta with the mountains as a backdrop and a large map showing hiking and skiing trails. Anyone wanting to go on to the Kebnekaise mountain hotel 19km (12 miles) further up the valley will have to do so on foot using the marked trail that winds its way through skinny looking birch trees following the green glacial water of a mountain river and in summer 5km (3 miles) of the distance is covered by boat. But remember to check on the seasonal operating times and conditions before setting out even on a ramble as apparently simple as this one. Although only accessible on foot or on skis, the mountain hotel is a comfortable base with a licensed restaurant, self catering facilities and a food shop. It is also a centre from which to further explore the mountains. Even Kebnekaise

One of the many walking trails through the Abisko National Park

itself can be 'conquered' with the help of a guide. 'Trips to the Top', glacier walks and more serious mountain climbing are organised at the hotel with special classes for beginners.

This itinerary continues from Kiruna heading north-west along the E10 towards Narvik. Until recently Kiruna was literally the end of the road and anyone wanting to travel on to the Norwegian border had to do so by train. There was considerable debate about the detrimental effects a new highway would have on the sensitive Arctic landscape. It was however finally completed in 1982, knocking 400km (248 miles) off the previous motoring distance. The road has since become a popular, well-used highway and the accidental nadir of some 500 unfortunate reindeer who get run over there every year. A plastic bag tied to a post means there are herds in the vicinity and that motorists should take extra care, but accidents are inevitable. Note that at the time of writing there were no fuel stations between Abisko and Narvik, a distance of about 70km (43 miles).

The road follows the railway line, first crossing a flat region of mainly boggy marshland sprinkled in late summer with ripe Arctic cloudberries. Most of the tiny settlements along the way have grown around the railway line. The 168km (104 miles) stretch to Narvik was completed in 1902 providing a vital transport link from Kiruna's ore fields. It was a considerable engineering feat — during the final leg to the Norwegian coast trains descend 520m (1,706ft) over 39km (24 miles) and pass through twenty-one tunnels. The road reaches the shores of Sweden's seventh largest lake, Torne Träsk some 60km (37 miles) north-west of Kiruna. On a sunny day during the brief Arctic summer the water looks so blue that it almost seems artificial. But storms can whip up 2m (7ft) high waves and for much of the year it is covered in thick ice. The dark snow-streaked fells to the north are roadless and untouched by all except a few Sami moving with their reindeer herds across the tundra. South of the lake mountains rise to 1,700m (5,576ft) and include one of Lappland's most familiar images, Lapporten meaning literally The Lapp Gate. The natural mountain U-shape can be seen to the left of the main road from a variety of vantage points, but is at its most symmetrical when viewed from near the **Abisko National Park**.

Abisko has been protected since 1909 and is one of Sweden's oldest and most popular National Parks. In spite of lying 250km (155 miles) north of the Arctic Circle, it is also one of its most accessible. Unlike some of the more rugged offerings, you do not have to be super-fit or an outdoor type to enjoy a visit here. There is a large and comfortable mountain hotel called the Abisko Turiststation just off the main road with a fully licensed restaurant as well as self-catering facilities, a shop and holiday cottages for rent. Prices are remarkably reasonable. The reception desk has literally dozens of leaflets suggesting activities, walks, guided tours and courses. To give just a few examples they range from the obscure 'how to die knitting wool with fungi' to watercolouring, photographic and ornithological tours and parascending. Some can be fairly expensive. Staff can also arrange equipment hire; skis in winter, rucksacks and walking shoes in summer, and there is a 'Naturum' housing an exhibition about the local flora and fauna.

The park covers a 77sq km (30sq miles) river valley, chosen not only for its natural beauty but for the enormous variety of highland flowers, trees and shrubs that grow there. The terrain varies from thick birch forests, to windswept mosses, heathland, rocky highland and of course Lake Torne Träsk in the north. Among the flowers are mountain violet, creeping azalea, saxifrage, bright yellow globe flowers, moss campion and Arctic heather. The most colourful time is in June and July, the ground becomes drier in August and in September the park puts on a spectacular show of autumn colours. The whole area lies in a rain shadow and is said to have the lowest precipitation in Sweden.

Keen walkers know Abisko as the start of **Kungsleden**, the King's Route, a marathon 500km (310 mile) trail through some of Sweden's wildest regions. But there are plenty of short walks ranging from an hour to a whole day that start and end at the hotel or the nearby railway station. Each route is meticulously marked, planks are laid across marshy sections and you may well find a manmade windbreak with a camp fire or picnic spot along the way. You are also more than likely to come across herds of reindeer as Abisko has always been a traditional pasture ground for the Sami who have a small display of Lapp dwellings in a clearing a few minutes from the railway station. Aross on the other side of the river a chairlift negotiates part of the mountain called Njulla generally regarded as a good spot from which to view the Midnight Sun (visible betweeen 30 May to 16 July).

From Abisko the main road passes avalanche warning signals as it edges along the lakeside. This stretch was built on an area of permafrost which started to melt under the weight of traffic, causing a major headache for construction engineers. Additional hardcore and sand was added to stabilise the ground. Nine kilometres (6 miles) on is **Björkliden**, a small ski resort with a modern hotel, caravan site and a large batch of well-equipped if not exactly beautiful cottages for rent. It also boasts 'the world's most northerly golfcourse' whose tricky nine holes offer superlative views of the lake and Lapporten beyond. The golf season may be short up here, but you can make up for that by playing round the clock. High above Björkliden at an altitude of over 1,200m (3,936ft) is a well-known mountain hotel and restaurant called Låktatjåkko.

The E10 leaves Torne Träsk behind at Tornehamn in whose churchyard lie many of the labourers that worked on the infamous Narvik to Kiruna railway line. They include the cook, a woman nick-named 'Black Bear' who became a living legend. The road climbs through a bleak and rugged landscape of barren rocks and small dark lakes. The stunted birch trees have virtually given up the ghost as it passes the Sami's holy mountain, Vuottassrita. There is usually snow up here until the end of June — an irresistible draw for winter sports enthusiasts seeking new challenges including the chance to ski in the Midnight Sun on Midsummers Eve! The mountain resort of **Riksgränsen** — it literally means 'The Border' — understandably trades on this exotic quirk and usually keeps at least a couple of ski runs open until mid-summer. Lifts operate until midnight and beyond from mid-May until late June depending on snow conditions. Riksgränsen is one of the world's most northerly ski resorts and has been going strong since the beginning of the twentieth century. The ski season starts in February for anyone willing to don layers of thermal underwear while in June the sun can be warm enough for just tee-shirt and shorts. But it is worth mentioning that at these extreme latitudes an altitude of 1,000m (3,280ft) has conditions similar to a height of 2,500m (8,200ft) in the Alps and protective clothing could be necessary at any time.

The resort has a variety of runs and plenty of snow because, in contrast to Abisko, it has Sweden's highest annual precipitation. Hotel Riksgränsen includes a choice of accommodation from fully serviced rooms to self catering apartments and there is a restaurant, nightclub, disco, swimming pool, shop and ski hire facilities. Next door is a permanent show of work by Lappland photographer Sven Hörnell.

Motorists cross into Norway at a mountain border post just after Riksgränsen although it is unlikely that either set of passport or customs officers will put in an appearance. After the border the road descends quickly, winding past dozens of small rocky tarns and past isolated summer cottages. It is still 'winter' well into June up here but down by the ice-free fjords a few kilometres on, the gulf stream ensures that the seasons are well advanced. The contrast at certain times of year can be staggering.

Strictly speaking the most spectacular way to reach **Narvik** from the border is by rail. The track clings to the steep mountainside passing through tunnel after tunnel on its journey along the Rombak fjord. There are awesome views from the road too as it drops to the waters edge on the northern side of the fjord with the precipitous wall of Fagernesfjellet ahead. Turn left onto the E6, following the Narvik signs. The road crosses the water on a modern bridge and edges around the shoreline into the town. It is not the purpose of this book to provide a detailed guide to Norway so the itinerary will deal only briefly with Narvik. Anyone wanting to explore this side of the border in more depth will find the *Visitor's Guide to Norway* in the same series invaluable. The history of Narvik is firmly tied to the iron ore fields of Swedish Lappland. There were only a few farms here until the turn of the century when the railway finally linked the Norwegian coast with the giant ore deposits across the border. Narvik's ice free port became of immense importance for the shipping of ore and thus a primary strategic target during World War II. In April 1940 ten German destroyers entered the harbour, sank two Norwegian battleships and took the town. There was a fierce sea battle a few days later when the British Navy, supported by the French and the Poles annihilated the German fleet and recaptured Narvik. It was a great victory and a temporary morale booster, but the allied position was

Lappland is the great Swedish outdoors at its most majestic

untenable and they were ordered to abandon Narvik some weeks later. The Germans took the town again, but not before the all-important ore handling facilities had been destroyed. Narvik's harbour was a graveyard of tangled metal.

The Nordland Røde Kors Krigsminnemuseum (Nordland War Memorial Museum), in the centre of the town diagonally opposite the town hall attracts 50,000 visitors anually. It tells the story of those years with the help of an impressive and eclectic collection of mementos, photographs, contemporary documents and propaganda leaflets. Every inch of space is crammed with exhibits and the best way to make sense of them is to borrow an English language guide from reception. It makes fascinating reading. Among the items on display is a reconstructed German hide-out which remained hidden in the mountains for 39 years until it was found, with contents intact, by grouse hunters. The town itself is dotted with statues and plaques commemorating the soldiers and sailors of many nationalities who lost their lives there.

A couple of minutes from the War Memorial Museum on the other side of the main Kongens Gate road is the Ofoten Museum. It is devoted to local cultural history including the earliest traces of human settlement going back to the Stone Age. There is a rock carving of an elk believed to be 3,000 years old at Brennholtet in the northern part of the town.

The railway line effectively slices Narvik in two and ends in massive shipment docks where ore is automatically unloaded from a steady stream of wagons. The operators, LKAB Malmhavnen (Ore Harbour) offer tours of the harbour and there are rail excursions to the Swedish border. Visitors looking for a 'photo opportunity' in Narvik town centre tend to gravitate to the bright yellow signpost near the War Museum which marks the distance to almost two dozen places including the North Pole (2,420km/1,500 miles). The rather dull looking, main street is brightened up by dozens of souvenir trolls leering from their shop windows. For a good view of the surrounding fjords and mountains try the Narvik Gondolbane, a cablecar rising from near the Narvik Sportell hotel to a mountain restaurant 650m (2,132ft) above.

Narvik is also a good starting point for an excursion to the extraordinary Lofoten Islands whose jagged profile can sometimes be glimpsed across Ofotfjorden. The tooth shaped mountains rising straight out of the sea shelter small picturesque fishing communities at their base. In summer regular catamaran services cover the distance at speeds of 70kph (43mph) leaving from the Dampskipskaia in Narvik harbour — south of the ore loading depot.

The drawback of any itinerary in this part of Scandinavia is the limited choice of roads. Anyone with plenty of time to spare can continue north along the main E6, then south on the E78 through Finland to cross back into Sweden at Karesuando, the country's northernmost parish. As the detour is long and the scenery relatively unremarkable the route outlined in this chapter will now double back along the E10 to Kiruna and past the town to Svappavaara, another mining community. Branch left onto route 45 signposted Karesuando, Vittangi and Pajala.

With the mountains now far behind it is the turn of the lowland birch and fir trees to make their presence felt. One tree in particular was of special significance to those travelling regularly, on horseback or by carriage, between Vittangi and Kiruna. The tall pine on the left about 15km (9 miles) east of Svappavaara looks ordinary enough. But an official signpost marks it out in local Finnish dialect as *Ryyppö Talli* 'Sup Tallen' in Swedish, which liberally translated means the 'Boozers' Pine'. The tree acquired the name because it was used as a pit-stop during these journeys and a glass of snaps would be drunk under its branches. It was apparently so much a part of the routine that the horses stopped there automatically. There is a picnic spot even today, although current Swedish drink-driving laws mean motorists are ill-advised to down anything stronger than a fruit juice.

Vittangi is a sleepy rural community straddling the ragged banks of the Torne river along one of its more peaceful stretches. There is a bird sanctuary here but not much else. Ignore the main road signposted Karesuando and follow the 395 towards Pajala. White water rafting, fishing and canoeing can be organised at the 'Wilderness Centre' at Laino 30km (19 miles) from the road.

The road continues south-east through flat forested countryside to an old mining village called **Masugnsbyn** where the local council has done its best to turn the remnants of its old iron workings into a local attraction. The former blast furnace has been restored and is open to visitors although the remains of the ore roasting pits leave a lot to the imagination. Just the other side of Masugnsbyn the road leaves Lappland and passes into its next-door province, Norbotten. It meets the broad Torneälv river again at Junosuando and follows it as the calm water upstream turns into powerful rapids. There are a couple of good picnic and barbecue spots at Tornefors just east of Junosuando where an automatic machine sells 'do-it-yourself' fishing licences. The licence entitles holders to fish from the shore with a rod — the idea of going out in a boat on the rapids is unlikely to appeal anyway! The wooded riverbank has the remains of some more ore roasting pits.

The lush Torne valley with its mild summer climate is a sharp contrast to the bare, uninhabited tundra further north. Suddenly settlements seem to multiply and gardens are filled with fruit bushes and vegetables. Although most of the larger communities have a hotel, there are not many in between and the accommodation gap is filled by *stugor* which may be private cottages for rent or complete holiday villages with a sauna, pool and canoe hire. **Tärendö**, 15km (9 miles) from the main road is a tranquil little backwater at the confluence of two other sizeable Arctic rivers, Kalixälven and Tärendöälven. The latter is deemed an oddity because it links Kalixälven and Torneälven in what is known as a bifurcation. The

scattered village is linked by three bridges and there is a Hembygdsgård

(Homestead Museum) incorporating twenty-two old buildings from the Torne valley. Local reindeer roundups and marking takes place in the area during summer.

Back on the main 395 is the larger community of **Pajala** — a fairly uninspiring but locally important commercial centre on the banks of the Torneälv. Small factories make rocking chairs and wall clocks, but Pajala is perhaps best known for its association with temperance preacher Lars Levi Laestadius who died here in 1861. His movement, Laestadianism, spread through Lappland, neighbouring Finland and even to the USA. Laestadius began his mission to save the souls of local settlers and Sami in Karesuando but spent his last 12 years in Pajala where his former home, Laestadipörti is open to visitors.

Just the other side of Pajala is **Kengis Bruk**, the most northerly manor in Sweden and once the site of an important iron and copperworks using locally mined ore. There is not much to see today, but a pleasant kilometre long walk follows the river as it roars over some rapids. The Russians, who once lurked on the other side of the river burnt Kengis factory and chapel to the ground in 1717 temporarily leaving 200 angry locals without a job.

Shortly after Kengis Bruk the river turns south to form the boundary between Sweden and Finland. Relations between the Nordic neighbours are close and cordial. Every year there are 'international weddings' as boy meets girl across the river and the two communities have a joint celebration. Finnish signs appear on Swedish roads and neighbours hop across to each other by boat. You can take a brief excursion into Finland by turning left on road 402 toward Pello, crossing the bridge and then turning right to follow the E78 south on the other side. It does not look much different of course, but try reading some of the unpronounceable signs such as '*Luonnonnähtävyys Jääkauden Ajalta*', meaning 'Natural Ice-Age Site' or '*näköalapaikka*' meaning simply 'View'. There are a number of pleasant picnic spots along the road, but signs remind drivers that this is also an area of reindeer husbandry.

The E78 crosses the Arctic Circle ('Napapiiri' in Finnish) at **Juoksenki**, ❉ and the enterprising locals have made the most of it. A white line traces the invisible landmark across the parking area of a cavernous souvenir shop which itself straddles the circle. So too do foreigners who pose one foot either side for the standard photo. It may be unashamedly commercial, but the shop does sell a vast range of souvenirs and has an airy and reasonably priced cafeteria with chunky furnishings made out of local timber. There are even a couple of reindeer outside for added atmosphere.

Continue south on the main road with the river on the right and alternating agricultural land and forest on the left. It passes the small community of Kaulinranta, then near Aavasaksa it signposts 'Ruotsi' to the right. The word may look unfamiliar, but in fact it means 'Sweden' in Finnish. Suffice to say that Finland is really called Suomi — just as confusing! Turn right across the bridge to the said 'Ruotsi' and follow signs to the village of **Övertorneå** on the Swedish side. The village is

Kukkulaforsen rapids, a must for the amateur fisherman

Playing chess in the main shopping street at Luleå

rightly proud of its red timber church which dates from 1617 and houses Sweden's oldest organ, a 1608 hand-me-down from the German Church in Stockholm. There is a richly worked pulpit and a series of wooden sculptures from the fourteenth and fifteenth centuries. The most noteable is the so-called 'Mantle Madonna' whose cloak opens to reveal religious figures inside. The sculptures originally adorned an older chapel but both they and the building were washed away by a disastrous spring flood in 1615. Fortunately a group of haymakers working near the river found the artefacts caught on the bank downstream.

Follow route 400 from Övertorneå. A few kilometres on at Luppio there is a rounded rocky outcrop to the right of the road called Tomteberget or 'Father Christmas Mountain'. But if you drive to the top you will find that it is not Father Christmas but his 'mother' who claims to have set up shop there. A small cafeteria bearing the name 'Santa's Mother's Coffee Cottage' (Tomtemor's Kaffe Stuga) offers wonderful views across the Torne valley and even a glimpse of the Midnight Sun from its terrace — but alas no Santa's toy factory. The proprietors however dutifully don red tunics and pom-pom hats when a group of young visitors are expected. Unlike Santa they seem to work only in summer! It has to be said that although generally translated as Father Christmas, the Swedish 'Tomte' is a rather different character. There is not one but several 'Tomtar' and they are not large and portly but small, jolly and mischevious — with a particular liking for rice-pudding!

The river meanders on south through alternating farmland and forest. The road follows its path, passing Hietaniemi and then Karungi before arriving at **Kukkolaforsen**, the Kukkola Rapids. This is a must for ama- teur fishermen with a yen to try something different. The rapids have for centuries been famous for whitefish caught not by rod and line but by long handled dip-nets which are used to scoop them out of the water. The technique is apparently matched only in the Amazon and as the spring floodwater subsides a precarious rickety fishing pier is edged bit by bit into the middle of the rapids. A similar construction emerges from the Finnish side and the survival chances of the local whitefish diminish accordingly. Dip-net licences are purchased by the hour, but on a good day the fish are so plentiful that even an inept novice can bag a few in that time. The neighbouring restaurant specialises in whitefish (known as *Sik* in Sweden) and there is a small Fishing Museum nearby. The centre also organises 50-minute rubber-raft trips down the rapids and offers three types of sauna. There are holiday cotttages for rent and a campsite.

Fifteen kilometres (9 miles) further south, at the mouth of Torneälven are the twin towns of Haparanda on the Swedish side and Tornio (Swedish spelling, Torneå) in Finland. **Tornio** is the larger of the two, a modern looking border town with a tourist and information centre. The Aine Art Museum on Länsiranta has a good collection of Finnish works from the beginning of the 1800s to contemporary and the Historical Museum of the Tornio River Valley on nearby Keskikatu tells the story of the region. The most attractive of the churches is the seventeenth-century timber Tornio church and the town can be seen from above at the Water Tower Cafe.

A golf course called The Green Zone is a good indication of the cordial relations governing the two Nordic neighbours — half of it is in Sweden and half in Finland. With a one-hour time difference between them you can tee-off in Sweden and watch the ball land in Finland 60 minutes earlier. Alternatively it can take over an hour to sink a put! The scorecards all have customs regulations printed alongside local rules.

Haparanda is a smaller low-key place with the feeling that it has seen more exciting times. It was founded as a substitute for Tornio which, although initially Swedish, was lost to the Russians during a conflict in 1809. The Swedish-Russian war divided the linguistically and culturally homogeneous Torne valley along the river and to this day Finnish is commonly spoken even on the Swedish side of the border. Haparanda became an important border town during the World War I and the scene of countless prisoner-of-war exchanges. Some 75,000 wounded prisoners and a fair number of black marketeers, spies and other dubious characters are said to have passed through its railway station. The oversized station terminal and a churchyard monument to the wounded remain as permanent reminders of those days.

The Torne valley and its surrounding countryside is uniformly low and flat as the river finally flows out into the Bay of Bothnia between Tornio and Haparanda. This northern seaboard is sometimes called 'the low coast' and offshore, stretching southward for 200km (124 miles), are hundreds of equally low-profile islands. Most are small and wooded, barely rising more than a metre out of the sea. Only a few are inhabited. The waterbus *M/S Sandskär* does regular trips and private charters to the local archipelago departing from a quay off Strandgatan in Haparanda or Hallituskato in Tornio.

It has to be said that there are relatively few good bathing beaches just here. The best place to go if you want to swim in the northernmost part of the Bay of Bothnia is the larger island of Seskarö 25km (15½ miles) south of Haparanda and linked to the mainland by a 500m (1,640ft) long bridge. It has a sizeable sandy beach as well as a swimming pool, minigolf, boat, fishing and cycle hire. Seskarö Camping has holiday cottages and a caravan site. To get there follow the main E4 in the direction of Kalix and Luleå; it is well sign-posted to the left.

To continue the itinerary, stay on the E4. It may look like a coast road on the map, but sadly it offers only fleeting glimpses of the sea. The Viking burial mound some 50m (164ft) off to the right just east of Sangis is worth a mention. The warrior's sword and shield were originally buried with him but can now been seen in Norbotten's Museum in Luleå. **Kalix**, the next sizeable community, lies at the mouth of one of Norbotten's many great fishing rivers, Kalixälven. The local authorities are hoping to turn it into one of the best salmon rivers in northern Europe and a large new 'fishing camp' has been established on its banks. Kalix church dates from the 1400s but has since suffered the ravages of fire and eighteenth-century looting by Russian soldiers. The local beach, recreation and camping area, Frevisören, lies just off the E4 some 20km (12 miles) to the east of the community.

Shortly after Kalix the main road passes signs warning that you are entering a zone 'prohibited' to foreigners. As 'foreigners' are unlikely to have time to read the small print while keeping up with the traffic flow, most are probably unaware that they are in a Military Protection Zone. But do not worry about covering up the 'alien' licence plate. The restrictions mean that foreigners may drive through although they are not supposed to stop there without special permission.

The E4 speeds on through mixed agricultural land and forest to **Luleå**, ✳ the principal city and commercial centre of Norbotten province. Luleå's population is a modest 70,000, but it seems a major metropolis compared with most other communities on this northerly itinerary. It has a spacious, modern centre with broad, straight streets and water on three sides making them feel pretty draughty at times. A good pedestrian shopping area is based around Storgatan including the usual chain stores, a handicraft boutique and, if you do not want to be tempted to spend money, a popular pavement chess-set to help pass the time. Beware of cyclists though. The local council may have banned cars from the main shopping streets but for some reason decided to put a cycle lane right down the middle instead. There is a fairly good variety of restaurants and several large hotels, reflecting Luleå's commerical importance as a centre for both traditional industries and new technology. At one end of the shopping centre is the railway station and at the other, the provincial museum, Norbottens Museum. It houses a much admired collection of Sami arte- 🏛 facts, tools and clothes. Other exhibits, including a fully equipped 'cottage', trace the history of the region and of the city itself. The provincial administrative headquarters are just across the road while the tourist office can be found back towards the shopping centre on Rådhusgatan. 🛆 Luleå's red brick cathedral, Dom Krykan was built in the late 1800s after the previous one burnt down and nearby, on Rådhustorget, is a statue of the modern city's founder, King Gustav II Adolf.

Rather less worthy but a lot more fun is Teknikens Hus (the House of Technology), situated on the university campus at the edge of the city in ✳ the direction of Haparanda. It concentrates on technical developments, especially those within the great northern industries like mining, forestry, pulp and paper. That may sound dull, but there are plenty of buttons to press and expensive equipment to 'play' with. You can make paper, pan for gold or 'detonate' charges in a mine with special effects to make the floor shake under your feet. Kids love it and entrance is free.

Also not to be missed, 10km (6 miles) north-west of the modern city and well signposted from the main road is Gammelstad (the Old Town). This ✳ is the largest church village in Sweden with a jumble of 425 tiny wooden cottages grouped haphazardly around a large medieval stone church. It

The Dead Falls, a natural beauty spot to be enjoyed at leisure

Arctic river deltas are spectacular but remote

The Sami

The Lapps or Sami as they prefer to be called are the oldest inhabitants of northern Scandinavia although their ethnic roots are thought to lie further east. Their traditional homeland is called Sapmi and stretches across the borders of northern Sweden, Finland, Norway and onto the Kola Peninsula in Russia. They have their own language, cultural heritage and have adopted their own flag.

About 17,000 of the estimated 60,000 Sami live in Sweden. They are spread from the province of Dalarna in the south to the extreme north although the largest concentration of all is said to be in Stockholm! The idea of a city-dwelling Lapp fits uneasily with the picture-postcard image of a Nomadic reindeer herder wearing a bright woollen tunic and pom-pom hat. But the Sami have moved with the times while at the same time strengthening their sense of identity as an indigenous minority.

About 2,500 Swedish Sami are still directly involved in managing Sweden's 250,000 reindeer. Virtually none are Nomadic in the old sense of the word, preferring to live much of the year in ordinary houses. Traditional round-up methods have given way to the use of helicopters, snow-scooters and motor-cycles while colourful Lapp costumes are generally worn only on special occasions. In other words it can be rather difficult these days to determine whether someone is a Lapp at all.

Traditionally the Sami can be divided into the 'Forest Sami' and the 'Fell Sami'. The former always had a fairly settled lifestyle within the wide boundaries of Sami 'villages', keeping their reindeer in the forested lowland areas all year round. Their dwellings, known as *kåtor* were therefore permanent constructions made out of wood or even turf. The 'Mountain Sami' on the other hand move their herds to highland pastures for the summer where until fairly recently, they lived with their entire families in portable teepee-shaped *kåtor* made out of skins and poles.

But today the majority of Sami make their living outside the traditional areas of reindeer husbandry, hunting and fishing. Many work in industry and administration while tourism and handicrafts made of wood and bone bring in extra money. Look out for the beautifully patterned Lapp knives and coffee cups, but be prepared for a shock to the tastebuds if you are offered a Lapp coffee, it is served with salt! You may also get a chance to hear traditional Sami music or 'Jojk', a kind of 'oral literature' used to pass on stories, historical events and beliefs through the generations. Among those old beliefs was a faith in the spiritual side of nature and the powers of 'Noaidi', a kind of Sami medicine man who could contact the spirits with his drum and thus cure the sick.

was also the forerunner of modern Luleå, founded in the 1400s at what was then a strategic point near the water. The land has since risen and when the harbour failed to meet the demands of growing trade the king forced its reluctant inhabitants to move to a new site. Church villages like this developed because distant parishioners dotted around the vast tracts of forest needed somewhere to stay when they went to church; and there were strict attendance rules if you wanted to be sure your soul would be saved. Someone living 10km (6 miles) away was expected to be in his pew every Sunday, parishioners whose homes were 20km (12 miles) away should be there every other Sunday and so on. When the rules got stricter, more cottages sprung up.

People from the same village would tend to build houses in the same group, an ownership pattern broadly reflected even today. The cottages are still used in connection with church festivals, especially in the run-up to Midsummer when youngsters stay there before a big confirmation ceremony. The most authentic of the old church village buildings are in an area south-west of the church. There is also an inn serving local specialities and a cafeteria housed in a building called 'The Captain's Residence'.

The church was consecrated in 1492 and is the largest medieval church in northern Sweden. The local farmers and fishermen must have been doing pretty well for themselves. They are said to have paid 900 silver marks in cash for the beautiful altarpiece from Antwerp. Admittedly Stockholmers paid 1,000 marks for their famous *George and the Dragon* statue in the capital's cathedral, but they had 10 years in which to settle the bill. The elaborate pulpit is also worth a mention.

Luleå is fortunte in having dozens of archipelago islands on its doorstep. In summer there are a variety of boat excursions including occasional trips to attend a service at one of the tiny island chapels that were originally built for local fishermen. The programme will vary from week to week so it is best to contact the tourist office. A seasonal coastal service runs between Luleå and Kemi in Finland (the journey takes 5 hours) and there are departures from Norra Hamnen (the Northern Harbour) for trips along the Lule river to the garrison town of Boden.

In June, July and August 'beach ferries' leave from Södra Hamnen (the South Harbour) to Klubbviken on the island of Sandön, a popular swimming and watersports beach with its own restaurant. There are sandy beaches on several other islands too although many remain inaccessible unless you have your own boat. That of course is not the case with the mainland beaches such as Lulviken, Gültzaudden near the town centre and Kängsö outside Råneå to the north. Leave Luleå on the E4 towards Piteå, turning right after 15km (9 miles) onto route 94 in the direction of Älvsbyn. The road climbs imperceptibly away from the coast passing forest and farms and then descends gently into the broad Piteå (Pite River) valley. **Älvsbyn**, a sizeable community set on pleasantly undulating land has its own 'church village' with forty old cottages grouped on a low grassy hill near an eighteenth-century church. Next to them is a heritage and bakery museum. The latter is not as odd as it sounds because commercial baking is still an important part of the local economy along with forestry and timber products. The community tourist office next to the church village can give advice on some of the first rate fishing waters to be found in the area.

But the main reason tourists come to Älvsbyn lies some 40km (25 miles) further on to the north-west. **Storforsen** meaning 'the Big Rapid' is Scandinavia's largest natural waterfall. The powerful unharnessed Pite river falls 80m (262ft) over a 5km (3 mile) stretch with the final and most impressive section, Storforsen itself, descending 60m (197ft) over a turbulent 2km (1 mile). To get there take route 374 from Älvsbyn in the direction of Jokkmokk and, if the weather is good, pack a picnic — all the locals do. The road climbs steadily along the forested river valley and at first sight the giant rapid looks for all the world like a white 'ski slope' complete with foaming moguls. Storforsen is not a straight drop, but a long slide of roaring white water which is at its most impressive in spring when melting snow adds to the volume. There is a good camping and even swimming area at Bredsel directly opposite the fall. A left turn from the main road takes you to the Storforsen Nature Reserve and to a large parking area with a small gift shop and, a few metres further on, a restaurant. To get to the main rapids you have to cross an area of flat rocks, pools of water, natural cauldrons and canyons called the Dead Falls. They were the unexpected result of attempts to divert the river for logging purposes and today provide a first rate subathing and picnic spot. Wooden bridges link the islands of rock and in fine weather you will usually see some brave soul taking a dip in one of the pools of water in between. Special barbecue spots have been arranged in sheltered areas with firewood conveniently stored in a nearby shed.

Just a few metres from the Dead Falls is the real thing, a roaring mass of water that makes normal conversation impossible. There are wooden walkways along some of the most impressive parts. Unlike many other rivers, the Pite river has not been shackled for hydro-electric power projects and was used for log floating until 1984. It is a transportation method that has now completely died out in Sweden, but the old times are remembered in the small log floating and forestry museum near the carpark. Among the flora to be found in the reserve are Arctic raspberries and the Calypso and Lady's Slipper orchid, but remember this is a nature reserve and it is illegal to pick them.

White water rafting, on a rather less daunting stretch of river, horse riding and fishing trips can be booked in summer at the reserve or with the help of the Älvsbyn tourist office.

The circuit is now virtually complete and all that remains is the final leg back to Arvidsjaur. Return to the 374 after which there are two options. Either turn left towards Jokkmok followed by another left turn 30km (19 miles) on to join the main route 45 some 85km (53 miles) north of Arvidsjaur. Or, to avoid repeating the final stage of the journey, try turning right on the 374 and right again at the small riverside community of Vidsel. Cross the Pite river on a rather basic minor road and continue south through forest and past the tiny settlement of Manjärv. The road skirts its little lake passing the even smaller Edet, Muskus and an area of lake and marshes before joining trunk road 94 near Vistheden. Turn right for the final 80km (50 miles) into Arvidsjaur, crossing back into Lappland just after Grundsel.

Additional Information

Places to Visit

Arjeplog
Lapp Silver Museum
Open: daily June to mid-August 9am-6pm.
☎ 0961 11290

Arvidsjaur
Lappstaden (Lapp Town) and Arvas Samegård (Lapp Centre)
Situated just off Storgatan
☎ 0960 12525
Open: June to August. Guided tours of Lapp town.

Gamla Prästgården (Old Vicarage Homestead Museum)
Magnus Berlinväg 24
☎ 0960 12428
Open: June to September 10am-9pm (Saturday and Sunday 4pm-8pm) September to May 8am-4pm.

Björkliden
Björkliden Fell Centre (hotel, chalets, golf course)
9km (6 miles) west of Abisko
☎ 0980 40040

Gällivare
Gruvmuseet (Mining Museum)
Malmberget
☎ 0970 71337

Gällivare Hembygdsområde (Open-Air Museum)
Next to the river
☎ 0970 15509
Buildings open mid-June to mid-August 8am-11pm.

Kåkstan — The Shanty Town
Open: mid June to mid August 11am-7pm.
☎ 0970 18396/18361

Jokkmokk
Ájite Swedish Fell and Sami Museum
Kyrkogatan 3
☎ 0971 17070
Open: daily 9am-4pm, weekends 12noon-4pm. Longer hours in summer.
Closed on Mondays October to April.

Jukkasjärvi
Hembygdsgård (Homestead Museum)
Open: May to August 10am-6pm.
☎ 0980 21190

Kiruna
Kiirunavaara (Iron Ore Mine)
Daily tours of the mine are organised June to September by Kiruna tourist office. Children must be aged 10 or over.

Samegården
Brytaregatan 14
☎ 0980 17029
Open: summer daily 10am-6pm, winter Monday to Friday 8am-5pm.

Hjalmar Lundbohmsgården
Ingenjörsvägen 2
☎ 0980 70110
Open: summer daily 10am-8pm, winter Monday to Friday 10am-4pm.

Kukkolaforsen
Fishing Museum
Open: June to August 11am-8pm. (Other times can be arranged).

Luleå
Norbottens Museum
Hermelinsparken
☎ 0920 220355
Open: Monday to Friday 10am-4pm, weekends 12noon-4pm.

Teknikens Hus (House of Technology)
Högskoleområdet, Porsön (just north of
Luleå)
☎ 0920 72200
Open: Tuesday to Friday 9am-4pm
(mid-June to mid-August 11am-5pm)
weekends 12noon-5pm.

Narvik (Norway)
*Nordland Røde Kors Krigsminnemuseum
(Nordland War Memorial Museum)*
Kongensgate/Torghallen
☎ 082 44426
Open: summer 10am-10pm, shorter
hours spring and autumn.

Ofoten Museum
Parkhallen
☎ 082 44732
Open: Monday to Sunday 10am-4pm.

Narvik Gondolbane (cablecar)
Skistuaveien
☎ 082 44744
Open: summer Monday to Sunday
10am-12midnight.

Porjus
Between Jokkmokk and Gällivare
☎ 0973 77100
Open: daily 15 June to 15 August.

Riksgränsen
Winter Sports Complex just before the
Norwegian border
☎ 0980 40080

Storforsen
Forestry Museum
Guided tours in summer.
☎ 0929 31091

Tornio (Finland)
Aine Art Museum
Torikatu 2
☎ 9698 432438
Open: Tuesday to Friday 11am-7pm,
weekends 11am-5pm.

Historical Museum of the Tornio Valley
Keskikatu 22
☎ 9698 432451
Open: Tuesday to Friday 12noon-7pm,
weekends 12noon-5pm.

Tourist Information Centres

Abisko
Tourist Centre and National Park
(90km/56 miles west of Kiruna)
☎ 0980 40000
Hotel and tourist centre open summer
and winter seasons.

Arvidsjaur
Garvaregatan 4
☎ 0960 17500

Gällivare
Storgatan 16
☎ 0970 16660

Haparanda (Sweden)
Storgatan 92
☎ 0922 15045/15046
Winter ☎ 11480

Jokkmokk
Stortorget 4
☎ 0971 12140

Kiruna
Hjalmar Lundbomsvägen 42
☎ 0980 18880

Kukkolaforsen
☎ 0922 31000

Luleå
Rådhusgatan 9
☎ 0920 93829/93746

Narvik (Norway)
Kongensgate 66
☎ 082 43309

Tornio (Finland)
Lukiokatu 10
☎ 9698 40048/432/441

Vuollerim
Archaeological site and tourist information
Murjeksvägen 31
☎ 0976 10788

Älvsbyn
Summer only
Storgatan 6
☎ 0929 17200

Sweden Fact File

Accommodation

Most Swedish towns and cities have a good selection of hotels. Standards are generally high and a buffet breakfast is almost always included in the price. At the other end of the holiday budget is an enormous array of self-catering accommodation with enviable locations and facilities. But until recently there was something of a gap in the middle. Sweden does not have a long tradition in bed and breakfast, family run 'pensions' or budget hotels. Fortunately that gap is now being filled as private entrepreneurs respond to the growing demand for reasonably priced accommodation. Visitors can therefore expect to see dozens of signs advertising RUM (Rooms) along popular tourist routes and functional, no-frills cut price hotels are beginning to appear. Tourist Tax during 1993 brought average hotel prices down by 10 per cent.

It must be remembered that large parts of the country are sparsely populated. In these areas accommodation can be trickier to find and you may have to drive many miles to see a house, let alone a hotel! Check on the whereabouts of hotels, hostels and other accommodation with the local tourist office if venturing off the beaten track in remote parts of the country.

Hotels

Swedish hotels are not classified by star ratings so if you are simply looking for a night's accommodation you may have to let the price and the look of the place be the deciding factor. As with everywhere else you tend to get what you pay for, and depending on the hotel and the time of year it can be a lot. Larger towns however generally have a range of possibilities from modern luxury establishments to small suburban inns with just a few rooms. For something with a bit more character it is worth trying one of the many converted manor houses that have been turned into country hotels while small communities tend to have just one offering, almost inevitably called the 'Stads' or 'Town' hotel and impossible to miss right in the centre. Ask the local tourist office to recommend something that suits your budget and if that is closed, try the railway station where reservations staff are used to helping visitors.

The big hotel chains tend to rely heavily on business clients and their room rates often reflect expense account budgets. Fortunately these plummet in summer when the executives are on holiday and hotel managers have to look elsewhere to fill their beds. They therefore give sizeable summer discounts and year-round weekend rates to tourists, knocking up to 50 per cent off the normal overnight price. Most of the leading chains such as Best Western, Scandic and RESO offer special deals to summer visitors through 'hotel cheques' or other discount schemes. These usually involve paying for a series of vouchers in advance.

The Countryside/Romantik chain, a consortia of privately owned predominantly rural hotels also gives incentives while holders of 'city cards' such as the Stockholm or Göteborg Card are generally entitled to reduced room rates.

A new chain of special budget establishments called Welcome Hotels was opened in 1992. They rely on automation to cut costs. Four-bedded rooms are priced at a fixed charge regardless of how many sleep in them. All have a shower, toilet and TV, but breakfast comes out of the vending machine!

In Swedish hotels overnight rates include VAT, service charges and usually breakfast as well. Expect a single room to cost up to 80 per cent of the double room rate. In general half-board and full-board arrangements are available for stays of three or more days. With one of the highest standards of living in the world Sweden subjects its service industry to strict controls. Even the cheapest hotels should therefore be clean and comfortable. A free 'Hotels' booklet is available from major Swedish tourist offices and contains information about the facilities, prices, telephone numbers and addresses of more than 850 hotels.

The Gästgivaregård or Värdshus

The Värdshus (Host's House) is a pleasant contrast to the identikit executive hotels that have sprung up in recent years. Many are centuries old and their creaking floorboards have seen the comings and goings of generations of travellers. As old inns they cannot compete with their modern rivals in terms of size and facilities and many no longer have rooms for rent. Those that do offer a predictably high standard of accommodation. Swedes often choose a Värdshus if they are going out for a special meal. Many have fine restaurants often specialising in local specialities and *smörgåsbord*.

Motels

Swedish motels tend to be of a high standard and are usually located on busy routes in and out of major towns. Many have swimming pools, a gymnasium and saunas, restaurants and self-service cafeterias. They are often cheaper than the large hotels and a good bet for families with children.

Budget Accommodation

It is becoming increasingly popular for private individuals to rent out rooms in Sweden. The local tourist office should have a list of addresses, but you may simply see a pleasant looking place on your travels. Look out for the word *Rum* (Rooms). Breakfast is not normally included in the price but you may well get mod-cons such as a colour TV.

Farms sometimes offer overnight budget accommodation or full-scale holidays and once again the local tourist office should be able to give advice. A hearty farm breakfast is usually included here. Additional information from LRF (Lantbrukarnas Riksförbund), Klara Ö Kyrkog. 12, S-105 33 Stockholm ☎ 08 787 5000.

Maximum and minimum daily temperatures

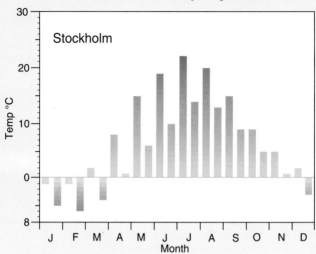

Average monthly rainfall

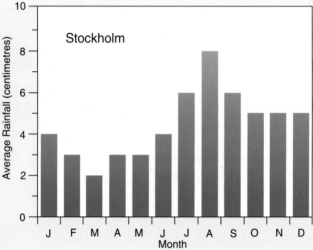

Climate

Thanks to the Gulf Stream much of Sweden enjoys a temperate climate with surprisingly warm summers and cold, crisp winters. The length and intensity of each season rather depends on where you are. In the south 'summer' effectively begins at the end of May and temperatures often reach the high 20s centigrade while in winter they tend to hover a few degrees either side of zero. The snow and ice does not lose its grip on the north until May but the short intense Arctic summer can rival that of the south. Because of the tilt in the earth's axis and its rotation around the sun, Sweden's far north has extreme contrasts between the long summer days and the equally long winter nights. The Midnight Sun can be seen above the Arctic Circle be-

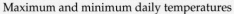
Maximum and minimum daily temperatures

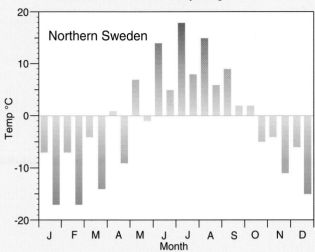

Average monthly rainfall

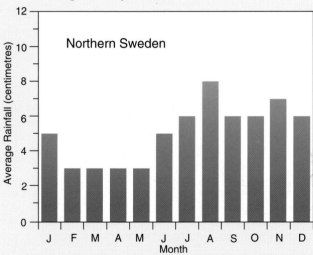

tween mid-May and mid-July and even as far south as Stockholm summer nights have only a few hours of semi-darkness. The opposite is of course true in winter when the Arctic is plunged into 24-hour darkness and temperatures drop well below freezing.

Not surprisingly the best time to visit Sweden is in summer; from May and June onwards for the south, a little later for the north. Many agree that late August and September with their vivid autumn colours are the best months in the Arctic. In general you should pack the same clothes as you would for a holiday in the British Isles although protective clothing is advisable if you are going to the mountains in the north. The winter sports season lasts between February and April.

Camping

Sweden has some 750 officially approved and classified campsites. Most are in picturesque surroundings by a lake or the seaside and they often have facilities such as boat, canoe and cycle hire, minigolf, tennis, riding and saunas. A large number are adapted for handicapped visitors. Campsites are generally open from 1 June to 1 September although some accept guests in April and May too. The 'early birds' might however have to make do without services such as the shop or post office which open only in peak season. About 200 sites, especially in winter sports areas, remain open through the winter.

To stay at an approved camp site you need a Camping Card, valid for 12 months. The card can be purchased when you check into your first campsite and is not necessary if you have a Camping International card.

Many campsites also have a compliment of camping chalets; small wooden huts with bunk beds that can sleep two to six people. They are a little more expensive but come fully equipped with a cooker and cooking utensils and are a handy alternative to canvas. You do have to bring your own sheets though.

Campers should be aware that only propane (eg primus) gas is normally obtainable in Sweden. It is therefore important to ensure that equipment designed to burn butane is not refilled with propane. Propane and associated cooking, heating or lighting equipment is widely available and relatively inexpensive in Sweden. The Swedish Travel and Tourism Council should be able to provide more detailed information about campsites. (see Tourist Information Centres, p261 for address).

Self Catering Accommodation

Self catering chalets known as Stugor and holiday villages (Stugby) are more luxurious and therefore more expensive than camping chalets. They are designed as a comfortable 'home from home' with a living room, two or three bedrooms, a well equipped kitchen and a separate bathroom and shower. There is usually a pleasant verandah and of course a colour TV. Although blankets and pillows are provided, guests have to bring their own towels and sheets. The cottages are usually situated in attractive lakeside, forest or mountain surroundings and many chalet villages have amenities such as grocery stores, leisure centres, swimming pools and so on. Swedish families will often book into one for a week's holiday but many cottages can also be rented for an overnight stay. You are expected to clean the chalet when you leave, ready for the next guest.

Private individuals sometimes rent out empty cottages and it is not unusual to see homemade signs for 'Stuga' along busy roads. The standards may not be as high as in the purpose-built versions, but the accommodation on offer is usually clean, comfortable and the prices are reasonable.

Youth Hostels

It is significant that the Swedish word for Youth Hostel is Vandrarhem meaning 'Wanderer's Home'. Firstly you do not need to be in the flush of youth to stay in one and secondly these comfortable establishments bear little relation to a 'hostel'.

Sweden has 280 *vandrarhem* from Karesuando in the far north to Smygehuk in the south. They range from mansion houses to converted prisons, farms, an old lighthouse and in Stockholm, a 100-year-old sailing ship with prime moorings opposite the Royal Palace. Standards of accommodation are generally regarded as among the best in the world. Visitors sleep in two or four bedded rooms with reading lights, wardrobes and a sink. There are even hostels where the rooms have private toilets. Self catering facilities are laid on but many serve breakfast and some provide full meals.

This is definitely a genteel form of youth-hostelling and clients range from jeans-clad back-packers to families on motoring holidays and the odd business traveller trying to cut down on expenses. Obviously some youth hostels are better than others and the most popular, like the Stockholm sailing ship, the *AF Chapman* can be booked up weeks in advance. All the hostels are open in summer and more than 100 keep open all year. Booking is essential in winter and advisable at peak times in summer.

You can get a full list of youth hostels with opening times and local details from STF (Svenska Turist Föreningen), Box 25, S-101 20 Stockholm ☎ 08 790 3100. Members of the International Youth Hostelling Federation or of STF pay the basic price, non members pay extra per night. If you are planning on staying in several hostels it is worth asking for an international stamp on each visit as six of them will entitle you to temporary membership and thus the reduced rate.

Mountain Hotels and Huts
The network of mountain hotels and huts are outlined in more detail in the section on walking. The hotels, or 'Fjällstationer' are often located in remote mountain areas accessible only on foot and provide rustic but comfortable accommodation at reasonable prices. The huts, operated by STF, splay out along hiking routes and run on the same principle as a youth hostel. If there is no host resident during your stay, you are expected to post the fee later. For more details contact the STF at the address above.

Crime

Sweden is rightly regarded as one of the safest countries in the world and crime is not a serious problem for tourists. Obviously there are incidents of petty theft but they are few and far between and in general you can feel pretty confident that you will return with all your belongings intact. The biggest problem anyone is likely to encounter is being pestered by a congenial drunk who wants you to buy half a bottle of *renat* (snaps) on his behalf because the shop refuses to serve him. Nevertheless, the usual advice holds true. Lock the car, try not to leave anything valuable on view when you leave it and take good care of handbags and other personal possessions.

Currency and Credit Cards

The Swedish *krona* (plural *kronor*) is usually abbreviated to 'kr' in shops or to 'SEK' to distinguish it from the Norwegian and Danish *krone*. The *krona* is split into 100 *öre*. Inflation has long since wiped out the one *öre* coin and the 10 *öre* has gone the same way. Coins are now issued to the value of 50 *öre*, 1 *krona*, 5 and 10 *kronor*. Bank-notes are printed in values of 10, 20, 50, 100, 500, 1,000 and 10,000 *kronor*. Travellers cheques in Swedish currency are not issued abroad but travellers cheques in other currencies can be exchanged without difficulty at banks all over Sweden. About 500 post offices also have a foreign exchange service. Eurocheques backed by a guarantee card are also accepted in banks, restaurants and shops.

Banks in Sweden are open Monday to Friday between 9.30am and 3pm although branches in larger cities may stay open until 5.30pm. Banks are closed on Saturdays. You can change money outside banking hours at major post offices or large hotels and at foreign exchange centres called 'Forex'. Stockholm's Arlanda Airport and Landvetter Airport, Göteborg have 7 day exchange facilities.

Major credit cards are widely accepted just about everywhere. Shops, restaurants, hotels and garages usually display signs showing which cards they take.

Disabled

Sweden has taken the lead in catering for disabled travellers and physical handicap should be no deterrent to a visit there. Many hotels have specially adapted rooms for guests with mobility or allergy problems. Access to public transport generally takes account of the needs of the disabled and a large number of campsites and holiday chalets also have wheelchair access.

The free Swedish 'Hotels' guide mentioned in the accommodation section lists hotels with rooms adapted for handicapped guests. An English language *Holiday Guide for the Disabled* is also available from the Swedish Travel and Tourism Council. It lists suitable accommodation, sightseeing and activities throughout the country.

Dress

You are unlikely ever to need formal clothes on a Swedish holiday. Casual dress is very much the order of the day. The best advice is to allow for the vagaries of the northern European weather when packing. If you are going in summer take light-weight sweaters, tee-shirts, cotton trousers and skirts and a pair of shorts. But pack a thicker sweater or jacket too for good measure and something rainproof. A pair of sensible low-heeled shoes is always a good idea because sightseeing inevitably involves a good deal of walking and many old town centres have cobbled streets. If you plan more serious hiking then walking or wellington boots are advisable.

Protective rainproof clothing is more important the further north you go and essential if you are in the mountains where temperatures and weather conditions can change rapidly. A couple of pairs of thick socks and a warm pair of trousers could come in handy even in mid-summer.

The Swedes tend to spend every spare minute they can on the beach or lakeside — so do not forget the swimming costume. Topless bathing is virtually the norm on public beaches.

Anyone going to Sweden in winter will predictably need to take warm clothing, a hat, gloves, scarf and ideally a pair of boots or shoes with thick insulated soles. The further north you go, the more important this becomes. The only way to remain comfortable in below freezing temperatures is to wear layers of thermal clothing, a down anorak and several pairs of socks inside thick-soled boots.

Drink

Sweden has a restrictive policy towards alcohol dating back to the days when alcoholism was such a problem that rationing had to be enforced. This thankfully is no longer the case today but you can still only buy wine, spirits and strong beer through state controlled shops known as Systembolaget. Prices are high. If you enjoy a tipple it is worth buying your full duty-free allowance. Systembolaget is open Monday to Friday and closed at the weekend. Be prepared for a long queue on Friday afternoons or before a public holiday and note that the minimum age for buying alcohol is 20.

The main drink is beer. It is of the lager or pilsner type and comes in three strengths; light beer (known as Class 1 or *lättöl*) with a maximum alcohol content of 1.8 per cent, ordinary beer (Class II or *mellanöl*) with 2.8 per cent alcohol and export beer (Class III or *starköl*) for anything stronger. The first two can be bought in supermarkets, the last only in Systembolaget. The local spirit, snaps or *akvavit* is made from potatoes or grain and sometimes doctored with herbs and spices. It looks innocent enough but can take your breath away as can the price because it is subject to the same taxes as imported alcohol. Snaps is usually served chilled in small glasses and often accompanies dishes of herring. When mixed with lemonade it becomes a *grogg*. At Christmas Swedes drink a hot spiced wine called Glögg which is laced with almonds and raisins and served in small cups.

Systembolaget has an excellent selection of wines, all well displayed with informative labels although the actual wares are kept behind the counter. On the whole wine is probably the best value and some prices came down recently with the introduction of a new tax system based on alcohol content. The high cost of alcohol is naturally reflected in bar and restaurant prices.

Electricity

The electricity supply in Sweden is 220 volts and adaptors are needed for appliances not fitted with two-pin plugs.

Embassies

The main Embassies in Sweden are:

UK	USA	Canada	Australia
Skarpögatan 6-8	Strandvägen 101	Tegelbacken 4	Sergels Torg 12
S-115 93 Stockholm	115 27 Stockholm	Box 16129	Box 7003
☎ 08 6670140	☎ 08 7835300	103 23 Stockholm	103 86 Stockholm
		☎ 08 6139900	☎ 08 6132900

Other Swedish Embassies are:

UK
11 Montagu Place
London W1H 2AL
☎ 071 734 2101

USA
Watergate 600
Suite 1200
600 New Hampshire Avenue NW
Washington DC
20037-2403 USA
☎ 202 944 5600

Canada
377 Dalhousie Street
Ottawa
Ontario
KIN 9N8 Canada
☎ 613 236 8553

Australia
5 Turrana Street
Yarralumla
Canberra ACT 2600
☎ 6 273 3033

Emergencies

To summon the police, fire brigade or ambulance dial 90 000. The number is free and no coins need be inserted in a callbox. Radio Sweden on KHZ 6065 broadcasts urgent messages for travellers, but only in cases of serious illness or death.

Entertainment

Most sizeable towns have a concert hall and theatre and in summer many groups organise outdoor performances too. Contrary to the gloomy Scandinavia of Ibsen and Strindberg, the Swedes have an apparently endless appetite for comedy and slapstick. Much of it can be seen in open-air performances but the dialogue is in Swedish. There are plenty of cinemas and as films are sub-titled rather than dubbed they may be a better bet.

Swedish state television has two channels. There is also one commercial and one pay channel. Depending on where you are you may be able to see Danish, Norwegian or Finnish television too.

Stockholm and Göteborg both have large-scale amusement parks with music and dancing late into the night. Older Swedes are still fond of traditional 'dance restaurants' while the younger ones flock to local discoteques, jazz or rock clubs on Friday and Saturday nights. Gambling is frowned on and the Government has outlawed one-arm bandit machines.

Festivals and Public Holidays

Festivals and public holidays usually go together in Sweden. There are plenty of them and it is worth noting that shop and office workers often take a half-day off before a public holiday, thus extending the break.

New Years Day (1 January) — Public Holiday
Epiphany (6 January) — Public Holiday
Good Friday — Public Holiday
Easter Monday — Public Holiday
Walpurgis Night (30 April) — Celebrations to welcome spring with

bonfires to chase away winter, songs and boisterous celebrations, especially among students in the university towns.

Labour Day (1 May) — Public Holiday. Students and workers join processions throughout the country although the collapse of Communism has removed much of the socialist fervour.

Ascension Day — Public Holiday

Whit Monday — Public Holiday

Swedish National Day (6 June) — Flags and festivities at Skansen open-air museum, Stockholm and patriotic celebrations elsewhere.

Midsummer — (around 21-22 June, the exact date varies) — This really is the most colourful of all the seasonal festivities, a boisterous climax to the year and a good time to visit Sweden. Maypoles clad with birch leaves and flowers are raised in parks, on village greens and in private gardens. In fact the word Maypole comes from an old Swedish word *maja* which means 'to make green'. Those who have a national costume wear it for games and dancing accompanied by traditional fiddle music while noisy parties go on right through the night. Among the best places to see the celebrations are the province of Dalarna, Nääs manor near Göteborg, Gammelgården in Bengtsfors, Dalsland, Högbobruk, Sandviken in Gästrikland and Fatmomakke in Lappland.

Crayfish time — Starts mid-August when Swedes are permitted to fish for the langoustine-like crustaceans. Paper hats and lanterns are essential accessories for the crayfish parties that follow. The crayfish are boiled in dill-seasoned water, piled high on a plate and washed down with snaps and beer. Unfortunately Swedish crayfish have become so expensive that only the most indulgent buy them these days while others make do with imports from Turkey, China or the USA.

The Stockholm Water Festival also in mid-August is a week of water-borne festivities in the capital.

All Saints Day (end of November) — Public Holiday

Nobel Day (10 December) — The annual Nobel Prizes are awarded by the Swedish king followed by a glittering banquet in Stockholm City Hall.

St Lucia's Day (13 December) — A girl dressed as St Lucia in white and wearing a 'crown' of candles traditionally appears at home or in the office, school, hospitals, hotels and public buildings. Sometimes there is a procession through town.

Christmas Day (25 December) — Public Holiday

Boxing Day (26 December) — Public Holiday

Food

The reputation of Swedish cooking has suffered unfairly from too many jokes about its dependence on raw herring and the much maligned meatball. In reality visitors will find an enormous variety of seafood, regional game and other delicacies culled from Sweden's many lakes and forest. The humble sandwich has been elevated to designer status and no day is complete without a pause for coffee and one of the endless varieties of cakes that grace the *konditori* shelves.

Breakfast usually consists of coffee, orange juice, two or three different sorts of bread, cheese, ham or sausage, marmalade and perhaps a boiled egg. Many Swedes have their main meal at lunchtime and this will usually be what is known as *husmanskost* (home cooking). As the name implies it tends to be fairly plain and simple; a chop or some other meat or fish with sauce, potatoes and perhaps a salad. It is often served by restaurants between 12noon and 2pm as Dagen's Rätt (Dish of the Day). Remember to look out for signs offering Dagen's Rätt' because the meal is likely to be unbeatable value by Swedish standards. For a fixed price you will get the main dish, a beer or soft drink, bread, butter and coffee.

Dinner is likely to come rather more expensive and an à la carte evening meal in a good restaurant with a decent bottle of wine can put a serious dent in the travel budget. Fortunately Sweden, like most other western European countries now plays host to a wide variety of reasonably priced pizzerias, Chinese, Indian and Mexican restaurants and of course McDonalds.

It is impossible to list all the local specialities in this section but here are a few of them.

Smörgås — It means sandwich, but expect a work of art piled with prawns, pâté or roast beef decorated with fresh fruit and salad. In fact it is usually hard to spot the bread underneath.

Smörgåsbord — Literally sandwich table but usually referred to as the 'cold table' in English. Guests help themselves as many times as they like and should always take a clean plate (a good waiter will constantly whisk away used ones). Start with the herring — usually served in many different flavoured marinades and absolutely delicious. Eat it with dark bread or potatoes and perhaps some soured cream and chopped onion. There may well be several kinds of salmon, smoked, *gravad* which means cured in dill and salt as well as fresh prawns and smoked eel — an expensive delicacy in Sweden. After the fish, try the cold meats such as roast beef, ham and turkey and then the hot food which is usually kept in warming dishes. That may consist of meatballs, small sausages, spare ribs or even a casserole. Those who still have the appetite can move on to the cheeses and dessert. The *smörgåsbord* is traditionally served at lunchtime and is washed down with beer and perhaps a snaps rather than wine.

Kräftor — Crayfish. Boiled in dill-flavoured water and piled high on serving plates they form the centrepiece of the crayfish season. In the old days it was customary to drink a snaps with every claw!

Ärtsoppa — Pea Soup with ham is a popular dish which should, according to custom, be served on Thursdays accompanied by a glass of warm punch and followed by pancakes.

Kåldolmar — This is real *husman's kost* and consists of minced pork and beef wrapped in cabbage leaves.

Jansson's Frestelse — It means Jansson's temptation and is a savoury mix of chopped potatoes, onions, anchovy and cream baked in the oven.

Surströmming — This is not for the faint-hearted. The literal translation is 'Sour Herring' which perfectly sums up this fermented fish sold in dangerously bulging tins. It is the object of desire of many northerners who hold great parties to celebrate the new 'vintage' on the third Thursday of

August each year. The smell of an open *surströmming* tin is not easily forgotten. It should be served with chopped onion, *tunnbröd* (thinbread) and special almond-shaped potatoes known as *mandel potatis*.

Game — Elk meat (*Älg*) is often served pot or oven roasted in good restaurants and is delicious. The meat is dark, rather like beef and tastes best with redcurrent or rowanberry jelly. Reindeer (*ren*) is also popular and tastes like venison. The meat is sometimes smoked and rolled into unlevened *tunnbröd* bread to form a snack known as a Renklämma or 'Reindeer Grip'. A few restaurants serve bear meat although it is so rare that the Swedes themselves regard it as exotic. It is also breathtakingly expensive and apart from the very best cuts, not all that good. Grouse and ptarmigen usually feature among the game birds while the lakes and rivers yield salmon, trout, Arctic char and whitefish.

Mushrooms — And toadstools are known as *svamp* in Swedish and can be found in vast quantities in the wild. Picking them is a favourite family pastime and in late summer and autumn special 'mushroom advisory centres' are set up to help people weed out the poisonous ones. Among the most prized are the Carl Johan cep and the orange coloured chanterel.

Hjortron — Cloudberries are much sought after for their distinctive peaty flavour. They look like orange raspberries and grow on marshy ground especially in the north. They make an absolutely delicious conserve and are unbeatable when served with whipped cream on freshly baked waffles. Other wild berries such as cranberry (*lingon*) and bilberry (*blåbär*) grow in great abundance and feature on many seasonal menus.

Konditori — The Swedes often refer euphemistically to 'coffee' when what they really fancy is a large cream cake. Konditori are to be found on every shopping street and provide the sort of social meeting place that pubs offer in England. '*Kaffe med bröd*' literally means coffee with bread but in this case the 'bread' is cake. Guests usually choose their cakes at the counter. Drinks are often self-service but at old fashioned *kondis* as they are affectionately known, the order may be taken at the table. Cakes include *Vetebröd*, a plain sweet loaf often filled with almond paste and topped with nuts; cinnamon buns known as *kanel bullar*, Danish pastries, which are confusingly called *Wienerbröd* (*Viennabread* in Sweden) and *småkakor* (small cakes) in a variety of shapes and flavours. The *konditori* will usually have an assortment of sticky cream cakes too and larger ones have open sandwiches or savoury flans. Coffee in Sweden is usually quite strong and very good while the tea can appear feeble to Anglo Saxon tastebuds. A second cup of coffee known as a *påtår* (refill) is often included in the price. *Konditori* serve soft drinks and beer but are not usually licenced for anything stronger.

Health Care

Anyone requiring medical treatment can either call a doctor — (*doktor* in Swedish) or go direct to a hospital casualty department known as 'Akutmottagning'. In remote areas the 'Vårdcentral' serves the same purpose. Most doctors and staff speak English. There is a reciprocal arrangement between Sweden and many European countries including the UK which entitles visitors to the same subsidised treatment as Swedish nationals. A similar agreement exists for Australian citizens but not for Canada or the USA whose nationals currently have to pay the full cost of care. If you do call a doctor (the hotel, campsite or youth hostel management will help) it is wise to check that he is affiliated to the Swedish National Health Service 'Försäkringskassan'. There is a standard fee for visits to the doctor, more if the doctor is called to the patient. Prescriptions are collected at the chemist 'Apotek' which are open during normal shopping hours. Note that chemists in Sweden do not normally sell items like cosmetics.

Dentists are called 'Tandläkare' and usually have an emergency out of hours service in larger cities.

Language

The Swedes are well aware that theirs is a minority language and set great store by learning others. Virtually everyone under the age of 50 speaks and understands English, often with remarkable degrees of fluency. They are usually delighted to test their linguistic skills on foreigners. Older people will probably understand English too but may be too shy or embarrassed to speak it.

Swedish is a teutonic language with many similarities to Danish and Norwegian. It is spoken in a range of dialects from the guttural, Danish sounding 'Skånska' in the far south to the so-called 'jingling' Stockholm accent and the soft sing-song tones of the north.

With English so widely spoken, communication is unlikely to be a problem. But it is always fun to be able to say a few words in the local language — even if your pronunciation is not quite what it should be! Remember that the Swedish alphabet has three extra letters. The å which is pronounced as the 'a' in 'law'; the ä, pronounced as the 'ea' in 'bear' and ö which sounds like the 'i' in 'sir'.

General
Mr/Mrs/Miss — *Herr/Fru/Fröken*
Yes/No — *Ja/Nej*
Thank you (very much) — *Tack (så mycket)*
Hello — *Hej or more formally God Dag*
Good Morning — *God Morgon*
Good Evening — *God Kväll*
Goodnight — *God Natt*
Goodbye - *Adjö*
Do you speak English? — *Talar du Engelska*
I do not understand — *Jag förstår inte*
I'm sorry — *Förlåt mej*
Where is? — *Var finns?*
May I have — *Kan jag få*
Help — *Hjälp*
How much is it? — *Hur mycket kostar det?*
Expensive — *Dyr*
Cheap — *Billig*

Accommodation
A single room — *Ett enkel rum*
A double room — *Ett dubbel rum*

With a bathroom — *Med badrum*
With a shower — *Med dusch*
Key — *Nyckel*
Postcard — *Vykort*
Stamp — *Frimärke*

Medical
Doctor — *Doktor*
Dentist — *Tandläkare*

Places
Bank — *Bank*
Chemist — *Apotek*
Church — *Kyrka*
Cinema — *Biograf*
Filling Station — *Bensin Station*
Hospital — *Sjukhus*
Library — *Bibliotek*
Museum — *Museum*
Police Station — *Polis Station*
Post Office — *Post*
Shop — *Affär*

Travel

Airport — *Flygplats*
Boat — *Båt*
Ferry — *Färja*
Bus/bus stop — *Buss/buss hållplats*
Customs — *Tull*
Taxi — *Taxi*
Ticket — *Biljett*
Train — *Tåg*
Railway Station — *Järnvägsstation*
Tram — *Spårvagn*
Underground — *Tunnelbana*

Food and Drink

The Bill — *Räkningen*
The Menu — *Menyn*
Tea — *The*
Coffee — *Kaffe*
Milk — *Mjölk*
Water — *Vatten*
Wine — *Vin*
Beer — *Öl/Pilsner*
Squash — *Saft*
Bread — *Bröd*
Butter — *Smör*
Eggs — *Ägg*
Cheese — *Ost*
Meat — Kött
Sausage — *Korv*
Ham — *Skinka*
Beef — *Oxkött*
Steak — *Biff*
Mince — *Köttfärs*
Lamb — *Lamm*
Pork — *Fläsk*
Veal — *Kalvkött*
Chicken — *Kyckling*
Duck — *Anka*
Turkey — *Kalkon*
Grouse — *Ripa*
Elk — *Älg*
Reindeer — *Ren*
Liver — *Lever*
Kidney — *Njure*
Rabbit — *Kanin*
Hare — *Hare*
Fish — Fisk
Haddock — *Kolja*
Herring — *Sill*
Prawns — *Räkor*
Crab — *Krabba*
Lobster — *Hummor*

Crayfish — *Kräftor*
Plaice — *Rödspätta*
Sole — *Sjötunga*
Halibut — *Helgeflundra*
Cod — *Torsk*
Mackerel — *Makrill*
Salmon/Smoked Salmon — *Lax/ Rökt Lax*
Eel — *Ål*
Trout — *Forell/Öring*
Whitefish — *Sik*
Char — *Röding*
Vegetables — Grönsaker
Potatoes — *Potatis*
Onions — *Lök*
Carrots — *Morötter*
Beans — *Bönor*
Peas — *Ärter*
Cauliflower — *Blomkål*
Cabbage — *Kål*
Lettuce — *Salad*
Cucumber — *Gurka*
Tomato — *Tomat*
Mushrooms — *Svamp*
Fruit — Frukt
Apple — *Äpple*
Orange — *Apelsin*
Grapes — *Druvor*
Plum — *Plommon*
Pineapple — *Ananas*
Lemon — *Citron*
Peach — *Persika*
Banana — *Banan*
Strawberry — *Jordgubbe*
Raspberry — *Hallon*
Gooseberry — *Krusbär*
Pear — *Päron*
Red/Black currents — *Röda/Svarta Vinbär*

Ice cream — *Glass*
Cream — *Grädde*
Gateau — *Tårta*
Cake — *Kaka*
Danish Pastry — *Wienerbröd*
Biscuit — *Kex*
Sugar — *Socker*
Waffle — *Våffla*
Boiled — *Kokt*
Fried — *Stekt*
Baked — *Bakad*
Grilled — *Grillad*

Maps and Brochures

There is no shortage of choice when it comes to maps and brochures on Sweden. The Swedish Travel and Tourism Council supplies free route planners called 'Discover Sweden' while the individual regions often hand out useful small-scale roadmaps or include them in their brochures. Many, such as the *South-West Sweden Road Map*, also mark out points of interest and suggested tours. The best bet is to contact the regional tourist office; relevant numbers and addresses are listed at the end of each chapter. Some of the giveaway maps are sponsored by Petroleum companies such as Q8 or Statoil and predictably also show the location of the sponsor's fuel stations.

More detailed maps such as the international Michelin series are of course available in Swedish bookstores. The *Nya Bil & TuristKartan* by Liberkartor can be a good value option. It splits the country into ten regions and each map marks places of interest, campsites, youth hostels and bathing beaches. Sweden has been changing the route numbers on some of its major roads and all but the most recent publications may well be out of date.

Many local tourist offices produce free brochures showing walking trails. Detailed maps with mountain trails can be bought at the regional tourist stations or contact The Swedish Touring Club (Svenska Turist Föreningen) Box 25, S101 20 Stockholm, Sweden ☎ 46 8 7903100 for further information.

Measurements

The metric system is used in Sweden. The following conversions apply:

1 kilogram (kg) = 2.2lb
1 litre = 1¾ pints
4.5 litres = 1 gallon
8 kilometres (km) = 5 miles

Newspapers and Magazines

British newspapers should be available on the day of publication in the major cities such as Stockholm, Göteborg and Malmö — elsewhere you may have to make do with yesterday's news. Sunday newspapers are also flown in on the day, but usually come minus the colour supplement. The *International Herald Tribune*, *The European* and weekly news publications such as *Time* and *Newsweek* are also readily available along with a wide range of English and American magazines. Good book shops generally have a large English language section, but be prepared to pay a hefty premium on the price of the same book back home.

Opening Hours

Banks — Banks are open Monday to Friday between 9.30am and 3pm. In some larger cities a few banks stay open till 5.30pm. All banks close on Saturdays and remember that on the eve of a public holiday they will probably close early. The bank at Stockholm's Arlanda Airport is open daily between 6.30am and 10pm and at Landvetter Airport, Göteborg between 8am and 8pm weekdays and during the afternoons on Saturdays and

Sundays. Forex foreign exchange offices in Stockholm, Göteborg, Malmö open 8am to 9pm. The company also has offices at the ferry terminals in Helsingborg, Ystad and Trelleborg.

Post Offices — Post Kontor open between 9am and 6pm on weekdays and from 10am to 1pm on Saturdays. Some branches may close on Saturdays in July. Post boxes in Sweden are painted yellow.

Museums and Monuments — Opening hours vary enormously depending on the season and the type of museum and it is almost impossible to generalise. In summer many attractions stay open from 10am until 6pm or even 7pm, while in winter the closing time is brought forward to 4pm. Some small museums open only for a few hours each week off-season and a few close completely. Many museums close on Mondays and have restricted hours at the weekends. A large number are open till late one evening each week, often Wednesdays.

Churches — As with museums, church opening times differ widely and some country churches may even be kept locked for much of the day. In these cases you may find instructions on where to collect the key, otherwise just ask at the nearest house, the occupant will probably know what to do. Most important churches are kept open until 4pm or 5pm although this is by no means a rule.

Shops — Shops in Sweden open between 9am and 6pm weekdays and until 1pm to 4pm on Saturdays. Some department stores in large towns stay open to 8pm and many are open on Sundays between 12noon and 4pm. Shops generally close early on days before a public holiday.

Passports

Visitors with a valid British passport or British Visitor's Passport can stay up to 3 months in Sweden. The same is true for other European citizens and for passport holders from the USA, Canada, Australia and New Zealand. There are no visa or vaccination requirements. Valid ID cards are accepted from Nationals of Belgium, France, Italy, Luxemburg, Switzerland, the Netherlands, Germany, Austria and Lichtenstein.

Religion

Sweden is a secular society and only about 5 per cent of the population attend church regularly. The vast majority (92 per cent) however belong to the protestant Church of Sweden for which a small annual subscription is automatically deducted in tax. They become members at birth and must 'opt out' if they wish to discontinue their membership. Few it seems bother to do so and therefore continue to contribute to the upkeep of the nation's churches even if they rarely set foot in one themselves.

Restaurants, Cafés and Bars

Much of the relevant information has been dealt with in the section on food. But it is important to say here that Swedes do not have a great tradition of eating out. High prices have been to blame and although things are begin-

ning to change visitors may find that rural restaurants often close early —
sometimes all evening. After serving a good value 'dish of the day' or
smörgåsbord at lunchtime there is not enough demand to make late opening
worthwhile.

Things are very different in the larger towns and cities where restaurants
stay open late. The most exclusive ones tend to be the haunt of business
people on expense accounts and anyone paying out of their own pocket
usually has something to celebrate. But there are plenty of cheaper and
equally congenial alternatives. Standards of both food and service are
generally high whichever you choose.

Swedes tend to eat fairly early and restaurants start serving lunch at
around 11am while small hotels may have the evening meal ready at 6pm.
Larger hotels, motels and city restaurants are far more flexible. Bars are
often linked to restaurants or hotels and spirits are sold in measures of 3cl.
With alcohol prices as they are there is no need to feel guilty about nursing
a drink for long periods — everyone does it! English style pubs have been
around for some years but are giving way to newer trendier social venues.
Among them are chic Brasseries attracting the local smart set. In summer
they combine with the *konditori* to provide a lively café life with tables and
chairs arranged on the pavement in continental style. For more information
about konditori, see the section on food.

The cheapest 'restaurant' in town is generally the aptly if unappetizingly
named Gatu-kök (Street Kitchen). These kiosks will not win any architectural awards but act as a magnet for local youngsters in the evenings. The
best selling line is usually a hotdog with mashed potatoes.

Right of Public Access (Allemansrätten)

The right to walk and camp almost anywhere in the Swedish countryside
is enshrined in this national law which literally means 'Everyman's Right'.
It allows you to pick mushrooms, wild berries and flowers (provided they
are not specifically protected) to swim and boat on rivers or lakes and even
camp for a brief period on privately owned land as long as you are well
away from houses and do not disturb anyone. The Swedes are very proud
of this law but stress that it also carries responsibilities. You are required to
show consideration to landowners, animals, plants and wildlife and to
acquaint yourself with local regulations — for example some areas may be
out of bounds during periods of animal husbandry. You must not leave
litter or cut down trees for firewood and when making a camp fire, try to
find a place that has already been used for one.

Shopping and Souvenirs

Shopping is a major leisure activity in Sweden and bargain hunters will
happily spend their day-off travelling dozens of kilometres in search of a
good buy. Large indoor shopping malls complete with cafés, fountains and
seductive birdsong have sprung up outside major towns while urban
centres usually have the ubiquitous Åhlens and Domus department stores
alongside outlets for popular clothing chains such as Hennes and Gullins.

Recently however there has been a perceptible trend towards smaller, more sophisticated shops providing plenty of scope for temptation in the average high street.

Fortunately for visitors, 90 per cent of Swedish shops are affiliated to the Sweden Tax-Free scheme which refunds about 15 per cent of the purchase price on an item. The percentage is a sizeable proportion of the VAT, known as MOMS in Sweden. Overseas customers receive a refund 'cheque' when they make their purchase and the item is sealed. They get the money back when they leave the country and must be prepared to show the sealed packet to officials. There are Tax Free refund offices at airports, border crossings and ferry terminals although the money is often paid back on the ferries themselves.

Clothing tops the tax-free purchase table. It is a popular buy in Sweden because it is relatively inexpensive, well designed and temptingly displayed. Swedish crystal and glassware has long been high on the real 'souvenir' shopping list. Few people who visit the glass factories of Småland come away without some small purchase and queues at the packing and shipping desks tell their own story. The best known names for crystal are Orrefors and Kosta Boda. The two companies now belong to the same group but have retained their distinct features ranging from traditional deep-cut crystal to avant-garde coloured glassware. For a good selection, try the 'Duka' chain of tableware stores. Sweden also produces some top quality porcelain. The names to look out for are Rörstrand and Gustavsberg while Boda Nova specialises in modern cutlery and other household design. In the far south, the town of Höganäs is famous for its rustic ceramics.

The wooden painted Dala Horse is of course an abiding symbol of Sweden and you do not have to go to Dalarna to get one — they are on sale in just about every souvenir shop although prices are high. Other wooden souvenirs include hand-turned candle sticks, lamps, beautifully grained bowls, cutting boards and larger items for the home. Textiles, whether expensive hand-woven and embroidered table cloths or avant garde design are also popular.

Sami handicraft is among the most sought after and expensive of souvenirs. The Sami also make decorated wooden coffee cups similar to those carried strung from the belt, bowls, pewter and leather objects and of course items made out of reindeer skin such as rugs.

Most sizeable towns and cities have a local handicraft shop called 'Hemslöjd' and it is usually well worth a visit.

Sports and Activities

Sport is enormously popular in Sweden. Hours of television air-time are devoted to it as are pages of newsprint and endless animated discussions. In common with most other countries the fortunes of the national football team, the 'Blue and Yellows' are avidly followed along with those of the 'Tre-Kronor' (Three Crowns) ice hockey team. In summer Swedes take to the water to sail, swim and windsurf. Golf has become immensely popular with new courses opening every year and even the tiniest community has its walking and jogging tracks.

257

There are tens of thousands of amateur fishermen who make the most of the rich lakes, rivers and offshore waters. Orienteering and rambling in the mountain regions also attracts large numbers although there is little really rugged rock climbing to be found in Sweden. Skiing, both alpine and cross country, is popular in winter.

Climbing

Sweden has plenty of mountains but most of them are more suited to rambling than to rock climbing. The country's main 'alpine' centre is the Kebnekaise Fjällstation, S-980 24, Abisko ☎ 0980 18184. Guides are on hand to take visitors across local glaciers and on climbing trips. Several mountain centres in the north run climbing courses and more information can be obtained from the Swedish Climbing Association ☎ 08 695 8000.

Cycling

Sweden's low traffic density and good road network make it a popular destination for cyclists. Although there are relatively few designated cycle tracks most provinces have special cycle routes chosen for their scenic qualities and to avoid busy roads. Twenty-six separate areas link together to form the marked Sverigeleden (the Swedish Route), which stretches the length of the country from Helsingborg in the south to Karesuando in the north. You would have to be a pretty keen cyclist to cover the whole distance — more than 2,500km (1,550 miles)! Regional tourist offices have maps and information. Alternatively contact Cykelfrämjandet, Torsgatan 31, Box 6072, 102 31 Stockholm ☎ 08 321680 or Svenska Cykelsällskapet, Box 6006, 164 06 Kista ☎ 08 7516204.

Fishing

Sweden has some of Europe's finest fishing waters and therefore attracts amateur anglers from all over the world. The great salmon rivers such as Mörrumsån in Blekinge and Ätran in Halland are easy to reach while further north the cold mountain water also yields Arctic char and, in coastal areas, whitefish. You can cast a line with a fair chance of success virtually anywhere in Sweden, even in the centre of Stockholm. Regular sea fishing trips are run from most major ports.

A permit 'Fiskekort' is usually obligatory for anyone fishing in Sweden's lakes and rivers. They can be obtained from local tourist offices, mountain hotels and even at certain shops and fuel stations. For further information contact the Swedish Sport Angling and Fishery Conservation Association, ☎ 08 795 3350 or the Swedish Forest Service, Domänverket ☎ 023 84000 for fishing permits in their waters. Regional tourist offices also have information and often produce special maps showing the best waters.

Golf

Golf is a boom sport in Sweden. It may not quite boast the climate of Portugal and Spain but the southern province of Skåne alone has more than fifty courses. Golfers can also play, albeit during a limited season, in the Arctic. Björkliden near Abisko claims to offer the world's most northerly golf while courses at Boden, Gällivare and Luleå all permit 'Midnight Sun' tee-offs. The Swedish and Finnish towns of Haparanda and Tornio have an 18-hole course that straddles the border with a one-hour time difference.

Green fees in Sweden are very reasonable by today's standards and guests are usually welcome although there may be restrictions at weekends or peak times. Most, but by no means all clubs require an official handicap. For further information contact Svenska Golf Förbundet, Box 84, 182 11 Danderyd ☎ 08 6221500.

Gold Panning

Panning for gold has become an increasingly popular tourist attraction in Lappland with several 'gold camps' offering package deals. For more information contact the Swedish Gold Panners' Association ☎ 0750 25886.

Hiking and Mountain Touring

The entire length of Sweden is criss-crossed by hundreds of walking and hiking trails. Some circuits can be covered in an afternoon stroll while others, of which the 500km (310 mile) long Kungsleden is the most famous, stretch hundreds of kilometres across rugged wilderness. The trails are usually well marked and mapped. Walking is immensely popular in Sweden and even tourist offices in the most unpromising areas will dig out maps showing local forest trails. The Swedish Touring Association (STF), Drottninggatan 33, Box 25, 101 20 Stockholm ☎ 08 790 3100 and the Swedish Walking Association ☎ 063 605 6000 can give more details. Alternatively contact the tourist office in the area to which you are going.

Information about mountain touring, accommodation and special activities can also be obtained from the major mountain stations operated by STF. They include Kebnekaise (see Climbing section), Abisko Turiststation, S-980 24, Abisko ☎ 0980 40000, Storulvåns Fjällstation, S-830 15 Duved ☎ 0647 74020 and Sylarnas Fjällstation, S-830 15 Duved ☎ 0647 75010. For details about the most popular areas read the special section on mountain touring.

Riding

Although most cities have well-managed riding stables, the best way to see Sweden on horseback is to trek through the mountains on one of the small sturdy Icelandic horses ideally suited to the terrain. You do not need much experience and equipment is usually provided. Contact the National Association of Swedish Riding Camp Operators, Box 30013, S-104 25 Stockholm. The STF (see address above) also arranges weeklong excursions.

Swimming

Sweden has miles of sandy beaches and thousands of lakes suitable for swimming — although the weather does sometimes dampen enthusiasm to take the plunge. Campsites, holiday hotels and beach resorts often have swimming pools with waterslides and most larger towns have indoor pools. The best areas for sandy beaches are the west coast province of Halland and Skåne in the south, but you can safely swim all along the coast. There are so many lakes that bathers are quite likely to have one to themselves. Good swimming areas are marked from the road.

Watersports

Sailing is immensely popular and on fine summer weekends it can look as if literally everyone owns a boat. Visitors can rent yachts and dinghies but local conditions vary — the best bet is to contact the local tourist office. The archipelago coastline can be complex for inexperienced navigators. Many of the rivers and lakes are best explored by canoe. Most suitable areas have canoe hire and local tourist offices should be able to give telephone numbers and prices. Dalsland and Värmland are good for canoe safaris while those looking for more demanding conditions may prefer the rugged north. The Swedish Canoe Association ☎ 0155 69508, has information.

Whitewater rafting is becoming popular in Sweden and tourist resorts such as Åre in Jämtland and Jukkasjärvi or Laino in Lappland are starting points for regular trips. Contact the STF or the local tourist office for names of individual operators.

A more sedate way of seeing the river is to gently drift along the old logging routes by raft. You effectively camp onboard and the journey can take several days. The river Klarälven in Värmland is one of the best places and participants can either 'build-their-own' raft or rent a ready-made one. Contact the Karlstad tourist office, Tingvallagatan 1D, S-651 84 Karlstad ☎ 054 195901 or Värmland's Turistråd, Box 323, S-651 08 Karlstad ☎ 054 102160.

Wintersports

Although its roots lie in Nordic style cross country skiing, Sweden now has a number of 'Alpine' centres with a variety of lifts and runs. The foremost of them, Åre in Jämtland, is a passable version of its rivals further south. There are some fairly hair-raising downhill runs at Riksgränsen, high in the Arctic and Sweden's most northerly ski resort. It is usually open until midsummer when the lifts run all night.

There are cross country trails all over the country — winter tracks are marked with a red cross. Ski touring is a popular family sport, especially during the schools 'winter sports holiday' in early spring. The mountains of Jämtland and Härjedalen are among the best areas and have a network of huts and mountain stations — but you will find winter tracks in country areas right down to Skåne. The season begins in February or even earlier in central and southern Sweden but not until mid to late March in the far north. For further information contact; Swedish Mountain Resort, c/o SLAO, Box 582, 831 27 Östersund ☎ 063 132395.

Telephone and Postal Services

Sweden's telephone system is efficient and, best of all, most of the telephone boxes work. A large number have however been switched over to telephone cards and it can sometimes be difficult to find one that takes real money. Cards can be bought from kiosks such as Pressbyrån and ordinary shops. The minimum payment for a call from a pay-phone is 2kr and as none to date take 10kr pieces long-distance conversations require a large stack of *kronor* or five *kronor*. For more information contact Televerket on 08 7131000

Post offices do not have telephone facilities but there are special 'telegraph offices' marked 'Tele' or 'Telebutik'. There are usually public telephones in restaurants, bars and some shops. Fuel stations may not have one but will often allow customers to use their private line for a local call in return for a small charge.

The international dialling code from Sweden is 009 followed by the country code; then wait for a second dialling tone before adding the subscriber's number. The international code for Sweden is 46. The emergency number is 90 000 and is free.

Tipping

A 10 per cent service charge is usually included in restaurant prices so there is no need to give an extra tip. Many people will however round up the total to give a helpful waiter a few extra *kronor*. Taxi drivers expect a tip of about 10 per cent and cloakroom attendants will be fairly unhappy if they do not receive at least 7 *kronor* for each coat. In hotels tipping is generally at the guest's discretion. It is not necessary to tip the chambermaid.

Toilet Facilities

Public toilet facilities are surprisingly poor for a country with Sweden's reputation for hygiene and cleanliness. The problem is not so much that they are dirty but that they are few and far between. Restaurants and department stores often have just one or two toilets while there are comparatively few public conveniences. Toilet facilities along main roads are sign-posted by an endearing little hut with a heart on the door.

Tourist Information Centres

Britain
Swedish Travel & Tourism Council/
Next stop Sweden
73 Welbeck Street
London W1M 8AN
☎ 071 487 3135/6
24-hour brochure service
☎ 0891 200280

USA
Swedish Travel and Tourism Council
(Head Office USA)
655 Third Avenue
New York, N.Y. 10017
☎ 1 212 9492333

Canada
Consulate General of Sweden
1 Queen Street East
Suite 2010
Toronto
☎ Canada 416 3678768

Australia
Embassy of Sweden
5 Turrana Street
Yarralumla
Canberra A.C.T. 2600
☎ 61 6 2733033

There are about 400 local Tourist Information Centres in Sweden. Some are open all year round, others only in summer. They are identified by the international 'i' sign. The main ones for areas covered in this book are listed in the 'Additional Information' section at the end of each chapter. The old Swedish Tourist Board has been privatised and is now called The Swedish Travel & Tourism Council/Next Stop Sweden. Its head office is:

Arenavägen 41
Box 10134
121 28 Stockholm-Globen
☎ 46 8 725 5500

Travelling to Sweden

Sweden is surprisingly quick and easy to get to by air, ferry, car or train from other parts of western Europe and is linked by daily flights to Canada, the USA and Australia.

Air

The Scandinavian airline SAS and British Airways operate frequent daily flights from London Heathrow to Stockholm and Göteborg. Stockholm is also served from London Gatwick by Transwede Airways. A new service from Gatwick to Malmö was launched in 1991 by Malmö Aviation. Services to Malmö are available via Copenhagen with an onward 'flight' by SAS hovercraft or rail and ferry connections to other parts of southern Sweden. SAS has daily connections to a large number of cities in the USA and Canada in partnership with Continental Airlines and to Australasia in conjunction with Thai International and All Nippon Airways. To make SAS reservations in Sweden ☎ 020 910110 (Euroclass) or ☎ 020 910150 (Tourist Class), calls are at local rate.

Britain
SAS Scandinavian Airlines
SAS House
52-53 Conduit Street
London W1R 0AY
☎ 071 734 2040

Malmö Aviation
Suite 217, Ashdown House
Gatwick Airport
West Sussex RH6 0EW
☎ 0293 568027

Transwede Airways
209 Edgware Road
London W2 1ES
☎ 071 706 2778

British Airways
PO BOX 10
Hounslow
Middlesex TW6 2JA
☎ 081 897 4000

USA
SAS Reservations, New York
☎ 1 800 221 2350 (toll free)
Ticket Office c/o Continental Air lines
100 East 42 Street
New York
☎ 212 682 3180

Canada
For reservations dial the US toll-free number (see above).

Australia
SAS Ticket Office
5th Floor
350 Kent Street
Sydney
☎ 02 299 6688

Air travel to Scandinavia from the UK has traditionally been expensive relative to the distance involved. Apex fares cut the cost by about 60 per cent and special low-price offers are sometimes available in summer. Several tour operators offer package holidays, adventure and city breaks. Low cost charter flights from London (Stansted) to Stockholm can be arranged by the UK based Strata Travel, 9 Central Parade, Green Street, Enfield, Middlesex EN3 7HG ☎ 081 805 1555.

By Coach

There is a daily coach service from London to Sweden via Amsterdam in summer. It is reduced to three times a week during the rest of the year. The journey time is 37 hours to Malmö, 41 hours to Göteborg and 47 hours to Stockholm and special youth fares are available. For further information contact Eurolines, 52 Grosvenor Gardens, London SW1 ☎ 071 730 8111.

By Rail

Rail services depart daily from London Victoria for the Dover-Ostend ferry service and from London Liverpool Street to link with the Harwich/Hook of Holland crossing. Connecting trains from the Dutch or Belgian ports go via Puttgarden/Rödby (carriages are loaded onboard the ferry for the hour long crossing) and on to Copenhagen. Through coaches for Sweden are then taken to the Elsinor/Helsingborg ferry (a 20 minute crossing) but it may be necessary to change at Copenhagen. For details contact;
   British Rail, European Rail Departure Office,
   Victoria Station, London SW1 ☎ 071 834 8511

Norwegian State Railways, NSR, act as agents for Swedish State Railways (SJ) in London. They can be contacted at:
   21-24 Cockspur Street, London SW1Y 5DA ☎ 071 930 6666

Discount fares for young people under 26 are available from:
   Eurotrain, 52 Grosvenor Gardens, London SW1 ☎ 071 730 8111

By Ferry

Geography currently dictates that the most direct routes to Sweden from the UK or mainland Europe require at least one ferry crossing. The plan to build a new road and rail link between Copenhagen and Malmö by the end of the twentieth century may eventually change that, but until then, ferries will feature prominently in many travel itineraries. There are sea routes to Sweden from the UK, Denmark, Germany, Finland and an increasing number across the Baltic from the new democracies of Eastern Europe, Russia (St Petersburg) Estonia, Latvia and Poland.

From the UK

The most direct sea route to Sweden is the 24 hour crossing from Harwich to Göteborg. Scandinavian Seaways operates regular services all year using large, comfortable car ferries complete with swimming pool, two cinemas and a choice of restaurants. The company operates a second scheduled service from Newcastle to Göteborg in summer. A third Scandinavian Seaways ferry route goes from Harwich to Esbjerg in Denmark from where boat trains take passengers without cars direct to Copenhagen and connecting rail or ferry services to Sweden. Motorists heading further north may prefer to drive up to Fredrikshavn and take the Stena Line ferry to Göteborg (see section on Stena). Scandinavian Seaways also arranges good-value package holidays in Sweden, city breaks and mini-crusies. For more information contact at the following address:
   Scandinavian Seaways, Scandinavia House, Parkeston Quay
   Harwich, Essex CO12 4G ☎ 0255 240240 or
   15 Hannover Street, London W1R 9HG ☎ 071 493 6696

Tyre Commission Quay, North Shields
Newcastle-upon-Tyne, NE29 6EE ☎ 091 2936262

Through fares to Sweden via the continent are available from Olau Line. Passengers use the Olau Line car ferry service from Sheerness to Vlissingen in the Netherlands, then connect with TT Line ferries that operate from Travemünde in Germany to Trelleborg in the south of Sweden. The crossing takes 7 hours. For information contact:
Olau Line UK Ltd, 104 Anchor Lane, Sheerness
Kent ME12 1SN ☎ 0795 666666

Stena Line has several useful ferry services for journeys to Sweden. The company runs daily sailings from Harwich to the Hook of Holland and from there it is possible to connect with another Stena Line service from Kiel in northern Germany direct to Göteborg (14 hours) or Fredrikshavn on Jutland. Alternatively take the 7 hour TT crossing from Travemünde to Trelleborg. Stena also operates a well-used regular link between Fredrikshavn and Göteborg. The 3 hour journey is a popular 'shopping route' for locals. More information about Stena services from:
Sealink-Stena Line, Charter House, Park Street
Ashford, Kent TN24 8EX ☎ 0233 647047

The busiest ferry route is between Elsinor in Denmark and Helsingborg. Car ferries operated by Scandinavian Ferry Lines, Swedish and Danish railways make the 25 minute crossing at least twice an hour. Anyone travelling by road from Germany will find it cheaper to buy a through ticket covering these ferries and the Puttgarden/Rödby crossing. The Öresund route is also plied by small, foot-passenger only boats called 'sound buses'. Scandinavian Ferry Lines also operate twenty daily services from Dragør near Copenhagen to Limhamn by Malmö. The crossing takes just under an hour. Foot passengers can cut the journey time by taking a hydrofoil direct from the Danish capital to Malmö.

Other Ferry Services
Euroway operates a daily service between Travemünde in Germany and Malmö. Two ferry companies, Silja Line and Viking Line have regular sailings between Stockholm and Helsinki in Finland while Baltic Express operate twice weekly from Stockholm to St Petersburg. All three routes take about 15 hours, but passengers are rewarded with wonderful views of the Stockholm archipelago which seems to stretch half-way across the Baltic. Estline has three or four weekly sailings between Stockholm and Tallinn in Estonia and Pol-Line operate one sailing a week between Gdansk and Ystad in Skåne. For Estline and Silja Line information contact Scandinavian Seaways. Viking Line can be contacted at:
8 Spring Gardens, Trafalgar Square, London SW1A 2BG ☎ 071 839 2927

Ferry prices vary but not always in direct relation to the crossing time. A short popular route may well be more expensive than a longer one so it is always worth checking the alternatives. Anyone taking a vehicle should also look at the car costs. Sometimes what appears to be a bargain passenger fare is offset by high vehicle rates and vice versa. Ferry fares and schedules can be almost as complicated as the well-known air fares labyrinth.

Travelling in Sweden

It would be fair to say that travel in Sweden is about as hassle-free as travel can be anywhere in the world. The roads in general are good and relatively uncrowded, there is an efficient internal flight network and an express bus service between the larger towns and cities. Swedes complain bitterly about the state railway system but most well-travelled visitors will wonder what the fuss is about. It is clean, efficient and generally runs on time. Rail travel also offers some good value off-peak fares. Meanwhile regular boat and ferry services link the offshore islands and inland lakes and waterways. Many serve isolated island communities so fares are kept as low as possible and those operated by the Ministry of Transport are free.

By Air

Sweden is a large country and air travel can save a good deal of time for those heading up north. It need not be as expensive as it sounds and may be worth investigating. Internal flights are operated mainly by SAS Scandinavian Airlines and Linjeflyg in a network that covers more than forty destinations. Half-price fares are available on both airlines for off-peak so-called 'red departures' while return 'micro-fares' can knock 60 per cent off the normal rate. Unfortunately the latter can only be bought in Sweden and must be booked and paid for 14 days in advance. These conditions tend to make them unsuitable for foreign holidaymakers on short visits. The airlines also offer 'mini-price' family fares in which the first passenger pays the basic price but other members of the family pay a discounted fare. Children under 11 pay less and under the age of 2 they travel free. 'Mini-price' fares require at least a two night stay at the destination unless the departure is on a Saturday or Sunday.

Young people under the age of 25 can fly remarkably cheaply on a 'stand-by' basis. Senior citizens are also entitled to special concessionary rates. For more information about internal flights contact:

Linjeflyg, Box 550, S-190 45 Stockholm Arlanda ☎ 08 797 5000
SAS Arlanda, Box 54,, S-190 45 Stockholm Arlanda ☎ 08 797 5050

Alternatively contact the local SAS office (the address of SAS, London is given above). It should be mentioned that a few of the inter-city air services are operated by small independent airlines.

By Boat

There are so many local boat services in Sweden that no travel section can adequately deal with the variety. Most are small archipelago boats or inshore ferries and the best bet is often to let the weather and the mood decide which route to take. Large car ferries operate regularly to the Baltic island of Gotland from Nynäshamn and Oskarshamn on the east coast. Tickets can be booked through Scandinavian Seaways and the journey takes 5 hours. In summer you can also take the car ferry from Oskarshamn to Byxelkrok on Öland even though the island is now linked to the mainland by Europe's longest roadbridge. Anyone who wants to explore the archipelago off Stockholm can buy the 'Båtluffarkort' which entitles them to island hop for up to 16 days on the picturesque white painted island ferries.

Contact the Stockholm Tourist Office for more information. There are of course archipelagos all along Sweden's coast, each one with its own ferry services and each one claiming to be more beautiful than the last. The west coast islands are renowned for their barren appeal and small fishing communities, islands along the east coast are greener and more lush. Remember that a few areas are out of bounds to foreigners especially the islands off the naval town of Karlskrona in Blekinge and one or two in the Göteborg and Stockholm archipelagos.

The Göta Kanal is a popular tourist route linking the Baltic with the North Sea via Sweden's two largest lakes, Vänern and Vättern. There are regular departures along the canal between mid-May and early September and the journey from Göteborg to Stockholm takes 3½ days. For more information contact the Göta Kanal Steamship Company at P.O. Box 272, S-401 24, Göteborg ☎ 031 806315, or in the UK, Scantours ☎ 071 839 2927, Scanscape ☎ 0293 599922 or NSR Travel ☎ 071 930 6666.

By Rail

Swedish railways are called Statens Järnvägar or SJ for short. As in many other countries there has been fierce competition between internal rail and air services resulting in SJ smartening up its image to attract lucrative business custom. Virtually all long-distance trains have a restaurant or buffet car, seating compartments and overnight sleepers and couchettes are of a generally high standard. The network covers the whole country from Malmö in the south to Kiruna in the north with hourly services on the 'trunk route' between Göteborg and Stockholm. New high speed trains have cut the journey time to 3 hours. Services marked with an 'R' or 'IC' require seat reservations which can be made up to the time of departure.

SJ operates a variety of concessionary fares. Some weekday services described in the timetable as 'red departures' or 'low price' cost just 50 per cent of the normal fare. The only restriction is that passengers cannot make stopovers and must pay a minimum fare. Students and children under 16 travel at half the reduced fare and up to two children under 12 accompanied by an adult are free. Passengers with a European senior citizen's railcard qualify for a 50 per cent reduction in fares and there is a special summer 'offer' under which second class ticket holders can travel first class for a small supplement.

SJ accepts three concessionary rail cards, Interrail available throughout Europe, the Nordic Railpass; a 21 day ticket valid in Sweden, Norway, Denmark and Finland and purchased in any of those countries and Eurailpass, valid throughout Europe but available only to non-Europeans. In Sweden the Eurailpass can be bought through SJ Stockholm Central. Remember that concessions come and go and each year brings out a new crop of incentives so it is worth checking on the latest 'offer'.

For further advice and information contact SJ in Sweden ☎ 020 757575 or their British agents, Norwegian State railways (NSR) whose address and number is listed in the Travelling to Sweden (By Rail) section.

Motorail

A limited motorail service runs in summer from Malmö, Göteborg and Västerås to Kiruna and Luleå.

Inlandsbanan

The 'inland railway' has a special place in Swedish hearts, not least because it has been hanging on under threat of closure for several years. It covers 750km (465 miles) from Östersund to Gällivare in Lappland passing some of Sweden's most sparsely populated wilderness. Although it lost its commercial value as a railway long ago, it has become a major tourist attraction, offering glimpses of wildlife and nature as it chugs between small northerly towns and villages. The driver is quite likely to stop the train if he spots and elk or otter so that his passengers can see it too. Reindeer on the line are a great photo-opportunity as is the obligatory stop on crossing the Arctic Circle. There are effectively two services on this line. The old Inlandsbanan railcars are fairly basic and without restaurant cars although food is generally available at stations along the way. In 1993 the new 'Wilderness Express' was introduced on the stretch between Östersund and Arvidsjaur. It uses luxurious old carriages and has multi-lingual guides on board. It also has a restaurant car serving regional specialities. A number of 'package tours' are available on this service. Contact: Inlandståget AB, Kyrkgatan 56, Östersund ☎ 063 127695 or SJ for further information. A 14 day go-as-you-please pass is available for unlimited travel. Note that Inlandsbanan does not run in winter.

By Car

Sweden's uncrowded roads make it ideal for motoring holidays. Traffic density decreases from low to minimal north of Stockholm and in remote parts of Lappland you are as likely to meet a reindeer as another car. In spite of this, Sweden has more than 80,000km (49,600 miles) of good trunk road ranging from four lane motorways on the busiest stretches, fast highway known as *motorled* and conventional two-lane roads. Venture off the beaten track however and you will probably come across a few *grus* (gravel) roads winding a bumpy and often picturesque path through the countryside. Even these should present no difficulty although visitors with caravans and large campervans should perhaps ask about the suitablility before they head off down one.

Motorways in Sweden are toll free and mainly concentrated in the south. The motorway network is not all that extensive—some 1,200km (744 miles) in all. The *motorled* effectively reaches the parts that motorways do not! They are broad two lane highways with hard shoulders wide enough to constitute a second lane on each side. Vehicles move in to the hard shoulder when being overtaken, effectively turning it into an extra lane. Speed limits outside built-up areas vary from 110kph (68mph) to 90kph (56mph) or 70kph (43mph) depending on the road width and traffic density. In built up areas the limit is usually 50kph (31mph), going down to 30kph (18mph) near a school. Give way to traffic coming from the right unless road signs or markings indicate otherwise.

Swedes in common with other Europeans drive on the right and vehicles must have at least dipped headlights during the day. Headlights set for left-hand traffic must have the relevant portion taped over to avoid dazzling oncoming drivers. All the occupants must use seatbelts.

It is very important to remember that Sweden has one of the strictest

Drink-Driving laws in the world and that police have the power to stop a motorist at any time and take a breathalyzer test. This is no idle threat. Tiny amounts of alcohol in the bloodstream can lead to prosecution. The legal limit is 20mg/100ml, the equivalent of less than one can of beer.

Petrol (fuel) is sold in 95 octane lead-free (*Blyfri* in Swedish), 96 octane (three-star), 98 octane (four-star) and diesel fuel. Most filling stations are self-service, indicated by the sign Tanka Själv. Some have automatic pumps with signs saying '*Sedel automat*'. They accept 100kr notes and can be used when the service station is otherwise closed. Pumps with the sign '*konto*' are for local account holders. Nearly all filling stations accept credit cards and many have shops selling basic foodstuffs, newspapers and confectionery. There are plenty of filling stations along the main roads and many have late or even 24-hour opening.

Parking can be expensive if you get it wrong! A circular sign with a red cross on a blue background means parking prohibited — if a yellow plate with a red border is added below it means there are restrictions only during the time indicated. Anyone leaving a vehicle parked overnight would be wise to check which night the street is being cleaned because a car left in the path of the council cleansing department is likely to have a ticket on the windscreen next morning. Town centres have plenty of meters, 'P-automat' ticket machines and in larger cities, 'P-hus' — multi-story car parks.

Sweden has a relatively low accident rate. The standard of driving is good and could even be described as cautious compared with many other parts of Europe. In case of an accident or breakdown contact either the police or the 'Larmtjänst' organisation which is run by the Swedish insurance companies and operates a 24-hour service. The address is; Tegeluddsvägen 100, 115 87 Stockholm ☎ 08 7837000. It is not mandatory to call the police but drivers must give their name and address to the other party involved, even in the case of slight damage. Vehicles must have valid international insurance, anyone who does not can buy temporary insurance cover at the border.

The major car hire companies have offices in most cities and at the airports. Charges can be high but special rates are usually available in summer and it is worth shopping around.

Although most road signs are international and easily recognised one or two common signs and abbreviations are worth a special mention here;

Common Road Signs

1 A triangular warning sign showing an elk should be taken seriously. Wild animals, especially elk can (and do) cause serious accidents if they run out onto the road. Most care should be taken at dawn and dusk. Reflective posts along the verges are an attempt to frighten them off while plastic bags flapping along the road in the far north mean there are reindeer herds in the area.

2 A square symbol made of four loops marks a sight of interest near the road.

3 A black 'door' with a white heart indicates a public convenience.

4 A square sign with a small hut indicates holiday cottages for rent. They may also be marked with the sign 'STUGBY' or in the case of a single (often privately owned) cottage 'STUGA'. A horn and crown means post office.

5 A hut with a tree means Youth Hostel.

6 A triangular 'tent' means campsite.

7 A fish on a line indicates the sale of fishing licences.

8 A head and two wavey lines means swimming area.

K:A — Church
JVSTN — Railway Station
M — Meeting place (on narrow road)
G:A — Old (as in G:A K:A — old church)
FÄB — Fäbod, meaning hill farm
HPL — Bus or coachstop
Lanthandel — Rural general store
Hembygdsgård — Heritage Museum

Dangerous road conditions are marked with clear international warning symbols or flashing lights. A particularly sharp bend may have an additional sign saying 'Farlig Kurva'. Snow and ice are a problem in winter and snow chains or winter tyres plus a shovel are essential for anyone heading north. Many municipalities have stopped clearing snow from all but the most major roads, allowing it to pack hard under the weight of traffic instead. They have discovered that drivers who might be tempted to put their foot down if the road appears clear are more cautious when they can actually see the hazard.

By Coach
A network of express bus services link the larger towns and cities in southern and central Sweden. There are also regular bus services between Stockholm and the coastal towns in the north. The main operators are Swebus and Linjebuss. Several other private coach companies have weekend services and tours and in the north there is service run by none other than the Swedish Post Office. Many operators have special offers at weekends. Information is available from local tourist offices. Swebus can be contacted at:

Gullbergs Strandgata 34, S-41104 Göteborg ☎ 031 103820

Urban Public Transport
Most towns and cities have an efficient and relatively cheap public transport system. Göteborg and Norrköping have hung onto their trams and Stockholm is served by an extensive underground system called T-banan. Otherwise urban bus services are the mainstay of local transport. Customers can usually buy multiple tickets or cards as well as single use tickets. Taxis are widely available but fairly expensive.

INDEX

Page numbers in **bold** type indicate maps
The Swedish language has three additional vowels, which appear
at the end of this index